With All My Heart

AUTHORS
Rabbi Yosi Wolf
Rabbi Baruch Shalom Davidson
Rabbi Lazer Gurkow

Printed in the United States of America

822 Eastern Parkway, Brooklyn, NY 11213

Cover Art: The Exacting Potion Nº 9 (detail), Sara Richardson; encaustic wax, pigment, and encaustic medium on a cradled birch panel, United States.

(888) YOUR-JLI/718-221-6900
WWW.MYJLI.COM

ב"ה

With All My Heart

The Jewish Art of Prayer and Spiritual Experience

STUDENT TEXTBOOK

The Rohr Jewish Learning Institute acknowledges the generous support of the following individuals and foundations:

PRINCIPAL BENEFACTOR

GEORGE ROHR
New York, NY

PARTNERING FOUNDATIONS

AVI CHAI FOUNDATION

CRAIN-MALING FOUNDATION

ESTATE OF ELLIOT JAMES BELKIN

GOLDSTEIN FAMILY FOUNDATION

KOHELET FOUNDATION

KOSINS FAMILY FOUNDATION

MEROMIM FOUNDATION

MYRA REINHARD FAMILY FOUNDATION

OLAMI—WOLFSON FOUNDATION

RUDERMAN FAMILY FOUNDATION

THE MAYBERG FOUNDATION

WILLIAM DAVIDSON FOUNDATION

WORLD ZIONIST ORGANIZATION

YEHUDA AND ANNE NEUBERGER PHILANTHROPIC FUND

ADVISORY BOARD OF GOVERNORS

YAAKOV AND KAREN COHEN
Potomac, MD

YITZCHOK AND JULIE GNIWISCH
Montreal, QC

BARBARA HINES
Aspen, CO

DANIEL B. MARKSON
S. Antonio, TX

DANIEL AND ROSIE MATTIO
Seattle, WA

DAVID MINTZ
Tenafly, NJ

DR. STEPHEN F. SERBIN
Columbia, SC

LEONARD A. WIEN, JR.
Miami Beach, FL

PILLARS OF JEWISH LITERACY

KEVIN BERMEISTER
Sydney, Australia

PABLO AND SARA BRIMAN
Mexico City, Mexico

ZALMAN AND MIMI FELLIG
Miami Beach, FL

YOSEF GOROWITZ
Redondo Beach, CA

DR. VERA KOCH GROSZMANN
S. Paulo, Brazil

HERSCHEL LAZAROFF
Monsey, NY

JENNY LJUNGBERG
New York, NY

DAVID MAGERMAN
Gladwyne, PA

DR. MICHAEL MALING
Deerfield, IL

YITZCHAK MIRILASHVILI
Herzliya, Israel

BEN NASH
New Jersey

YAIR SHAMIR
Savyon, Israel

LARRY SIFEN
Virginia Beach, VA

SPONSORS

MARK AND REBECCA BOLINSKY
Long Beach, NY

DANIEL AND ETA COTLAR
Houston, TX

GORDON DIAMOND
Vancouver, BC

AMIR AND DAFNA ELYASHAR
Ramat Aviv, Israel

SHMUEL AND SHARONE GOODMAN
Chicago, IL

JOE AND SHIRA LIPSEY
Aspen, CO

ELLEN MARKS
S. Diego, CA

RACHELLE NEDOW
El Paso, TX

PETER AND HAZEL PFLAUM
Newport Beach, CA

FRANK (A"H) AND FRUMETH POLASKY
Saginaw, MI

MOSHE AND YAFFA POPACK
Fisher Island, FL

HERCHEL AND JULIE PORTMAN
Denver, CO

EYAL AND AVIVA POSTELNIK
Marietta, GA

DR. ZE'EV RAV-NOY
Los Angeles, CA

CLIVE AND ZOE ROCK
Irvine, CA

ZVI RYZMAN
Los Angeles, CA

ALAN ZEKELMAN
Bloomfield Hills, MI

MYRNA ZISMAN
Cedarhurst, NY

The Rohr Jewish Learning Institute
gratefully acknowledges the pioneering
and ongoing support of

George and Pamela Rohr

Since its inception, the Rohr JLI has been a beneficiary of the vision, generosity, care, and concern of the Rohr family.

In the merit of the tens of thousands of hours of Torah study by JLI students worldwide, may they be blessed with health, *Yiddishe nachas* from all their loved ones, and extraordinary success in all their endeavors.

DEDICATED IN LOVING MEMORY OF

David Rock

דוד שמואל ע"ה בן יבלחט"א זלמן גרשון

May the study of this JLI course
by thousands of students worldwide
be a source of merit to his soul
and a blessing to his entire family.

And in tribute to

Mr. Neil Rock

with deep appreciation for his partnership with JLI
in bringing Torah study to all corners of the world.

May he and his family go from strength to strength and
enjoy good health, happiness, *nachas* from his loved ones,
and success in all his endeavors לאורך ימים ושנים טובות.

Endorsements

For those who take prayer even only semi-seriously, it is unlikely they will be able to "stick with it" for long. Perfunctory prayer, wherein one has little idea of what they are doing, why they are doing it, and the meaning and purpose of the individual prayers, has a limited shelf life. For prayer to resonate and for those who engage in prayer to continue praying, the one praying needs to know the why's and the wherefores. Welcome to this wonderful endeavor by the Rohr Jewish Learning Institute to bring the spirit, soul, and purpose to prayer so that *tefilah* is embraced in its totality—out of knowledge, understanding, and fullness of devotion.

RABBI DR. REUVEN P. BULKA, PHD

Rabbi Emeritus, Congregation Machzikei Hadas,
Ottawa, Ontario, Canada.
Author, *What You Thought You Knew about Judaism*
and more than twenty-five other titles

The greatest problem of prayer for most people today isn't the "what" but rather the "how." How do we best link our souls to our Creator, express our deepest feelings to the Almighty, and put into words our needs, our dreams, and our desire to infuse our lives with meaning? Like the pious of old, we pray—that we learn how to pray. The difference between Torah and prayer, we've been told, is that in Torah G-d speaks to us; in prayer we speak to Him. Jewish prayer and its vehicles, the siddur, the blessings, the Shema, the silent prayer, all grant us the divine secrets for dialoguing with G-d. At last we have a JLI course that teaches how to achieve that goal.

RABBI BENJAMIN BLECH

Professor of Talmud, Yeshiva University
Author, *The Secrets of Hebrew Words* and fifteen other titles

Speaking to G-d is easy—or is it? The idea of prayer is simple, but praying the Jewish way takes training, insight, and practice. Through the wisdom of our sages, the prayer services have the power to break through all barriers between our world and the highest heaven. Through prayer, we can change our relationship with G-d and, perhaps, even change our destiny.

Prayer is not just a shopping list of requests; it is a union with G-d. We are spiritual beings in a physical world. Our job is to unite the two. If only we knew how much power is in our prayer! Everything can change in the moment of prayer, but if you want a truly spiritual experience in prayer, you have to do the work. JLI's course, *With All My Heart*, will show you how to bring that inner peace that comes through a personally meaningful relationship with G-d as you climb the ladder to the Infinite with the Jewish art of prayer.

RAE SHAGALOV

Author, *The Secret Art of Talking to G-d*
and *Create Your Joyfully Jewish Life!*

For most of its history, humanity was based in an agricultural environment. Our symbiotic relationship with nature brought us close to the Creator and imbued us with a humble spirit. Today, post-Industrial Revolution, when machine, computer, and man/robot synthesis is mooted, humanity is increasingly estranged from the natural world, and we are losing our sense of self, purpose, and mission. These losses are expressed most profoundly in our relationship with synagogue and prayer. The vast majority of Jews feel estranged, embarrassed, and unsure of themselves in the *shul*, if not finding the prayer experience utterly irrelevant. Talking to G-d, or discovering the deeper self, is not taught or experienced by most Jews in a lifetime. It is therefore heroic of JLI to tackle this gap and bridge it with an excellent course that includes experiential elements like meditation. This approach speaks to the contemporary condition while the content remains deeply loyal to the profound spiritual truths within Jewish prayer and the building blocks of personal growth that Jewish prayer is capable of providing. I commend both the courage of the course designers and the excellence of the content, and add my encouragement for Jews at all stages of development to give themselves the opportunity to enter the gates of higher consciousness that this new JLI course provides.

RABBI LAIBL WOLF
Founder and Dean, Spiritgrow
Author, *Practical Kabbalah*

If the Greek philosophical tradition defined the human being as a "rational animal," the Jewish tradition preferred to think of him as a "praying person." With this new course on the meaning, purpose, and dynamics of prayer, *With All My Heart*, the student is introduced to both key texts and themes on the power and efficacy of human prayer—all in an intimate but user-friendly forum. The sages rightly called prayer a "worship of the heart," and every worship that's worth its name demands a serious unsentimental but thoughtful approach to both the "big picture" of prayer and the seemingly more "mechanical" details that form the rhythm of the life of prayer. The Rohr JLI series has made a real contribution to the inner life of the modern Jew with this new course. Souls seeking a language of authentic dialogue with the Divine in an era of hiddenness and barren secularity now have a wonderful resource to turn to.

RABBI MARK GOTTLIEB
Senior Director, The Tikvah Fund
Dean, Tikvah Summer Institute at Yale University

I applaud the Rohr Jewish Learning Institute. . . . Its teachers present a wide range of Jewish topics with a depth that is both exciting and stimulating. I wish that such courses had existed when I started learning about Judaism. What a wonderful way for beginners, as well as people with much background, to expand their knowledge of Judaism.

LISA AIKEN, PHD
Author, *The Art of Jewish Prayer* and twelve other titles

Contents

Lesson 1

OUT OF THE FOXHOLE

A NEW PARADIGM FOR PRAYER

Behind the Siddur (Prayer Book), Toby Gotesman Schneier, Fort Lauderdale, oil on canvas.

Burdensome. Unrealistic. Superfluous. Boring. A staple of human routine for millennia, prayer is nowadays often viewed as irrelevant. This lesson dissolves these negative labels by explaining the ultimate goal of prayer. It demonstrates the real-time relevance and indispensability of prayer for every human. And it guides us toward personalizing our prayers for a deeply meaningful experience.

Exercise 1.1

1 Why do you pray?

2 What do you find difficult about prayer?

3 What are you looking for in this course?

"Should I Pray If I Don't Believe in G-d?" **Rabbis *David Aaron*** *and* ***Yitzchak Schochet*** *respond:*

MYJLI.COM//PRAYER

TEXT 1

I SAMUEL 1:1–2, 10–11, 13

וַיְהִי אִישׁ אֶחָד מִן הָרָמָתַיִם צוֹפִים מֵהַר אֶפְרָיִם, וּשְׁמוֹ אֶלְקָנָה . . . וְלוֹ שְׁתֵּי נָשִׁים, שֵׁם אַחַת חַנָּה וְשֵׁם הַשֵּׁנִית פְּנִנָּה, וַיְהִי לִפְנִנָּה יְלָדִים וּלְחַנָּה אֵין יְלָדִים . . .

וְהִיא מָרַת נָפֶשׁ, וַתִּתְפַּלֵּל עַל ה' וּבָכֹה תִבְכֶּה. וַתִּדֹּר נֶדֶר וַתֹּאמַר, "ה' צְבָאוֹת! אִם רָאֹה תִרְאֶה בָּעֳנִי אֲמָתֶךָ, וּזְכַרְתַּנִי, וְלֹא תִשְׁכַּח אֶת אֲמָתֶךָ, וְנָתַתָּה לַאֲמָתְךָ זֶרַע אֲנָשִׁים, וּנְתַתִּיו לַה' כָּל יְמֵי חַיָּיו" . . .

וְחַנָּה הִיא מְדַבֶּרֶת עַל לִבָּהּ, רַק שְׂפָתֶיהָ נָּעוֹת, וְקוֹלָהּ לֹא יִשָּׁמֵעַ.

There was a man from Ramataim-Tsofim, in the hill country of Ephraim. His name was Elkanah. . . . He had two wives: one named Chanah and the other Peninah. Peninah had children, but Chanah was childless. . . .

Chanah was embittered. She prayed to G-d* and wept profusely. She vowed, "G-d of the many heavenly and worldly beings! Look upon your servant's misery and remember me. Do not forget your servant, and give me a son. If you do this I will dedicate him to G-d all the days of his life. . . ."

Chanah was praying in her heart. Her lips were moving, but her voice was silent.

* Throughout this book, "G-d" and "L-rd" are written with a hyphen instead of an "o" (both in our own translations and when quoting others). This is one way we accord reverence to the sacred divine name. This also reminds us that, even as we seek G-d, He transcends any human effort to describe His reality.

TEXT 2

PSALMS 23

מִזְמוֹר לְדָוִד, ה' רֹעִי, לֹא אֶחְסָר. בִּנְאוֹת דֶּשֶׁא יַרְבִּיצֵנִי, עַל מֵי מְנֻחוֹת
יְנַהֲלֵנִי. נַפְשִׁי יְשׁוֹבֵב, יַנְחֵנִי בְמַעְגְּלֵי צֶדֶק לְמַעַן שְׁמוֹ. גַּם כִּי אֵלֵךְ בְּגֵיא
צַלְמָוֶת, לֹא אִירָא רָע כִּי אַתָּה עִמָּדִי. שִׁבְטְךָ וּמִשְׁעַנְתֶּךָ, הֵמָּה יְנַחֲמֻנִי.
תַּעֲרֹךְ לְפָנַי שֻׁלְחָן נֶגֶד צֹרְרָי. דִּשַּׁנְתָּ בַשֶּׁמֶן רֹאשִׁי, כּוֹסִי רְוָיָה. אַךְ טוֹב
וָחֶסֶד יִרְדְּפוּנִי כָּל יְמֵי חַיָּי, וְשַׁבְתִּי בְּבֵית ה' לְאֹרֶךְ יָמִים.

Historical insight: What led to a standardized liturgy? ***Rabbi Yossi Paltiel*** *explains:*

MYJLI.COM/PRAYER

A psalm of David:

G-d is my shepherd, I lack nothing.

He lies me down in green meadows; He leads me beside still waters.

He calms my soul; He leads me upon upright paths, to show His care.

Even when I walk in the shadow of death, I fear no harm, for You are with me. Your rod and Your staff, they comfort me.

I am confident that you will yet set a table before me, in front of my enemies. You have anointed my head with oil [meaning: granted me kingship]; you have filled my cup [meaning: assured me great power].

May only goodness and kindness follow me all the days of my life. May I sit in the house of G-d for many long years.

TEXT 3

RABBI YISRAEL BAAL SHEM TOV, *KETER SHEM TOV*, P. 57

מָשָׁל שֶׁהִכְרִיז הַמֶּלֶךְ בְּיוֹם שִׂמְחָתוֹ, כָּל מִי שֶׁיְּבַקֵּשׁ דָּבָר מִן הַמֶּלֶךְ יְמַלְאוּ לוֹ בַּקָּשָׁתוֹ. וְיֵשׁ מִי שֶׁבִּיקֵּשׁ שְׂרָרָה וְכָבוֹד, וְיֵשׁ שֶׁבִּיקֵּשׁ עוֹשֶׁר, וְנָתְנוּ לְכָל אֶחָד מְבוּקָשׁוֹ. וְהָיָה שָׁם חָכָם אֶחָד שֶׁאָמַר שֶׁשְּׁאֵלָתוֹ וּמְבוּקָשׁוֹ שֶׁיְּדַבֵּר הַמֶּלֶךְ בְּעַצְמוֹ עִמּוֹ ג' פְּעָמִים בַּיּוֹם, וְהוּטַב מְאֹד בְּעֵינֵי הַמֶּלֶךְ, מֵאַחַר שֶׁדִּיבּוּרוֹ חָבִיב עָלָיו מִן עוֹשֶׁר וְכָבוֹד, לָכֵן יְמוּלָּא בַּקָּשָׁתוֹ שֶׁיִּתְּנוּ לוֹ רְשׁוּת לִיכָּנֵס בְּהֵיכָלוֹ לְדַבֵּר עִמּוֹ, וְשָׁם יִפְתְּחוּ לוֹ הָאוֹצָרוֹת שֶׁיִּקַּח מִן עוֹשֶׁר וְכָבוֹד גַּם כֵּן.

A king once decreed that on his day of celebration, anyone who would request something from him would have their request granted. One person asked for power and glory; another asked for wealth. Each person's request was granted. There was one wise man who requested that he be given the opportunity to speak with the king three times a day. The king was very impressed that this man valued speaking with him more than riches and glory. The king therefore fulfilled this man's request and allowed him to enter his chamber thrice daily to speak with him. The king also gave the man access to his treasuries, bestowing him with riches and glory as well.

RABBI YISRAEL BAAL SHEM TOV (BESHT) 1698–1760

Founder of the Chasidic movement. Born in Slutsk, Belarus, the Baal Shem Tov was orphaned as a child. He served as a teacher's assistant and clay digger before founding the Chasidic movement and revolutionizing the Jewish world with his emphasis on prayer, joy, and love for every Jew, regardless of his or her level of Torah knowledge.

TEXT 4a

MISHNAH, KELIM 3:5

הַתּוֹפֵל כְּלִי חֶרֶס . . .

One who attaches (plaster to) a clay vessel . . .

משניות
סדר זרעים
ווארשא

MISHNAH

The first authoritative work of Jewish law that was codified in writing. The Mishnah contains the oral traditions that were passed down from teacher to student; it supplements, clarifies, and systematizes the commandments of the Torah. Due to the continual persecution of the Jewish people, it became increasingly difficult to guarantee that these traditions would not be forgotten. Rabbi Yehudah Hanassi therefore redacted the Mishnah at the end of the 2nd century. It serves as the foundation for the Talmud.

My Cup Floweth Over, Yehoshua Wiseman, acrylic on canvas, Jerusalem.

TEXT 4b

THE REBBE, RABBI MENACHEM MENDEL SCHNEERSON, *LIKUTEI SICHOT* 2, P. 410

דִי גֶענוֹיעֶ אִיבֶּערְזֶעצוּנְג פוּן "פְּרֵייעֶר" - אוֹיף לָשׁוֹן הַקוֹדֶשׁ אִיז - בַּקָשָׁה, אָבֶּער בַּיי אִידְן הֵייסְט עֶס נִיט מִיטְן נָאמֶען בַּקָשָׁה נָאר מִיטְן נָאמֶען תְּפִלָה. דֶער אוּנְטֶערְשֵׁייד פוּן בַּקָשָׁה בִּיז תְּפִלָה אִיז אוֹיךְ אַ הָפְכִּית'דִיקֶער:

בַּקָשָׁה מֵיינְט בֶּעטְן אוּן תְּפִלָה מֵיינְט בַּאהֶעפְטְן זִיךְ. בַּקָשָׁה אוּנְטֶערְשְׁטְרַייכְט - בֶּעטְן, מֶען בֶּעט בַּיי דֶעם אוֹיבֶּערְשְׁטְן עֶר זָאל גֶעבְּן - מִלְמַעֲלָה לְמַטָה - דָאס וָואס עֶס פֶּעלְט. בִּשְׁעַת עֶס פֶּעלְט נִיט אָדֶער עֶס אִיז נִיטָא קֵיין רָצוֹן אוֹיף אַ זַאךְ, אִיז נִיט שַׁיָיךְ קֵיין בַּקָשָׁה.

תְּפִלָה אוּנְטֶערְשְׁטְרַייכְט - בַּאהֶעפְטְן זִיךְ מִיטְן אוֹיבֶּערְשְׁטְן מִלְמַטָה לְמַעֲלָה. דָאס אִיז שַׁיָיךְ בַּיי אַלֶעמֶען אוּן אַלֶעמָאל . . .

דֶערְפַאר אִיז אוֹיךְ בַּיי דִי וֶועלְכֶע עֶס פֶּעלְט זֵיי גָארְנִישְׁט, פַארַאן - אוּן מִיט דֶער גַאנְצֶער שְׁטַארְקֵייט - דִי זַאךְ פוּן תְּפִלָה, וַוייל תְּפִלָה אִיז נִיט נָאר גֶעבֶּעט אוּן בַּקָשָׁה, נָאר דֶער עִיקָר - דֶער אָפְּפְרִישׁ פוּן דֶעם פַארְבּוּנְד אוּן דְבֵיקוּת פוּן אִים מִיטְן אוֹיבֶּערְשְׁטְן.

The English word "prayer" would be best translated into Hebrew as *bakashah,* a request. Yet, in Jewish tradition, the word *tefilah* is preferred. Indeed, these two words—*bakashah* and *tefilah*—imply two very different concepts of prayer:

While *bakashah* means "to request," *tefilah* means "to connect."

Bakashah implies that prayer is a request of G-d to grant us something we may be lacking. Were we to neither

Tefilah...
to cleave, attach, connect.

RABBI MENACHEM MENDEL SCHNEERSON 1902–1994

The towering Jewish leader of the 20th century, known as "the Lubavitcher Rebbe," or simply as "the Rebbe." Born in southern Ukraine, the Rebbe escaped Nazi-occupied Europe, arriving in the U.S. in June 1941. The Rebbe inspired and guided the revival of traditional Judaism after the European devastation, impacting virtually every Jewish community the world over. The Rebbe often emphasized that the performance of just one additional good deed could usher in the era of Mashiach. The Rebbe's scholarly talks and writings have been printed in more than 200 volumes.

lack nor desire anything, prayer in the sense of *bakashah* would have no place.

Tefilah, however, implies connecting with G-d. This is something applicable to all people, at all times. . . .

Even for a person who lacks nothing, prayer—in its fullest sense—is still relevant. For prayer isn't only about making requests. Rather, it is primarily about renewing the connection between an individual and G-d.

Why pray every day?
Rabbi Shmuel Kaplan
responds:

MYJLI.COM/PRAYER

Morning Prayer on Subway, Lori Grinker, gelatin silver print, 1984. (The Jewish Museum, New York)

Exercise 1.2

Below are a few statements written in the first person. Using the accompanying scale of 1–4 (never, occasionally, often, or always), rate how often these statements describe your attitude.

	1	2	3	4
I believe G-d is involved in what happens in the world. He is intimately involved in my life.				
I feel self-reliant and independent of G-d. I don't sense His relevance to my life.				
I believe there is more to life than material concerns. Ultimately, I seek purpose and meaning.				
I am more concerned with my material needs than my spiritual ones.				
I am not a selfish person. I enjoy giving to others.				
I struggle with being altruistic.				

TEXT 5

THE REBBE, RABBI MENACHEM MENDEL SCHNEERSON, IBID.

יֶעדֶער אִיד הָאט אַ נְשָׁמָה וָואס זִי אִיז פַארְבּוּנְדְן מִיטְן אוֹיבֶּערְשְׁטְן. אָבֶּער מִצַד דֶעם וָואס דִי נְשָׁמָה אִיז אַרָאפּ אִין גוּף אוּן פַארְבּוּנְדְן מִיט אִים, מוּז דִי נְשָׁמָה פַארְבִּינְדְן זִיךְ מִיט גוּפְנִיּוּת'דִיקֶע עִנְיָנִים אַזוֹי וִוי עֶסְן, טְרִינְקֶען אוּן דָאס גְלַייכְן, וָואס אִין דֶער צַייט וֶוערְט אָפְּגֶעשְׁוַואכְט אִיר פַארְבּוּנְד מִיטְן אוֹיבֶּערְשְׁטְן. אוּן אוֹיף דֶעם זַיינֶען פַארַאן גֶעוִויסֶע צַייטְן אִין טָאג אוֹיף תְּפִלָּה, בִּכְדֵי צוּ בַּאנַייעֶן דֶעם פַארְבּוּנְד מִיטְן אוֹיבֶּערְשְׁטְן, אוּן פַארְשְׁטַארְקְן אִים.

Every Jew possesses a G-dly soul that is connected to G-d. But, due to the soul's descent and investment into the body, the soul becomes bogged down by the body's needs like eating, drinking, etc. Over time, this weakens the G-dly soul's connection with G-d.

The daily times of prayer, meaning connection, serve to renew and strengthen the G-dly soul's connection with G-d.

"Understanding Prayer: Heart, Mind and Soul"—a brilliant video series on prayer, by ***Rabbi Lord Jonathan Sacks****:*

MYJLI.COM/PRAYER

TEXT 6

RABBI SHNE'UR ZALMAN OF LIADI, *LIKUTEI TORAH*, P. 72, CITING THE *ZOHAR*

שַׁעַת צְלוֹתָא שַׁעַת קְרָבָא.

The time of prayer is a time of war.

RABBI SHNE'UR ZALMAN OF LIADI (ALTER REBBE) 1745–1812

Chasidic rebbe, halachic authority, and founder of the Chabad movement. The Alter Rebbe was born in Liozna, Belarus, and was among the principal students of the Magid of Mezeritch. His numerous works include the *Tanya*, an early classic containing the fundamentals of Chabad Chasidism, and *Shulchan Aruch HaRav*, an expanded and reworked code of Jewish law.

TEXT 7

RABBI SHALOM DOVBER SCHNEERSOHN, *KUNTRES HATEFILAH,* P. 20

אֲשֶׁר עַל זֶה הוּא תַּכְלִית יְרִידַת הַנְשָׁמָה בְּגוּף, בִּכְדֵי לְבָרֵר אֶת הַנֶּפֶשׁ הַבַּהֲמִית, לְזַכֵּךְ אֶת הַמִדוֹת הַטִבְעִיִּים . . . וְכַךְ נִקְצְבוּ לָאָדָם יְמֵי חַיָּיו בָּעוֹלָם הַזֶה, לְפִי הַבֵּירוּרִים שֶׁצָרִיךְ לְבָרֵר . . .

וְעִיקָר הַזִיכּוּךְ וְהַבֵּירוּר הוּא עַל יְדֵי עֲבוֹדַת הַתְּפִילָה דַוְקָא.

The purpose of the G-dly soul's descent into the body is to influence the animal soul and refine its natural habits. . . . The days of a person's life are numbered according to the time it takes to complete this job. . . .

The influencing of the animal soul occurs primarily through the service of prayer.

RABBI SHALOM DOVBER SCHNEERSOHN (RASHAB) 1860–1920

Chasidic rebbe. Rabbi Shalom Dovber became the fifth leader of the Chabad movement upon the passing of his father, Rabbi Shmuel of Lubavitch. He established the Lubavitch network of *yeshivot* called Tomchei Temimim. He authored many volumes of Chasidic discourses and is renowned for his lucid and thorough explanations of kabbalistic concepts.

TEXT 8

THE REBBE, RABBI MENACHEM MENDEL SCHNEERSON,
SEFER HAMAAMARIM MELUKAT (*TORAT MENACHEM* EDITION), 2, P. 1

דְהַטַעַם עַל זֶה שֶׁמִלְחָמָה נִקְרֵאת בְּשֵׁם קְרָב מִלָשׁוֹן קִירוּב (אַף שֶׁמִלְחָמָה הִיא הֵיפֶךְ עִנְיַן הַקִירוּב), הוּא, כִּי עִנְיַן הַמִלְחָמָה הוּא שֶׁכָּל אֶחָד מִשְׁנֵי הַלוֹחֲמִים רוֹצֶה לְנַצֵחַ אֶת הַשֵׁנִי וּלְהַכְנִיעַ אוֹתוֹ שֶׁיוּכְלָל בּוֹ, וּבִכְדֵי לִפְעוֹל בָּזֶה שֶׁלוֹחֵם כְּנֶגְדוֹ שֶׁיוּכְלַל בּוֹ, הוּא דַוְקָא עַל יְדֵי הַקִירוּב שֶׁמִתְקָרֵב אֵלָיו, קְרָב מִלָשׁוֹן קִירוּב.

וְעַל דֶרֶךְ זֶה הוּא בְּהַמִלְחָמָה דְנֶפֶשׁ הָאֱלֹקִית וְנֶפֶשׁ הַבַּהֲמִית, דְעִיקָר הַמִלְחָמָה הִיא בִּשְׁעַת הַתְּפִלָּה (שַׁעַת צְלוֹתָא שַׁעַת קְרָבָא), שֶׁבִּכְדֵי שֶׁהָעֲבוֹדָה (תְּפִלָּה) דְנֶפֶשׁ הָאֱלֹקִית תִּפְעוֹל בְּנֶפֶשׁ הַבַּהֲמִית שֶׁתּוּכְלַל בְּנֶפֶשׁ הָאֱלֹקִית [הַיְינוּ שֶׁגַם נֶפֶשׁ הַבַּהֲמִית תִּהְיֶה לָהּ אַהֲבַת ה', בְּכָל לְבָבְךָ בִּשְׁנֵי יְצָרֶיךָ] הוּא עַל יְדֵי שֶׁנֶפֶשׁ הָאֱלֹקִית מִתְלַבֶּשֶׁת בְּנֶפֶשׁ הַבַּהֲמִית, שֶׁהַהִתְבּוֹנְנוּת שֶׁל נֶפֶשׁ הָאֱלֹקִית הִיא בְּעִנְיָנִים כָּאֵלוּ וּבְאוֹפֶן שֶׁגַם נֶפֶשׁ הַבַּהֲמִית יְכוֹלָה לְהַשִּׂיג.

War is referred to as "*kerav,*" which shares the same Hebrew letters as the word "*kiruv*"—closeness. This is ironic, for war is the opposite of closeness.

The explanation is as follows: In war, each of the two sides wishes to triumph over the other and subject it to its rule. To do so, the two sides must come in close contact. This explains the connection between the words *kerav*—war—and *kiruv*—closeness.

The same is true of the war between the G-dly and animal souls, which happens primarily during prayer—hence, "The time of prayer is a time of war." For the G-dly soul to subjugate the animal soul, bringing it to a love of G-d—"Love G-d with both your hearts" (MISHNAH, BERACHOT 9:5)—the G-dly soul must take the animal soul into close consideration. This means meditating in a way that the animal soul will also understand.

Inner Struggle, Armando Alemdar, London, charcoal and conte crayon on paper.

TEXT 9

RABBI YOSEF YITSCHAK SCHNEERSOHN, *SEFER HASICHOT* 5701, P. 54

רַבִּי גֶרְשׁוֹן בֶּער . . . פְלֶעגְט פַארְטַייטְשְׁן אַלְץ אוֹיף אִידִישׁ . . .

עֶר הָאט אַמָאל גֶעפְרֶעגְט בַּא הַחָסִיד רַבִּי פֶּרֶץ, רָב פוּן נֶעוֶועל און דֶערְנָאךְ אִין טְשֶׁערְנִיגָאװ, אוֹיבּ עֶר מֶעג פַארְטַייטְשְׁן דֶעם דַאוְוענֶען . . . הָאט אִים רַבִּי פֶּרֶץ גֶעזָאגְט, "צוּלִיבּ וָואס דַארְפְסְטוּ דָאס?"

הָאט עֶר אִים גֶעעֶנְטְפֶערְט, "מַיין נֶפֶשׁ הַבַּהֲמִית פַארְשְׁטֵייט בֶּעסֶער אוֹיף אִידִישׁ!"

Rabbi Gershon Ber . . . had a habit of translating prayers into Yiddish. . . .

He once asked Rabbi Perets, the rabbi of the city of Nevel and later of Chernigov, whether it was permissible to pray both in Hebrew and in Yiddish by translating the prayers as he went along. . . .

Rabbi Perets asked him, "Why would you want to do this?"

He responded, "My animal soul understands Yiddish better!"

RABBI YOSEF YITSCHAK SCHNEERSOHN (RAYATS, FRIERDIKER REBBE, PREVIOUS REBBE) 1880–1950

Chasidic rebbe, prolific writer, and Jewish activist. Rabbi Yosef Yitschak, the sixth leader of the Chabad movement, actively promoted Jewish religious practice in Soviet Russia and was arrested for these activities. After his release from prison and exile, he settled in Warsaw, Poland, from where he fled Nazi occupation and arrived in New York in 1940. Settling in Brooklyn, Rabbi Schneersohn worked to revitalize American Jewish life. His son-in-law, Rabbi Menachem Mendel Schneerson, succeeded him as the leader of the Chabad movement.

Chassidic Prayer: ***Professor Glenn Dynner*** *on its history; Dr.* ***Tali Lowenthal*** *on its contemporary relevance:*

MYJLI.COM/PRAYER

TEXT 10

ELOKAI NESHAMAH, MORNING PRAYERS

אֱלֹקַי, נְשָׁמָה שֶׁנָתַתָּ בִּי טְהוֹרָה הִיא.

אַתָּה בְרָאתָהּ, אַתָּה יְצַרְתָּהּ, אַתָּה נְפַחְתָּהּ בִּי, וְאַתָּה מְשַׁמְּרָהּ בְּקִרְבִּי, וְאַתָּה עָתִיד לִטְּלָהּ מִמֶּנִי, וּלְהַחֲזִירָהּ בִּי לֶעָתִיד לָבוֹא.

כָּל זְמַן שֶׁהַנְשָׁמָה בְּקִרְבִּי, מוֹדֶה אֲנִי לְפָנֶיךָ ה' אֱלֹקַי וֵאלֹקֵי אֲבוֹתַי, רִבּוֹן כָּל הַמַּעֲשִׂים אֲדוֹן כָּל הַנְשָׁמוֹת.

What is your favorite Jewish prayer? Five major Jewish scholars share theirs:

MYJLI.COM/PRAYER

My G-d, the soul You have placed within me is pure.

You created it, You formed it, You have breathed it within me, and You preserve it within me. Ultimately, You will take it from me and restore it to me in the Time to Come.

As long as the soul is within me, I thankfully acknowledge You, G-d, my G-d and G-d of my ancestors, Master of all works, L-rd of all souls.

Exercise for the Week

Connecting. This week, set aside sixty seconds for a brief prayer, with your focus exclusively on seeking to connect with G-d through this exercise. It can be done at home, in a synagogue, or at any location or setting that you consider conducive and appropriate.

We'll discuss how it went during the next lesson.

KEY POINTS

1 Prayer is deeply personal and profoundly individualistic. It is the way a person expresses their deepest thoughts and feelings, in conversation, to G-d. The rituals associated with prayer aren't intended to diminish this.

2 The word *tefilah* implies that there is more to prayer than just asking G-d for things. Prayer is also a time to connect. Even if a person feels that there's nothing they need to tell G-d, prayer, in the sense of connection, is still relevant to them. This—developing one's connection with G-d—is one of the goals of daily prayer.

3 Each individual possesses two souls: one G-dly and the other animalistic. These souls are extremely different in nature. Prayer—connecting with G-d—is for both of them.

4 The G-dly soul is a stranger in this world. It yearns for spiritual experience and closeness to G-d. Prayer is its chance. Prayer nourishes the G-dly soul and fills it with spiritual stamina.

5 The G-dly soul has a mission: to elevate the animal soul it shares the body with. This is primarily achieved through prayer. Simply put, this means thinking about

G-d in practical and relevant terms, which resonate with the animal soul.

6 The prayer book is intended to facilitate—not replace—personal prayer. It is meant to guide our thoughts and articulate our feelings. When we use it properly, its words become our own.

Appendix

TEXT 11

ECCLESIASTES 3:21

רוּחַ בְּנֵי הָאָדָם הָעֹלָה הִיא לְמָעְלָה, וְרוּחַ הַבְּהֵמָה הַיֹּרֶדֶת הִיא לְמַטָּה לָאָרֶץ.

While the soul of the human ascends upward, the soul of the animal descends downward, toward the ground.

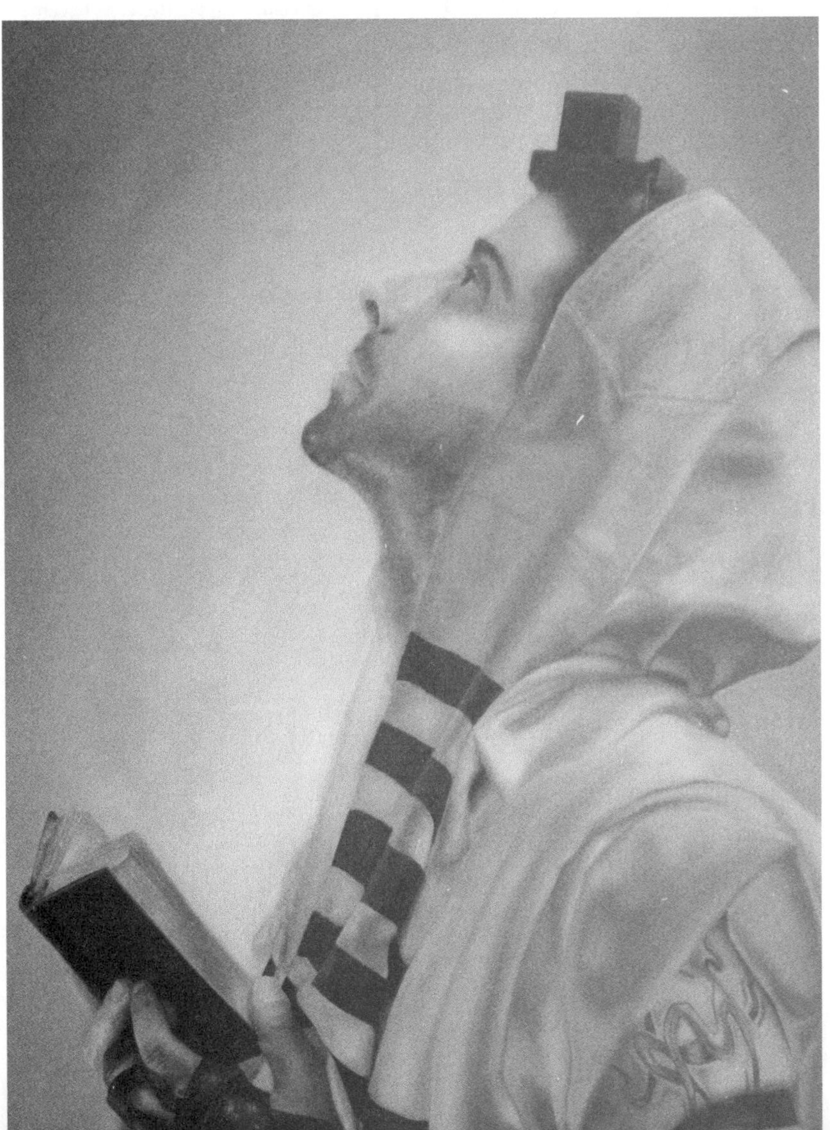

Calling G-d, Avital Abergel, oil on canvas, London.

TEXT 12

MAIMONIDES, *MISHNEH TORAH,* LAWS OF PRAYER 1:4–6

כֵּיוָן שֶׁגָּלוּ יִשְׂרָאֵל בִּימֵי נְבוּכַדְנֶצַּר הָרָשָׁע, נִתְעָרְבוּ בְּפָרַס וְיָוָן וּשְׁאָר הָאֻמּוֹת, וְנוֹלְדוּ לָהֶם בָּנִים בְּאַרְצוֹת הַגּוֹיִם. וְאוֹתָן הַבָּנִים נִתְבַּלְבְּלָה שְׂפָתָם, וְהָיְתָה שְׂפַת כָּל אֶחָד וְאֶחָד מְעֹרֶבֶת מִלְּשׁוֹנוֹת הַרְבֵּה. וְכֵיוָן שֶׁהָיָה מְדַבֵּר, אֵינוֹ יָכוֹל לְדַבֵּר כָּל צְרָכוֹ בְּלָשׁוֹן אַחַת אֶלָּא בְּשִׁבּוּשׁ, שֶׁנֶּאֱמַר: "וּבְנֵיהֶם חֲצִי מְדַבֵּר אַשְׁדּוֹדִית, וְאֵינָם מַכִּירִים לְדַבֵּר יְהוּדִית, וְכִלְשׁוֹן עַם וָעָם" (נְחֶמְיָה יג, כד).

וּמִפְּנֵי זֶה, כְּשֶׁהָיָה אֶחָד מֵהֶם מִתְפַּלֵּל, תִּקְצַר לְשׁוֹנוֹ לִשְׁאֹל חֲפָצָיו, אוֹ לְהַגִּיד שֶׁבַח הַקָּדוֹשׁ בָּרוּךְ הוּא בִּלְשׁוֹן הַקֹּדֶשׁ, עַד שֶׁיְּעָרְבוּ עִמָּהּ לְשׁוֹנוֹת אֲחֵרוֹת.

וְכֵיוָן שֶׁרָאָה עֶזְרָא וּבֵית דִּינוֹ כָּךְ, עָמְדוּ וְתִקְּנוּ לָהֶם שְׁמוֹנֶה עֶשְׂרֵה בְּרָכוֹת עַל הַסֵּדֶר: שָׁלוֹשׁ רִאשׁוֹנוֹת שֶׁבַח לַה', וְשָׁלוֹשׁ אַחֲרוֹנוֹת הוֹדָיָה, וְאֶמְצָעִיּוֹת יֵשׁ בָּהֶן שְׁאֵלַת כָּל הַדְּבָרִים – שֶׁהֵן כְּמוֹ אָבוֹת לְכָל חֶפְצֵי אִישׁ וָאִישׁ, וּלְצָרְכֵי הַצִּבּוּר כֻּלָּן.

כְּדֵי שֶׁיִּהְיוּ עֲרוּכוֹת בְּפִי הַכֹּל, וְיִלְמְדוּ אוֹתָן, וְתִהְיֶה תְּפִלַּת אֵלּוּ הָעִלְּגִים תְּפִלָּה שְׁלֵמָה כִּתְפִלַּת בַּעֲלֵי הַלָּשׁוֹן הַצָּחָה.

When the Jewish people were exiled in the times of the wicked Nebuchadnezzar, they became interspersed in Persia and Greece and other countries. The children they raised in these foreign countries weren't proficient in any single language; their language was a concoction of many. In the words of the verse, "And their children spoke in both Ashdodit and in other languages. They did not know how to speak the Jewish language" (NEHEMIAH 13:24).

Consequently, when it came to prayer, these people were unable to adequately request their needs or praise G-d

RABBI MOSHE BEN MAIMON (MAIMONIDES, RAMBAM) 1135–1204

Halachist, philosopher, author, and physician. Maimonides was born in Córdoba, Spain. After the conquest of Córdoba by the Almohads, he fled Spain and eventually settled in Cairo, Egypt. There, he became the leader of the Jewish community and served as court physician to the vizier of Egypt. He is most noted for authoring the *Mishneh Torah,* an encyclopedic arrangement of Jewish law, and for his philosophical work, *Guide for the Perplexed.* His rulings on Jewish law are integral to the formation of halachic consensus.

in Hebrew unless they would complement their prayers with other languages.

When Ezra and his court saw this, they established the Amidah prayer, which consists of eighteen blessings. The first three blessings are praises of G-d, and the last three are thanksgiving. The intermediate twelve blessings are requests for all types of matters. They serve as general categories for all the specific requests of both the individual and the community.

The people could thus easily learn these prayers and recite them fluently, enabling them to pray with the same degree of eloquence as those people who did have command over the language.

TEXT 13

RABBI BACHYA IBN PAKUDAH, *CHOVOT HALEVAVOT* 8:3

וְדַע, כִּי הַמִּלּוֹת תִּהְיֶינָה בַּלָּשׁוֹן וְהָעִיּוּן בַּלֵּב, וְהַמִּלּוֹת כְּגוּף לַתְּפִלָּה וְהָעִיּוּן כְּרוּחַ. וּכְשֶׁיִּתְפַּלֵּל הַמִּתְפַּלֵּל בִּלְשׁוֹנוֹ, וְלִבּוֹ טָרוּד בְּזוּלַת עִנְיַן הַתְּפִלָּה, תִּהְיֶה תְּפִלָּתוֹ גוּף בְּלֹא רוּחַ וּקְלִיפָּה בְּלֹא לֵב, מִפְּנֵי שֶׁגּוּפוֹ נִמְצָא וְלִבּוֹ בַּל עִמּוֹ עֵת תְּפִלָּתוֹ . . .

וּלְפִי שֶׁהָיְתָה מַחְשֶׁבֶת הַלֵּב מִתְהַפֶּכֶת הַרְבֵּה, וְאֵין לָהּ קִיְּמָה לִמְהִירוּת עֲבוּר הַהִרְהוּרִים עַל הַנֶּפֶשׁ, הָיָה קָשֶׁה עָלֶיהָ לְסַדֵּר עִנְיָנֵי הַתְּפִלָּה מֵעַצְמָהּ, תִּקְּנוּ אוֹתָם רַבּוֹתֵינוּ זִכְרוֹנָם לִבְרָכָה בְּמִלִּים מְתוּקָּנוֹת, יְסַדְּרֵם הָאָדָם בִּלְשׁוֹנוֹ, מִפְּנֵי שֶׁמַּחְשֶׁבֶת הַנֶּפֶשׁ הוֹלֶכֶת אַחַר הַמַּאֲמָר וְנִמְשֶׁכֶת אֶל הַדִּבּוּר.

וְהָיְתָה הַתְּפִלָּה מִלּוֹת וְעִנְיָנִים, וְהַמִּלּוֹת צְרִיכוֹת אֶל הָעִנְיָן וְהָעִנְיָן אֵינוֹ צָרִיךְ אֶל הַדִּבּוּר.

Know that the words of prayer should be on the tongue and its correlating meditation in the heart. For, while words are the body of prayer, meditation is its spirit. But when one prays with just their tongue, and their heart is distracted, the prayer is like a body without a spirit; a shell without a kernel. For, during this person's prayer, the body is present, but the heart is not. . . .

Maintaining focus during prayer is difficult, and it is for this reason that the rabbis established the liturgy of the prayer book. The words of the prayer book engage a person's thoughts and thus help the individual to maintain focus.

Prayer is a composite of words and the content they express. The words need the content, but the content does not need the words.

RABBI BACHYA IBN PAKUDA
11TH CENTURY

Moral philosopher and author. Ibn Pakuda lived in Muslim Spain, but little else is known about his life. *Chovot Halevavot* (*Duties of the Heart*), his major work, was intended to be a guide for attaining spiritual perfection. Originally written in Judeo-Arabic and published in 1080, it was later translated into Hebrew and published in 1161 by Judah ibn Tibbon, a scion of the famous family of translators. Ibn Pakuda had a strong influence on Jewish pietistic literature.

TEXT 14

RABBI YOSEF YITSCHAK SCHNEERSOHN, *KUNTRES TORAT HACHASIDUT*, PP. 6–7

עוּבְדָא הֲוָה בִּימֵי מוֹרֵנוּ הַבַּעַל שֵׁם טוֹב נִשְׁמָתוֹ עֵדֶן, אֲשֶׁר הָיָה קִטְרוּג שֶׁל כְּלָיָה רַחֲמָנָא לִצְלָן עַל אַחַת הַקְּהִלּוֹת, וּכְשֶׁרָאָה מוֹרֵנוּ הַבַּעַל שֵׁם טוֹב אֶת כּוֹבֶד הַמַּצָּב הִרְבָּה בִּתְפִלָּה וּבְתַחֲנוּנִים בְּרֹאשׁ הַשָּׁנָה וּבְיוֹם הַכִּפּוּרִים. וַיְהִי בְּעֵת תְּפִלַּת נְעִילָה הִכִּירוּ הַתַּלְמִידִים הַקְּדוֹשִׁים בִּתְפִלַּת מוֹרֵנוּ הַבַּעַל שֵׁם טוֹב אֲשֶׁר מַצָּבוֹ שֶׁל הַקִּטְרוּג רַחֲמָנָא לִצְלָן הוּא רְצִינִי בִּמְאוֹד, וְיִתְאַמְּצוּ גַּם הֵם בִּתְפִלּוֹת תַּחֲנוּנִים בִּבְכִיּוֹת עֲצוּמוֹת מֵעוּמְקָא דְלִיבָּא.

כִּרְאוֹת מִתְפַּלְּלֵי בֵּית הַכְּנֶסֶת בְּעֶזְרַת יִשְׂרָאֵל וּבְעֶזְרַת נָשִׁים אֲשֶׁר מוֹרֵנוּ הַבַּעַל שֵׁם טוֹב וְתַלְמִידָיו הַקְּדוֹשִׁים עוֹדָם עוֹמְדִים עַל עָמְדָם מִתְחַזְּקִים וּמִתְאַמְּצִים בִּתְפִלָּתָם, הֵבִינוּ כּוּלָּם כִּי הַמַּצָּב נוֹרָא הוּא, וַיִּבְכּוּ הָאֲנָשִׁים וְהַנָּשִׁים מֵעוֹמֶק נְקוּדַּת לְבָבָם בִּבְכִיּוֹת עֲצוּמוֹת וַיְהִי רַעַשׁ גָּדוֹל.

זֶה אֵיזֶה שָׁנִים, אֲשֶׁר בָּחוּר עִבְרִי בֶּן כְּפַר רוֹעֶה צֹאן וּבָקָר, בָּא לוֹ לְיָמִים הַנּוֹרָאִים לְבֵית הַכְּנֶסֶת שֶׁל מוֹרֵנוּ הַבַּעַל שֵׁם טוֹב, וּבִהְיוֹתוֹ בּוּר גָּמוּר הָיָה עוֹמֵד מַקְשִׁיב וּמִסְתַּכֵּל בִּפְנֵי הַחַזָּן בְּאֵין אוֹמֵר וּדְבָרִים. כִּכְפָרִי הָיָה רָגִיל בְּקוֹל בְּהֵמוֹת, הָעִזִּים, הַכְּבָשִׂים, הַצִּפּוֹרִים, וְהָעוֹפוֹת, וְהֶחָשׁוּב בֵּינֵיהֶם הָיָה אֶצְלוֹ קוֹל הַתַּרְנְגוֹל בִּקְרִיאָתוֹ. וּבִרְאוֹתוֹ הַהִתְרַגְּשׁוּת הַגְּדוֹלָה אֲשֶׁר בְּבֵית הַכְּנֶסֶת, וּבְשָׁמְעוֹ הַבְּכִיּוֹת בְּעֶזְרַת יִשְׂרָאֵל וּבְעֶזְרַת נָשִׁים, הַצְּעָקוֹת הַנּוֹרָאוֹת הִנֵּה גַּם לְבָבוֹ נִשְׁבָּר בְּקִרְבּוֹ, וַיִּקְרָא בְּקוֹל גָּדוֹל, "קוּקִי-רֶעקָא-הָאן, גָ-ט הָאב רַחֲמָנוּת!"

בְּהִשָּׁמַע בְּבֵית הַכְּנֶסֶת קוֹל הַקּוֹרֵא כְּתַרְנְגוֹל, נִבְהֲלוּ הָעוֹמְדִים בְּעֶזְרַת יִשְׂרָאֵל, וְנִפְחֲדוּ הַשּׁוֹמְעוֹת בְּעֶזְרַת נָשִׁים, וְלֹא יָדְעוּ מִי הוּא הַקּוֹרֵא, וּכְשָׁמְעָם הַצְּעָקָה "גָ־ט הָאב רַחֲמָנוּת", רָאוּ כִּי הַבָּחוּר הַכַּפְרִי הִשְׁמִיעַ קוֹלוֹ. אֲחָדִים מֵהַמִּתְפַּלְּלִים אֲשֶׁר עָמְדוּ אֵצֶל הַכַּפְרִי, גָּעֲרוּ בּוֹ לְהַשְׁתִּיקוֹ, וְחָפְצוּ לְגָרְשׁוֹ. וַיֹּאמַר אֲלֵיהֶם, "גַּם אָנֹכִי יְהוּדִי, וֶאֱלֹקֵיכֶם הוּא גַּם אֱלוֹקַהּ שֶׁלִּי". הַשַּׁמָּשׁ הַזָּקֵן רַבִּי יוֹסֵף יוֹזְפָּא הִרְגִּיעַ אֶת רוּחָם שֶׁל הַמִּתְפַּלְּלִים, וַיֹּאמַר לְהַכַּפְרִי כִּי יִשָּׁאֵר עַל מְקוֹמוֹ כְּבַתְּחִלָּה.

כַּעֲבוֹר רְגָעִים אֲחָדִים אַחַר הַמְאוּרָע עִם בֶּן הַכַּפְרִי, נִשְׁמַע קוֹלוֹ שֶׁל מוֹרֵנוּ הַבַּעַל שֵׁם טוֹב, וְאַחֲרָיו הַתַּלְמִידִים הַקְּדוֹשִׁים הַמְמַהֲרִים לְסַיֵּים תְּפִלַּת הַשְּׁמוֹנֶה עֶשְׂרֵה בִּנְעִילָה, וּפְנֵי קֹדֶשׁ הַבַּעַל שֵׁם טוֹב נָהֲרוּ מִגִּיל. בִּנְעִימָה מְיוּחָדָה הִתְחִיל מוֹרֵנוּ הַבַּעַל שֵׁם טוֹב חֲזָרַת הַשָּׁלִיחַ צִבּוּר בִּתְפִלַּת נְעִילָה, וּבְהִתְעוֹרְרוּת מְיוּחָדָה אָמַר פְּסוּקֵי הַיִּחוּד שְׁמַע יִשְׂרָאֵל, בָּרוּךְ שֵׁם, ה' הוּא הָאֱלֹקִים. וַיָּשִׁיר מוֹרֵנוּ הַבַּעַל שֵׁם טוֹב שִׁירֵי שִׂמְחָה.

כְּשֶׁבֶת מוֹרֵנוּ הַבַּעַל שֵׁם טוֹב עִם תַּלְמִידָיו הַקְּדוֹשִׁים בִּסְעוּדַת מוֹצָאֵי יוֹם כִּפּוּרִים הוֹאִיל לְסַפֵּר כָּל פְּרָטֵי עִנְיְנֵי הַקִּטְרוּג רַחֲמָנָא לִצְלָן שֶׁהָיָה – לֹא עָלֵינוּ – עַל עֵדָה בְּיִשְׂרָאֵל, וְכַאֲשֶׁר הִתְאַמֵּץ בִּתְפִלָּתוֹ לְעוֹרֵר רַחֲמֵי שָׁמַיִם עַל הָעֵדָה, הִנֵּה פָּגַשׁ רַחֲמָנָא לִצְלָן קִטְרוּג גָּדוֹל עָלָיו, עַל אֲשֶׁר מִשְׁתַּדֵּל לְהוֹשִׁיב בְּנֵי יִשְׂרָאֵל בַּכְּפָרִים וּבְפָרָשַׁת דְּרָכִים, אֲשֶׁר יְכוֹלִים הֵם לִלְמוֹד חַס וְשָׁלוֹם מִשְּׁכֵנֵיהֶם.

כְּשֶׁהִתְחִילוּ לִבְדּוֹק בְּמַעֲשֵׂיהֶם וּמַצָּבָם שֶׁל אַנְשֵׁי הַכְּפָר, רָאִיתִי אֲשֶׁר הַמַּצָּב הוּא קָשֶׁה בִּמְאֹד וְהָיִיתִי בְּכָל רָע, אַךְ לְפֶתַע פִּתְאוֹם נִשְׁמַע בַּמָּרוֹם קוֹל קְרִיאָתוֹ שֶׁל בֶּן הַכְּפָר הַתָּם, "קוּקוּ־רֶעקָא־הָאן, גָ־ט הָאב רַחֲמָנוּת!" אֲשֶׁר קְרִיאָה תְּמִימָה זוֹ גָּרְמָה קוֹרַת רוּחַ לְמַעְלָה עַד רוּם הַמַּעֲלוֹת. וּבִטְלוּ הַקִּטְרוּגִים מֵעַל הָעֵדָה וּמֵעָלַי.

Once, in the times of the Baal Shem Tov, a heavenly decree of destruction was issued against a certain community. The Baal Shem Tov sensed the gravity of the decree and prayed fervently that year on Rosh Hashanah and Yom Kippur.

During the *ne'ilah* prayers [the concluding prayers of Yom Kippur], the Baal Shem Tov continued to pray intensely. His students sensed the desperateness of the situation, and they, too, prayed intensely, weeping from the depths of their hearts.

The rest of the congregants in the synagogue, both men and women, upon seeing the intensity of the prayers of the Baal Shem Tov and his students, understood that the situation was dire. They, too, burst into tears and cried out their hearts in prayer.

For the past few years, a certain Jewish farm boy from the countryside had been coming to the Baal Shem Tov's synagogue for the Days of Awe. This boy was completely illiterate (and unable to pray from the prayer book), so he would stand silently and listen, and he would watch the face of the cantor.

Being a farm boy, he was familiar with all kinds of animal sounds and had a particular liking for the rooster's cry. The great storm of emotion in the synagogue and the weeping of the men and women broke his heart. He called out aloud, "*Cuckoo-ree-koo-hon!* G-d have mercy!"

The men and women in the synagogue were taken aback. Who had called that out? But when they heard, "G-d have mercy!" they realized that it was the country boy.

Some of the congregants standing near the boy admonished him and tried silencing him. They wanted to remove him from the synagogue. The boy pleaded, "I, too, am a Jew, and we both have the same G-d." The old synagogue secretary, Rabbi Yosef Yozpa, calmed the congregants and allowed the boy to remain in his place.

A few moments after this incident, the Baal Shem Tov and his students proceeded to conclude the silent Amidah of the *ne'ilah* prayer. The Baal Shem Tov's face shone with joy. He began the repetition of the Amidah with a special melody. He recited the verses of *Hear*

O Israel, Blessed is the name, and *The L-rd is G-d* with great excitement. He followed these verses by singing joyous songs.

At the meal to break the fast after Yom Kippur, the Baal Shem Tov explained the entire story to his students:

"There was a terrible decree against a certain community. When I tried to intercede, I discovered that I, too, was the subject of a negative heavenly decree, due to my initiative of creating Jewish communities in remote farm areas, where the members of these communities could be negatively influenced by their neighbors.

"When the heavenly court began to examine the conduct of the Jewish farm people, I realized that I was in trouble. But suddenly, the call of '*Cuckoo-ree-koo-hon!* G-d have mercy!' of this farm boy was heard on high. This wholehearted cry brought G-d tremendous pleasure, causing Him to nullify the decrees that hung over that community and over me."

Additional Readings

PRAYERS, SYNAGOGUE, WORSHIPPERS

BY HERMAN WOUK

A Visit to the Synagogue

Even the most convinced unbeliever is likely to have an occasional religious mood or fancy, no matter how much he may disapprove of it; as the most devoted husband feels an unwanted stir of pleasure now and then when a pretty girl passes by. Nature will win out. The human impulse—if the secularist prefers, the human weakness—that has created and perpetuated religion is not absent from any breast. In such a passing religious moment, the Jewish skeptic may go so far as to wander into a synagogue to see what the faith of his fathers has to offer him.

He is handed a prayer book that strikes him as a jumble, with English translations that for long stretches make little sense. He is apt to observe preoccupied and inattentive worshippers reeling off Hebrew with few external symptoms of devotion, or whispering together while a reader chants a long singsong. Now and then everybody stands, he cannot say why, and there is a mass chant, he cannot say what; or if he dimly recalls it from childhood, he cannot find it in the prayer book. The time comes when the Holy Scroll is taken from the Ark for a parade to the reading desk, the bells tinkling on its silver crown. The reading in a strange Oriental mode seems endless, and he observes that it seems endless to some other worshippers too, who slump in an unfocussed torpor, or chat, or even sleep. If there is a sermon, especially from a young rabbi, the chances are that it is a digest of articles from the past week's liberal newspapers and magazines, with a few references to the Bible. The skeptic leaves—early, if he can—well satisfied that his views are sound, that his religious fancy was a temporary touch of melancholia, and that if the Jewish G-d exists, there is no reaching him through the synagogue.

The experience will be somewhat different, probably, if he happens into a synagogue so old-fashioned that its rabbi is a bearded ancient who speaks Yiddish. In that case the worshippers may seem more fervid in their devotions, though no less apt to chat now and then. The sermon—if the visitor remembers his Yiddish—is likely to strike at least a momentary response from him with vivid racy imagery, with insights into life that are curiously phrased but dig deep. He may leave with a wisp of regret for days and ways that are done; for of course there is no reviving Yiddish as a community tongue or teaching it to his children, who probably attend a progressive private school.

All this presumes a visit to a traditional synagogue. Conservative and Reform temples, with some differences in manner and custom, offer parts of the same substance. When the whole has no good effect on him, we can assume that parts probably will not either.

A Night at the Opera

The reader will perhaps remember, in this connection, his first visit to the opera. The chances are that he went sometime in his late teens or early twenties, urged on by an enthusiastic companion, perhaps female. The chances are, too, that he was skeptical about

HERMAN WOUK, PHD, 1915–

American novelist and playwright. Wouk was born in New York City to a Jewish-Russian immigrant family. When the U.S. entered World War II, he joined the Navy, serving in the Pacific Theater for four years. Wouk's wartime experiences gave him the material and background for his bestseller and Pulitzer-Prize-winning *The Caine Mutiny*. *This Is My G-d* was his best-selling affirmation of faith in traditional Judaism, penned after much self-examination and exposure to many secular influences. His later works include the novel *Inside, Outside*, which discusses Judaism in private life and in politics, and *The Will to Live On: This Is Our Heritage*.

grand opera and suspected it might all be an elaborate boring fraud, a dead transplanted art form which American snobs and phonies pretended to enjoy because going to the opera was a high-class European habit. For all I know, this is the present opinion of opera that many of my readers hold.

But those who have changed their minds will recall that they did not do so on their first visit. Then, on the contrary, they probably saw confirming evidence of their suspicions. Fat old men slumped asleep in the boxes, their stiff shirts buckling; their wives more interested in the clothes and faces in the other boxes than in the stage performance; soulful creatures needing haircuts standing in the back of the orchestra, or squatting on the floor, in self-conscious poses of rapture; on the stage a fat screechy woman pretending to be a demure little country bride, a little man with a potbelly and short jerking arms impersonating Don Juan, a chorus of aging painted ladies, and men with ridiculous matchstick legs in tight hose, making tired clumsy gestures at acting now and then; while the orchestra tootled and tinkled without cease one monotonous kind of sugary noise; that, in all likelihood, was his first impression of one of the miracles of human inspiration, Mozart's *Don Giovanni*.

Sir Thomas Beecham once said that *Don Giovanni* has never had an adequate performance—that is, a troupe of singers capable of singing it, and an audience equipped to hear it. The run of singing artists does not produce in one generation enough voices to match Mozart's demands. The people who fill an opera house on any night are—people; some wonderful, some ordinary, some stupid, some insufferable, some dragged there by wives, some coming there to prove they are intelligent, some coming out of habit, some to tell the folks back home that they saw a New York opera, and some who love Mozart as they love the sunlight, and who are willing to endure all the coarseness and failure of another performance for the sake of the shafts of lovely light that despite all will break through now and then.

As performers and audience cannot usually rise to Mozart, the rabbi and his congregation cannot usually rise to Moses. That does not mean that the law of Moses is less sublime than world opinion acknowledges it to be, or that the forms of popular worship it has inspired are not capable of carrying its message down the years. The fact is that the synagogue, for all its human weaknesses, has done so. Every synagogue at every service has worshippers to whom the words and the ceremonies are transfusions of strength and intelligence; perhaps a few, perhaps many. The visitor's quick look cannot go inside their heads and hearts; in the good phrase of the jazz addicts, he does not dig what he is seeing.

What the Synagogue Is

The synagogue began as a kind of popular law school well over two thousand years ago. In classic synagogue architecture there are always study tables placed where the light is best. The tables have become vestigial or have disappeared in many American structures, as the synagogue, with the rest of Judaism, has undergone the dislocation of a shift of hemispheres. It is a pretty good guess that where an old rabbi sermonizes in Yiddish the tables will still be found; and the old rabbi will be found at one or another table with his followers, expounding the law.

It is a social axiom of Judaism—like our American doctrine that all men are created equal, which we know to be romantic, but which nevertheless stands as our working ideal—that all Jews are law students, commencing their studies at five. From this course in Torah law nobody graduates. Advanced students become rabbis; that is, literally, teachers. But in the Jewish diction rabbis do not teach; they learn with their students. One says quite literally of a master of the Talmud, "He knows how to learn." The theoretical norm of Jewish conduct includes enough labor in the marketplace to support one's family, the rest of one's time going to the law. Since this norm operates for perhaps one percent of Jewry, it is a somewhat abnormal norm; admirably intellectual, perhaps, but not geared to the distribution curve of human traits. Nevertheless, as a working ideal it deeply stamps our institutions and our manners.

It determines, for instance, the liturgy and the atmosphere of the synagogue; what we do there, and the way we do it. The very heart of synagogue practice is the reading of the Torah, week by week, in fifty-two sections, so that once a year in perpetuity we review and discuss our whole statutory law.

When the First Temple fell and the great daily service in Jerusalem stopped, the vacuum at the core of the religion might have brought on a total collapse. But Jewry, with the regenerative power that is its magic, created a new institution. In the houses of law study that existed everywhere in Judea and Babylon, the Jews took to offering devotions like those that had gone with the priestly ceremonies, adding prayers for an end to the exile and a restoration of the Temple. The house of study evolved into a house of worship. It kept its character as the law school of the masses, but services became fixed in its pattern.

The Second Temple revived Jewish life in the Holy Land, but much of Jewry remained in Babylon. The synagogue held its place as a center of worship as well as of study. When the Romans levelled the Second Temple, the synagogue became the fortress of the faith, the place where Jews gathered, learned the law, and prayed; the intellectual fortress, and in times of attack often the physical fortress.

In this form, the institution successfully traversed twenty centuries.

Naturally, such an immense stretch of time left its marks. The liturgy kept gathering layers of new devotions. A simple structure became overlaid with additions from Bible and Talmud, and with fresh compositions by rabbis of different centuries. Copyists and printers tended to cut nothing that had once been added, for that approached sacrilege. The prayer books became steadily longer, the Hebrew more difficult—pure, clear Hebrew is usually ancient—and the forms more complicated. By the nineteenth century, a morning festival service contained enough material to take up, if spoken with due attention, six or seven hours. The habit of racing through prayers arose. When I was a boy, I marveled at the ability of the adults in the synagogue to proceed at such breakneck speed through difficult medieval poetry. I looked forward to the day when I too would have such mastery of Hebrew and such powers of concentration. Now I know that nobody has such powers.

A change in such a state of affairs had to come. The Reform movement tore the liturgy to bits, retained a few fragments translated into German—later into English—and that was that. The Conservatives kept more of the liturgy and more Hebrew, but drastically modified or cut out prayers and ceremonies going back to Temple times. In the traditional synagogue there has been a slow process of bringing the prayer book back to its classic form. More and more we tend to skip the cabalistic acrostics of the Middle Ages, which not one worshipper in a thousand can understand—though those who do maintain that they are deep and lovely—and to give more time and attention to the pure and transparent Hebrew of the prayers that come down from the oldest times, that are the core of the service, and that anyone who knows even a little Hebrew can easily say.

This process is not a smooth one. Old pietists naturally dig in against omission of any prayers they have come to know. Youngsters can hardly be trained to handle the essential liturgy in the time given to Hebrew study. The mere machinery of an American religious center—membership drive, building drive, committee meetings, men's club, sisterhood, youth league, and so forth—tends to overwhelm all. The young rabbi comes out of his ordination with a head full of Talmudic lore and plunges into a vortex where everybody is an authority: the synagogue's president, the chairlady of the sisterhood, or even a novelist who pokes into the Talmud now and then. He is told to comment on the news; not to comment on the news; that he speaks above the people's heads; that he is debasing himself to the popular level; that a modern rabbi must be a social leader, a fundraiser, an inspirational orator, a jolly good fellow, a passable card player, and a pious figure no less awe-inspiring than his bearded forebears in the old country; and in this whirl of contradictions and impasses he must spend his days and gain his bearings. The wonder is that we still have young rabbis, that the number of synagogues is increasing, and that the outlines of a stable modern service are appearing. The vitality of Judaism is the reason. While controversy waxes over the coming shape of the tree, the old tree slowly and steadily puts out its new branches. And as the French say, the more it changes the more it becomes what it was.

The Creed and the Service

At the heart of all our liturgies—the forty minutes of an ordinary Tuesday morning, as well as the twelve solid hours of the Day of Atonement—lie two devotions. I will call them the Creed and the Service, to indicate their nature. In the synagogue their names are the *Sh'ma* and the *Shmone Esrai*—that is, literally, Hear, and The Eighteen.

Around these two key prayers cluster excerpts from the classics of Jewish literature and law: the Torah, the Prophets, the Psalms, the Talmud: for the synagogue remains, as it always was, a study hall. The worshipper, repeating the day's prayers, traverses the main fields of Judaic learning, fulfilling his formal duty of perpetual study.

The two basic prayers are short. The Creed itself you can say in a few seconds, the Service in a few minutes. A worshipper pressed for time, reciting these two devotions, performs the ritual of Hebrew worship; for the Sh'ma is the essence of our law, and The Eighteen is the link between the synagogue and the ancient Temple. The full texts of both are in a note to this chapter, so the reader who is wholly strange to the prayer book can know what they are.

The Sh'ma contains the one verse of Scripture that probably every Jew in the world knows by heart, or has at least heard often, Deuteronomy 6:4:

> *Hear, O Israel, the L-rd our G-d, the L-rd is One.*

The observant Jew says it in the morning and at nightfall every day of his life, with three related passages from the Torah. It is the first Hebrew sentence a child learns, and it is the utterance with which every Jew is supposed to breathe his last.

On this point I will obtrude a short personal anecdote. I used to wonder whether, in the last extremity, a man could really call to mind and recite the Creed. Then once during a typhoon in the Pacific I was almost blown off the deck of a ship, and I remember quite clearly thinking, as I went sliding toward my fate, "Well, if l drown, let me say the Sh'ma as I go." Luckily for me the lifeline I grabbed happened to hold; and so I postponed the utterance, and the world has a few plays and novels it could well have wagged along without, and the patient reader is enduring the present harangue. I believe there are one or two literary critics who may wish I had gotten to say that watery Sh'ma, but I cannot help that, a man hangs on if he can.

The Service is an extremely old litany of eighteen blessings. A nineteenth was added in Talmudic times; and on Sabbaths and festivals there are only seven; but The Eighteen is still what everybody calls the devotion. There are three Eighteens, morning and afternoon and evening, to parallel the Temple rites.

Must Prayer Be in Hebrew?

The first tractate of the Talmud, Benedictions, fixes the times and customs of saying the Sh'ma, does the same for The Eighteen, and then develops the blessings for all occasions of life. The antiquity of the Creed and the Service is evident in the matter-of-fact way the Talmud discusses them.

Benedictions lays down the rule that one should bless the Creator for every good in this world; and it even contains a remarkable blessing on evil news. Perhaps the most startling passage in it, for a modern reader, is an open authorization to pray in English, that is, in any language one understands. The popular notion is that English prayer is a shattering heresy. Our common law allowed it two thousand years ago.

Despite that, the Jews have always clung to a Hebrew liturgy. In previous times it might have caused less trouble and disaffection if the prayers had been in Greek, Aramaic, Latin, Egyptian, Arabic, Spanish, French, Turkish, German, Polish, or Russian. But the community, by a continuing mass instinct, has held to the Scripture tongue. That instinct is asserting itself today in the United States, in the Reform and Conservative movements, which year by year bring back more Hebrew into their devotions.

Today we have printed translations. In olden times, when knowledge of Hebrew was sometimes scantier than it is today, there was an important synagogue officer, the *meturgeman*, or translator, who called out line by line the vernacular meaning of Torah readings. In certain Sefard prayer books you will still find interlinear Spanish. Our people have put themselves to all this awkwardness and difficulty and persisted in praying in Hebrew. My guess is that they will always do so.

A language has a genius. Some works translate well, others are untranslatable. Moliere is effective only in

French. Without knowing Arabic nobody has ever understood the Koran. Pushkin remains a possession of the Russian people, though the world has acquired Tolstoy. In general, the higher the charge of peculiarly national identity and emotion, the less translatable a work is.

The Hebrew Bible speaks with power in all the tongues of earth, but it sounds to nobody else as it does to the Jews. The Second Table of the Ten Commandments reads in Hebrew something like this: "Don't kill; don't be vile; don't steal; don't tell lies about others; don't envy any man his wife or house or animals, or anything he has." This sounds shockingly wrong in English. For the English genius, religion is solemn and stately; Canterbury Cathedral, not a shul. The grand slow march of "Thou Shalt Nots" is exactly right. Religion for the Jews is intimate and colloquial, or it is nothing.

Our liturgy, at least the classic part, is as colloquial and easy-flowing as the Torah. No adequate or even approximate translation of the prayer book exists (this situation is improving. -HW [1985]). The King James Bible serves as a mine for splendid translations of Psalms and other Scripture stretches. Even so, the change from Hebrew to English drastically alters the feeling. Translators of other sections use the King James diction—*wouldst* and *thou* and *vouchsafe* and *loving-kindness* and all the rest—and the tone and texture of our prayers nearly evaporate. People complain sometimes that praying in English makes them feel as though they were in a church. It is a just reaction. They experience the English genius, not the Hebrew.

All the same, half a loaf is assuredly better than none. If prayer in the current language resulted in a stronger and better-informed Jewry, whatever the watering down of meaning, every man of sense would be for it. But on that head we have twenty centuries of experimental evidence. Translated prayer has been, in the communities that have adopted it, a first step toward general loss of Hebrew. Loss of Hebrew has always been a long step toward loss of law, custom, and knowledge, and toward oblivion by absorption.

The fact is that Judaism always has worked by raising the small cadre of Jews to an extraordinary cultural level. The Jews to stay alive have had to know two or three languages. All of them have always had to read and write. It is everlastingly uphill work. Nothing else seems to answer.

During the war I led many services in English, and I have prayed in English. The Talmud surely is right to advise a man to pray in any language that he understands rather than to give up prayer because he does not know Hebrew. For all that, I do not imagine that I can spare my children the old Jewish task of mastering the holy tongue. This was true before the birth of Israel made it an important modern language. Goethe in his day, Edmund Wilson in ours, learned Hebrew to find out what the Bible was driving at. So in all times have many Christian scholars. We learn it to find out what our Torah is telling us and what we truly mean by our prayers. It is work. But any intelligent adult in a year can command the simple Hebrew of our liturgy if he wishes.

One worshipper becomes the prayer leader, or "messenger of the assembly." His special status lasts for one service, then he returns to his place. Anybody who can read Hebrew aloud correctly can take a turn at the reading stand. Most congregations use a prayer leader with a good singing voice—a cantor—on Sabbaths and festivals. The purpose is to add charm to the service and draw crowds. Of course, the piety of the cantor, who week after week leads the service, becomes a matter of concern. The mistaken impression thereby arises that a cantor holds some kind of religious office. He is, however, simply a Jew who knows Hebrew and can sing.

Every Jew has the same prayers to say. There is no intercession, no praying by proxy, and the most pious and world-revered rabbi has no different duties or offices to perform in worship than any thirteen-year-old boy.

The prayer leader keeps order by chanting the first and last lines of prayers. He repeats aloud the Eighteen Benedictions, with the congregation responding, "Amen." The task is an easy one. Many a neophyte who knows Hebrew goes confidently to the reading stand and leads the prayers, and nobody has anything but praise for him. After some attendance in the synagogue he realizes he is missing all the refinements of *nigun* (melody) and he becomes shaky and self-conscious. But in a lifetime of worship he will always encounter Jews who know nigun better than he does, so there is nothing for it but to plunge in and do his best. Any man who speaks the Hebrew loud and clear performs the office.

A truly necessary office is the *shamas*, or sexton. An expert in nigun, he is the factotum of the synagogue. He cares for the library, prayer books, and shawls, serves as prayer leader when no qualified worshipper appears, ensures a quorum of ten at all times, and reads the Holy Scrolls. A synagogue can get along without a rabbi and a cantor. But there must be a shamas, or some worshipper must do a shamas's work.

Some Major Variations

After the Roman dispersion, the Jews pulled together in two general communities: the Ashkenaz of North and East Europe, and the Sefard of the Mediterranean lands. They came to pronounce Hebrew differently. Their customs and their liturgies branched into distinct forms. This split exists today. Israeli Hebrew, for instance, is Sefard. It takes some relearning for a Jew who has the Ashkenaz education usual in America.

In New York there is an important Sefard congregation more than three hundred years old, founded by the first Spanish-Jewish settlers in the New World. In this charming Spanish-Portuguese Synagogue, at Seventieth Street and Central Park West, the Sefard liturgy lives on, different in rite and melody from the Ashkenaz worship that wholly surrounds it, and to some tastes more evocative and picturesque.

A number of the congregants bear old names of the original Spanish founders, whose families are a roll of honor in American history.

The interesting thing about Jewish worship, considering the long dispersion, the total absence of a governing religious body, and the difficulty of communications until recently, is not the variation in customs and text but the underlying sameness. One finds in the Talmud, written before the nations of Europe even existed, minute discussions of how to say prayers that Jews still recite today in Tokyo, Johannesburg, London, and Los Angeles. An American or British Jew wandering into a Sefard synagogue in Israel full of dark-skinned Yemenites will feel temporarily at sea; but once he is handed a book he can follow the service and say his prayers.

Utter silence during prayer is the rule, and words spoken during the Sh'ma and The Eighteen are especially serious violations. In the old-time East European synagogue this rule suffered partial eclipse.

The poverty of the ghetto forced synagogues to support themselves by auctioning off Sabbath and holy day honors. Calls to the Torah, opening of the Ark, and so forth, all went for a price. The auctions were colorful and exciting enough, but the mood of prayer naturally vanished while they went on. They were often quite long. During the reading of the Torah, moreover, it became the practice for each man, as he was called to his aliya, or reading turn, to announce his contributions to the synagogue's many charities. For each announcement he or his family received a public blessing by the shamas. Again, this was a process of high economic value, but not attuned to thoughts of the higher world.

These customs came to America with the great waves of Jewish immigrants at the turn of the century. They enabled many tiny congregations to survive and grow into majestic synagogues and fashionable temples. With the prospering of the Jewish community, these devices of desperation have gradually given way to conventional fund-raising. The auction atmosphere of the Torah-reading time, and the exodus of sidewalk gossipers during this part of the service, are only memories now. There has been a fairly effective restoration of the rule of silence.

I would not give up for anything, all the same, my remembrance of the mournful auction chant of the shamas: "*Finif Tollar um shlishi!* Five dollars for the third reading!" Nor do I want to forget the historic auction one Yom Kippur afternoon nearly forty years ago, in a synagogue in a Bronx cellar, when my father outbid men with far more money (though they were all poor struggling immigrants) for the reading of the Book of Jonah. One by one the competitors dropped out as the bidding went up past a hundred, a hundred twenty-five, to the incredibly magnificent sum of two hundred dollars, bid in one devastating leap by my father. I can still hear the crash of the sexton's palm on the table, and his shaken happy shout, "*Zwei hunderd tollar um maftir Yena!*"

My father made this tremendous and costly beau geste because his own father, a shamas in Minsk, had had the prerogative of reading the Book of Jonah, and he was determined to keep the custom in the family. He did, too. In that synagogue nobody ever seriously bid against him for the honor again. To this day my brother and I read the Book of Jonah at Yom Kippur services wherever we can. We have done so in places as far apart as Chicago, Hawaii, and Okinawa.

The auctions are a thing of the past and it is better so, but they served a purpose. Children in such synagogues learned unmistakably what a precious thing a call to the Torah was.

Some Difficulties

The newcomer in a synagogue will of course feel strange and ill at ease; he will be put off by the matter-of-fact manner of many of the worshippers; he will find the process hard to follow, and he will be an exceptional person not to feel discouragement at first. But persevering attendance, especially linked with any kind of elementary Hebrew training, will in a short time give him back the key to the storehouse of Jewish prayer. Then when he wants to, he will pray in the measured and fine words of the tradition; at the synagogue if he can go there, at home if he cannot.

The difficulties of a newcomer are matched, possibly overshadowed, by the problems that face the pious. If the newcomer is not at home, the novelty at least excites his attention. The synagogue-goer is too much at home. The prayers are too familiar. Years of repetition have grooved the words into his memory. If he is not at pains to concentrate, they slide by like water.

The fact is, prayer is never easy. True prayer is as demanding—at least as demanding—as the carrying on of a business conversation or the writing of a letter. It purports to be a communication with a Listener. The child and the newcomer struggle with their unfamiliarity. Devout worshippers struggle with their overfamiliarity. All men of any training or any faith are put to the greatest mental effort, I imagine, to get at any real sense of talking to G-d.

That being the case—since so much praying is, by the limits of human nature, doomed to fall short of what it sets out to be—the question arises, Is not prayer three times a day, in forms long fixed, mere empty machinery? It might be so, perhaps, except that the synagogue always remains what it was in origin: a study hall. One learns worship by worshipping or by trying to—there is absolutely no other way. The natural outpouring of the heart in moments of crisis is not, as the romantic would imagine, prayer at its best. Those who have been through such experiences know that they find themselves reduced to incoherent, shamefaced stammering. Improvised prayer is honored in Judaism, and some inspired improvisations have entered the liturgy. The fixed prayers are the base for a man to stand on, in everyday devotion and in extremity.

Daily prayer, at the very least, is a review of one necessary instrument of the good life as Judaism knows it. It is a duty done, a link in the chain going back to Abraham's acknowledgment of One G-d, a link we add as G-d adds a new day to time. And there is no such thing as wholly absent, wholly mechanical prayer. A glint of the light in the words and the thoughts of the Jewish liturgy falls at some instant, at several instants, into the mind of the most preoccupied worshipper. At least he is there, praying to G-d, so that the glints can come.

Perhaps for saints and for truly holy men fully conscious prayer is really an everyday thing. They live, in that case, in clarity that plain people do not know. For the ordinary worshipper, the rewards of a lifetime of faithful praying come at unpredictable times, scattered through the years, when all at once the liturgy glows as with fire. Such an hour may come after a death, or after a birth; it may strike after a miraculous deliverance, or on the brink of evident doom; it may flood the soul at no marked time, for no marked reason. It comes, and he knows why he has prayed all his life.

This Is My G-d: The Jewish Way of Life (Garden City, N.Y.: Doubleday & Co., Inc., 1959), pp. 92–108

PRAYER: OBLIGATION OR INSPIRATION

BY RABBI ELI SILBERSTEIN

It is dawn in Jerusalem. The light is clear. A bent woman lays her head upon the stones; the men are draped in a sea of undulating black and white prayer shawls. The morning service has begun.

Prayer is arguably the most powerful image of genuine religious experience. A theme richly developed in the sacred literature, the *Zohar* goes so far as to refer to prayer as the "spinal cord" of Judaism, for it suffuses our religious practice with life and movement, and gives structure to our spiritual development. *Kavanah*, intense mental concentration, is central to the prayer experience. The word for praying in Hebrew, *lehitpallel*, can also be translated as the reflexive form of the word *pillel*, meaning "self-reflection." Furthermore, the Torah refers to prayer as a service of the heart—not of the mouth. The rabbis teach that,[1] "Prayer without *kavanah* is like a body without a soul." Contemplation not only enhances prayer but is its most essential component.

Given the great emphasis by the rabbis on praying with *kavanah*, the routine prayer of many Jews seems disturbing, even jarring. Wedging the *mincha* prayer in between business calls, as many Torah-observant Jews tend to do, makes prayer seem less a spiritual service and more a chore to be dispensed with as quickly as possible.

And yet, *halakhic* sources describing the legal framework of prayer seem to feed this attitude by focusing primarily on its technical structure. The Jew's obligation to pray at specified hours three times a day while adhering closely to the prayer book text seems antithetical to a practice ostensibly driven by deep inner spiritual seeking. The laws that focus on the physical decorum of prayer would seem to engender an artificial and pretentious piety, for few people can fully meet these *halakhic* expectations. For example, we are enjoined to recite the silent prayer standing, feet together, like a servant before a master. The prayer is recited silently, prefaced with the words, "My master, open my lips and my mouth will utter your praises." The form of the prayer assumes that we are cognizant of G-d's greatness, and stand before him in such trepidation that it is only by His Divine assistance that we are able to speak. Realistically, can the law expect the average person to pray three times a day in a way that genuinely matches this description?

Halakhah seems to codify for all Jews the outer trappings of a meditative experience that they are unlikely to achieve. While strictly codifying the content and frequency of prayer can appear stultifying, dictating the protocol seems to force behaviors that are faked and disingenuous. Perhaps an alternative might have been to allow these prayer conventions to emerge spontaneously from the supplications of the righteous, while allowing others to engage in rites that more genuinely mirror their spiritual level.

In contrast to the unyielding rules of protocol regarding prayer, the sages seem disinclined to demand that they be validated by deep sincerity.

Rabbinic flexibility in regard to *kavanah* is so generous that it appears to rob the notion of prayer of its very heart. For example, initially the law deemed a prayer valid only if the person uttering it reflected on the meaning of the words. But the rabbis realized that if they invalidated the prayers of those who were distracted during prayer, few people would ever fulfill their obligation. So they ruled that as long as one focused on the meaning of at least the first of the nineteen prayers, there was no need to repeat the silent prayer.[2] Later, rabbis realized that even this diminished standard was too demanding. So they decided that even in the absence of reflection on the meaning of the text, the prayer need not be repeated.[3] They

RABBI ELI SILBERSTEIN, 1959–

Scholar of Jewish law, philosophy, and kabbalah. Rabbi Silberstein lectures widely on many Jewish subjects with a particular interest in the intersection between Jewish law and Jewish mysticism. He is the founding director of Chabad at Cornell University and is the author of several JLI courses.

settled on a much more basic definition of *kavanah*, in which the individual had to be aware that he or she was engaged in addressing G-d. We find, then, Maimonides[4] arguing that one who does not bear in mind that he is "standing before the Divine presence and beseeching him" is not considered to have prayed.[5] In his view, one's prayers are *halakhically* valid even if they are said without reflecting on the content. It is sufficient to be aware that one is engaged in prayer.

But normative Jewish practice does not seem to demand even this much-diminished standard.[6] For example, a number of Talmudic sages noted that they prayed on occasion while being distracted by surrounding sights.[7] The implication of these statements is that while this was not an ideal situation, the prayers were not deemed invalid.

Further evidence for the validity of distracted prayer can be found in the discussion of the laws regarding the recitation of the Shema. The Code of Jewish Law asks what is to be done if one is reciting the *Shema* and has reached the word "*ukshartam*" which appears twice in the text. It is imperative that each word of the *Shema* be articulated. But in this case, the supplicant, having been distracted in his prayers, is not sure whether he has reached the second instance of *ukshartam*, or whether he is only up to the first instance. Such thoughtlessness during the recitation of the *Shema* would seem to render the prayer unacceptable. Yet the law only requires that he assume that he is up to the first instance and that he continue from that point on, in order to ensure that no word of the prayer is missed.[8] This law derives from a narrower criterion than that of Maimonides (because the awareness that one is addressing G-d would never result in the dilemma of distracted prayers) and establishes a minimal requirement of *kavanah*. The definition of *kavanah* that seems to be operative in this case is that the supplicant started his prayer with the intention of fulfilling his obligation. So long as this initial thought is present, the prayer is valid.[9]

While prayer has the potential of embodying the most sublime religious dimensions, it also appears to be, in its *halakhic* formulation, an act more concerned with procedural technicality than spiritual contemplation.

The traditional notion of prayer, then, seems almost paradoxical in nature. While on the one hand it has the potential of embodying the most sublime religious dimensions, allowing us to "talk" with G-d, it also appears to be, in its *halakhic* formulation, an act more concerned with procedural technicality than spiritual contemplation. This perceived dichotomy between the legal and the spiritual is rooted in a common misconception about the nature of prayer. We view its reflective, emotional aspects as its heart. In fact, however, the mitzvah of prayer does not call upon us to undertake great spiritual journeys, and as such, a spiritual experience will not necessarily translate to a communication with G-d; it may be uplifting, but it is ultimately personal and subjective in nature. The essence of prayer is that it is an actual encounter between mortals and an infinite G-d.

Maimonides illustrates this distinction between a subjective and an objective encounter with G–d in his discussion of the nature of prophecy. Philosophers of the time argued that prophecy was the inevitable result of spiritual training, much as current practitioners of meditation claim to achieve spiritual enlightenment as a result of their ability to induce a state of heightened mental awareness. Maimonides disagrees with this view. While a certain mental frame of mind is a prerequisite for receiving prophecy, he believes that actual prophecy occurs only when G–d initiates this process by choosing to grace the prophet with revelation.[10] Similarly, the most notable aspect of prayer, as defined by Maimonides,[11] is that G-d commands us to appear before Him and to address Him. When we pray, it is our response to a genuine G–dly summons.

Prayer becomes a possible vehicle to connect the human with the Divine only because G–d has established it as the medium for this purpose, and not because of the individual's creative initiative. The holiest saint and the most ordinary of individuals, insofar as they both respond to the summons by "showing up" and uttering the words of the prayer text, are equally engaged in an encounter with G-d. *Kavanah*, then, does not constitute prayer itself, nor is it a means to the actualization of the prayer encounter. Rather, it is the result of the degree to which one is conscious that a meeting with G-d is in progress. To fully appreciate the nature of what transpires during this encounter, the individual must devote all of his emotional and intellectual energy. An appropriate reflection, according to Maimonides, includes extensive meditation on the endless greatness of G-d on the one hand, and the utter insignificance—by comparison—of the human being, on the other. The degree of appreciation for the prayer opportunity will be commensurate with the effort and inclination to engage in such meditation. Those with lesser spiritual qualities will appreciate prayer as an opportunity to ask G-d for one's physical and material needs. Those with greater meditative capacity will be thankful for the privilege to connect with the Divine. Judaism regards as reprehensible the absence of *kavanah* during prayer not because the prayer becomes invalid, but, on the contrary, because an encounter between human and G-d is in progress regardless of the degree of *kavanah* or lack thereof. Thoughtless prayers show disregard for the presence of the One being addressed, and are therefore offensive to G–d.

This aspect of Jewish prayer is well illustrated in a Talmudic anecdote about a sage in the times of Roman rulership over Israel.[12] The sage was traveling and when it was time for *mincha*, he stopped at the side of the road to pray. A Roman officer passed by and greeted the sage, but the sage did not respond. The officer waited until the sage finished his prayers and then said, "Why did you not respond to my greeting? As an officer of the crown, I have the power to kill you."

The sage responded, "If you were standing before the Roman emperor, and a fellow officer came to greet you, would you return the greeting?"

"I would not," replied the officer.

"And what punishment would you receive if you did respond to your friend's greeting while standing before the king?"

"Decapitation!" answered the officer.

"If the offense, when committed against a mortal king is so serious, imagine the gravity of this offense when committed against the immortal King of Kings!" concluded the sage.

The Roman official accepted this explanation, and cordially sent the sage on his way.

The story appears to make a rather obvious point. The officer knew that the sage was not ignoring him to be spiteful. Undoubtedly, he also knew that prayer constitutes communication between man and G-d. Why then, the analogy of the officer standing before a human ruler? If the officer respected prayer, he should not have become enraged at the sage's failure to return his greeting. If, on the other hand, he did not appreciate the concept, what additional insight did the words of the sage offer?

While the officer was aware of the sage's preoccupation with prayer, he perceived it as an arbitrary exercise—one that he ought to have abandoned in the face of what he understood to be a real encounter with the king's officer. The sage's words helped the officer understand that his prayers were no less an objective encounter with G-d than his meeting with the officer; just as the officer would not respond to a friend's greeting while standing before the Emperor, the sage could certainly not interrupt his audience with G-d to greet the officer.

The idea of prayer as an encounter with G–d demands a high degree of spiritual awareness, as the preceding story illustrates. By the same token, it highlights the indisputable spiritual value even of cursory prayers.

This contrast is wonderfully illustrated in a story about Rabbi Levi Yitzchak of Berditchev, known for his great love for every Jew, and his ability to positively interpret even their most blatantly negative behaviors.

R. Levi Yitzchak once saw a wagon driver leaving the synagogue in the middle of the service to grease the wheels of his wagon in preparation for an important journey. The man, apparently pressed for time, did not bother to take off his *tallit* and *tefillin* but rather continued to utter the words of prayer while greasing his wheels. When R. Levi Yitzchak saw this, he raised his eyes heavenward and said, "You see, Master of the Universe, how precious are Your people! This man loves you so much that he serves you not only inside the synagogue but also outside when he greases his wagon!"

To be sure, R. Levi Yitzchak was not endorsing the wagon driver's deplorable way of praying. What redeeming good did he perceive in this Jew's behavior to have praised him thus?

It is true that by his behavior, the wagon driver showed greater concern for his business than for engagement in prayer. At the same time, however, he was absolutely unwilling to abandon his spiritual obligations. The wagon driver's sensitivity of this awareness, so well illustrated by his contradictory behavior, was precious to R. Levi Yitzchak.

Rabbi Dov Ber, the Maggid of Mezerich, embraced the Chasidic tradition late in life. Previously, he devoted most of his day to Torah study, but from that point on he began to spend the better part of his day in devotional prayer. After many years, he met up with a friend from his youth who expressed surprise at Rabbi Dov Ber's new routine.

"Why does it take you so long to *daven*?" he asked. "I also meditate on the spiritual significance of prayer as described by the kabbalists, but I manage to finish in a much shorter amount of time."

"Tell me," said the Maggid, "How do you earn your living?"

"Actually most of the year, my wife runs a fabric stand, and I am able to devote almost all of my time to study. Once a year, I take off three weeks to travel to the fair in Leipzig, and there I buy the goods that she will need for the year."

"Why three weeks?" probed the Maggid. "I can trace the road to Leipzig in my mind in just a few moments."

"Come now," retorted his friend. "If you want to bring back merchandise, it is not enough to think about the route. You have to actually make the trip."

"Then you can understand why it takes me so long to *daven*," concluded the Maggid. "It is not enough to simply think about the mystical effects of an encounter with the Divine. To actually go there takes more time."

The words of the Maggid illuminate the Chasidic perspectives regarding prayer. It is not about conducting a mental exercise. It is about living a reality. And in the face of these words, we can imagine the Maggid's response to those who would question the value of *davening* a *mincha* by rote and then rushing back to business. He might well have said, "So what if your mind is a million miles away? You can still get to Leipzig, so long as you get on the train and make the trip."

Reprinted with permission of the author

Endnotes

1 See Rabbi Y. Emden's introduction to his Siddur; Tanya Ch. 38.
2 Berakhot 34b.
3 Tur, Orach Chaim 101.
4 Mishne Torah Hilkhot Tefilla 4:16.
5 See Chidushei Rabbi Chaim Halevi on Maimonides.
6 See Teshuvot Ubiurim p. 38.
7 Talmud Yerushalmi, Berakhot 1:4 Tosafot Rosh Hashana 16b. See Teshuvot Be'er Sheva for a different interpretation. Also see Chatam Sofer al HaTorah, parshat Shoftim.
8 See Rabbi Shlomo Zalman Auerbach in Minhat Shlomo no. 3. While the recitation of the Shema is a religious obligation distinct from the commandment of prayer, the Sages appended it to the general service, and it is considered an integral part of it. The concern about the value of words that are uttered without thinking applies to all mitzvot which involve speech. See Minhat Shlomo.
9 By this account, someone spontaneously singing the Shema while driving would not fulfill the prayer obligation because they did not engage in song in order to pray. The mere mouthing of the worlds in this context would be insufficient. However, if they intentionally initiated that same song while driving for the purpose of fulfilling their obligation and continued with the same level of rote chanting, they would not be required to repeat the prayers.
10 Guide to the Perplexed, vol. 2 ch. 32.
11 Hilkhot Tefillah 1:1.
12 Berakhot 32b.

Lesson 2

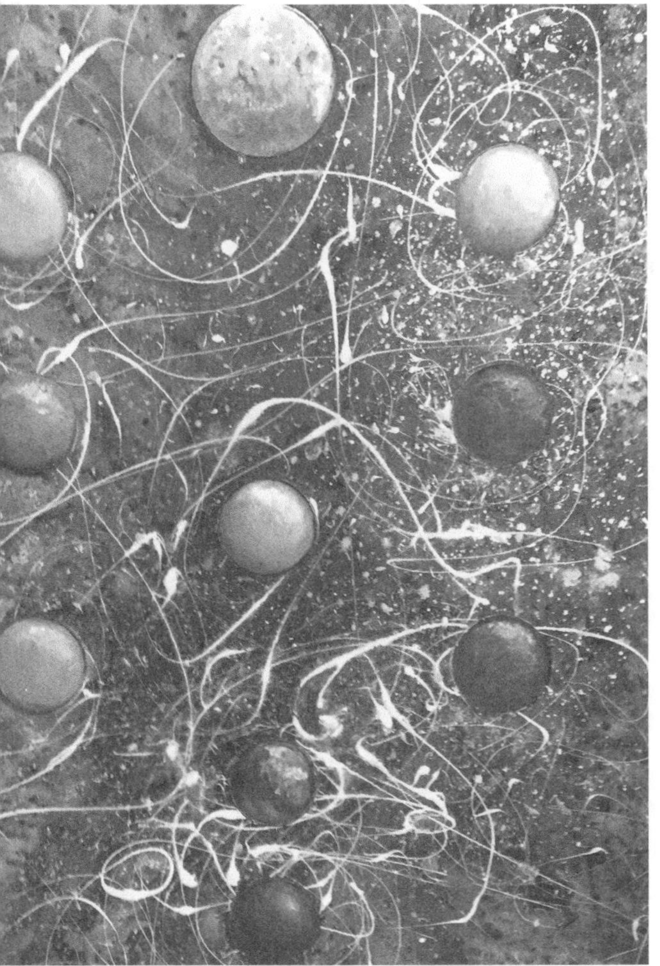

Sefirot (Revealed Symphony II), Fabian Lijtmaer, acrylic and mixed media on canvas, United States.

G-D PLANS AND MAN DEMANDS

UNDERSTANDING THE MECHANICS OF PETITION

Making personal requests of G-d sounds like trying to change G-d's decisions. Can we do that? This lesson explores the profound mystical workings of prayer, uncovering a complex process that G-d employs to orchestrate the minute details of this world, along with the means of effecting practical change. It guides us to the most beneficial state of mind during prayers and explains why an infinite G-d is waiting for us to pray for our mortal needs.

Exercise 2.1

List two recent occasions during which you prayed that something change.

1	
2	

How comfortable are you with praying to G-d for something you need?

Very comfortable	Comfortable	Ambivalent	Uncomfortable

"The Inner Dynamics of Prayer," by ***Rabbi Dr. Immanuel Schochet:***

MYJLI.COM//PRAYER

QUESTIONS FOR DISCUSSION

1 Hasn't G-d already determined my fate? Can my prayer modify G-d's decision?

2 If G-d is all-knowing, is He not aware of my needs without my informing Him?

3 Countless individuals benefit from many blessings in life without having prayed for them. Doesn't that indicate that praying for our needs is superfluous?

4 Many prayers appear to go unanswered. What, then, is the function of prayer?

5 If prayer is meant to be a spiritual exercise in transcendence, why do we taint this spiritual quest with petitions concerning material matters?

What's the point? G-d knows already! Can prayer change anything? ***Lisa Aiken, PhD****, and* ***Rabbi Yitzchak Breitowitz*** *respond:*

MYJLI.COM/PRAYER

TEXT 1a

REFA'EINU, EIGHTH BLESSING OF WEEKDAY AMIDAH

> רְפָאֵנוּ ה' וְנֵרָפֵא, הוֹשִׁיעֵנוּ וְנִוָּשֵׁעָה, כִּי תְהִלָּתֵנוּ אָתָּה. וְהַעֲלֵה אֲרוּכָה וּרְפוּאָה שְׁלֵימָה לְכָל מַכּוֹתֵינוּ . . .

Heal us, O L-rd, and we will be healed.

Help us, and we will be saved.

For You are our praise.

Grant complete cure and healing to all our wounds. . . .

TEXT 1b

BARECH ALEINU, NINTH BLESSING OF WEEKDAY AMIDAH

> בָּרֵךְ עָלֵינוּ ה' אֱלֹקֵינוּ אֶת הַשָּׁנָה הַזֹּאת וְאֶת כָּל מִינֵי תְבוּאָתָהּ לְטוֹבָה, וְתֵן טַל וּמָטָר לִבְרָכָה עַל פְּנֵי הָאֲדָמָה . . .

Bless for us, L-rd our G-d, this year.

And all the varieties of its produce for good.

And bestow dew and rain for blessing upon the face of the earth. . . .

Root, purpose, and practice of Jewish prayer: A four-part overview by ***Rabbi Lazer Gurkow:***

MYJLI.COM/PRAYER

TEXT 2

TALMUD, BEITSAH 16A

כָּל מְזוֹנוֹתָיו שֶׁל אָדָם קְצוּבִים לוֹ מֵרֹאשׁ הַשָּׁנָה וְעַד יוֹם הַכִּפּוּרִים.

All of our sustenance is allotted to us between Rosh Hashanah and Yom Kippur.

BABYLONIAN TALMUD

A literary work of monumental proportions that draws upon the legal, spiritual, intellectual, ethical, and historical traditions of Judaism. The 37 tractates of the Babylonian Talmud contain the teachings of the Jewish sages from the period after the destruction of the 2nd Temple through the 5th century CE. It has served as the primary vehicle for the transmission of the Oral Law and the education of Jews over the centuries; it is the entry point for all subsequent legal, ethical, and theological Jewish scholarship.

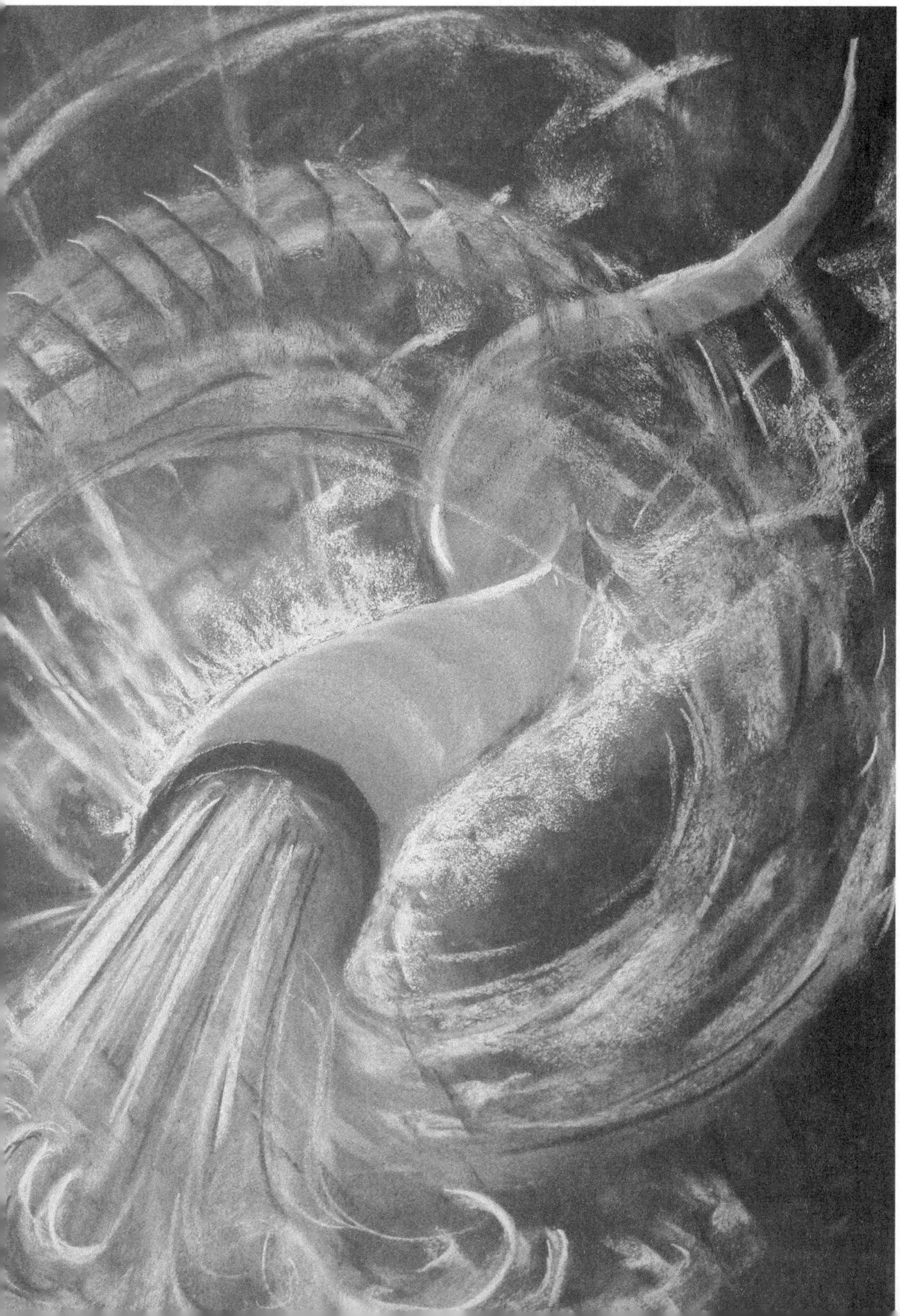

The Shofar Blast, Lillian Jane (Jay) Neal, painting.

TEXT 3a

RABBI MENACHEM MENDEL OF LUBAVITCH, *DERECH MITSVOTECHA* 106B

שֶׁבְּרֹאשׁ הַשָּׁנָה וְיוֹם הַכִּיפּוּרִים נִמְשַׁךְ חַיּוּת כְּלָלִי מֵאֵין סוֹף בָּרוּךְ הוּא לְהַחֲיוֹת הָעוֹלָמוֹת עַל שָׁנָה זוּ . . . הִנֵּה הַחֶסֶד הַזֶּה . . . הֲרֵי הוּא מְרוֹמָם וְנִשְׂגָּב מַעֲלָה מַעְלָה מֵהַשְׁפָּעַת טוֹבוֹת גַּשְׁמִיִּים שֶׁבָּעוֹלָם הַזֶּה כְּמוֹ בָּנֵי חַיֵּי וּמְזוֹנֵי, וּבִכְלָלָם כָּל הַטּוֹבוֹת גַּשְׁמִיּוֹת שֶׁהֵם טוֹבוֹת בָּעוֹלָם הַזֶּה. כִּי הֲרֵי . . . הַטּוֹב אֲשֶׁר הוּא לְמַעְלָה בַּאֲצִילוּת הוּא לְהַשְׁפִּיעַ גִילוּי אֱלֹקוּת . . . וְשֶׁגָבַהּ מַדְרֵיגַת טוֹב זֶה מֵהֱיוֹת נִמְשַׁךְ מִמֶּנּוּ עִנְיָנִים גַּשְׁמִיִּים שֶׁהֵם נֶחְשָׁבִים לְטוֹב בָּעוֹלָם הַזֶּה . . .

וְאֵין דֶרֶךְ לְהַמְשָׁכַת טוֹב וְחֶסֶד גַּשְׁמִי מִן חֶסֶד עֶלְיוֹן הַנִּזְכָּר לְעֵיל אֶלָּא עַל יְדֵי רִיבּוּי הַמְשָׁכוֹת וְהִתְלַבְּשׁוּת, שֶׁיִּתְלַבֵּשׁ הַחֶסֶד שֶׁבְּמַלְכוּת דַּאֲצִילוּת בִּלְבוּשִׁים . . . דִּבְרִיאָה יְצִירָה עֲשִׂיָּה, עַד שֶׁיִּהְיֶה מֵהַשְׁפָּעַת חַסְדּוֹ עִנְיָנִים גַּשְׁמִיִּים. וְיֵשׁ כַּמָּה וְכַמָּה הֵיכָלוֹת שֶׁדֶּרֶךְ בָּם עוֹבֵר שֶׁפַע הַחֶסֶד דַּאֲצִילוּת, עַד שֶׁמַּגִּיעַ בַּעֲשִׂיָּה לִהְיוֹת מִמֶּנּוּ הַשְׁפָּעוֹת גַּשְׁמִיִּים. שֶׁבְּעָבְרוֹ מֵהֵיכָל לְהֵיכָל, מִתְעַבֶּה הַשְׁפָּעָתוֹ לִהְיוֹת נִמְשַׁךְ מִמֶּנּוּ כְּפִי מַעֲלַת הַטּוֹב שֶׁבְּאוֹתוֹ הֵיכָל, עַד שֶׁכְּשֶׁמַּגִּיעַ לָעוֹלָם הַזֶּה, יוּמְשַׁךְ מִמֶּנּוּ טוֹב שֶׁלְּפָנֵינוּ בְּבָנֵי וְחַיֵּי וּמְזוֹנֵי, שֶׁבָּהֶם נִכְלָל כָּל טוֹבוֹת עוֹלָם הַזֶּה.

On Rosh Hashanah and Yom Kippur, an unspecified energy issues from G-d's infinite self to sustain the world during the upcoming year. . . . But this divine kindness in its initial state . . . is very distant from providing physical goodness in our world, like blessings of children, health, livelihood, and so forth. This is because . . . G-d's kindness in its pristine state in the highest spiritual world consists of a revelation of G-d . . . which transcends anything physical. . . .

G-d's kindness is converted into the material realm by passing through a lengthy chain of descents and concealments . . . through the various spiritual worlds

RABBI MENACHEM MENDEL OF LUBAVITCH (*TSEMACH TSEDEK*) 1789–1866

Chasidic rebbe and noted author. The *Tsemach Tsedek* was the third leader of the Chabad Chasidic movement and a noted authority on Jewish law. His numerous works include halachic responsa, Chasidic discourses, and kabbalistic writings. Active in the communal affairs of Russian Jewry, he worked to alleviate the plight of the cantonists, Jewish children kidnapped to serve in the Czar's army. He passed away in Lubavitch, leaving seven sons and two daughters.

until it can enter the physical realm. There are numerous and diverse chambers through which the energy must travel until it can reach our material world and assume the form of a physical blessing. As the energy passes through each chamber, it assumes a new identity and is converted to a form of goodness that is compatible with the parameters of that particular chamber. Finally, when it reaches our world, it is converted into tangible goodness that takes the form of family, health, livelihood, and all other matters that are considered positive in this world.

How does prayer turn our spiritual blessings into tangible benefits? ***Rabbi Yitzchak Schochet*** *explains:*

MYJLI.COM/PRAYER

Bereshit: Genesis (detail), Yehoshua Wiseman, painting, Jerusalem.

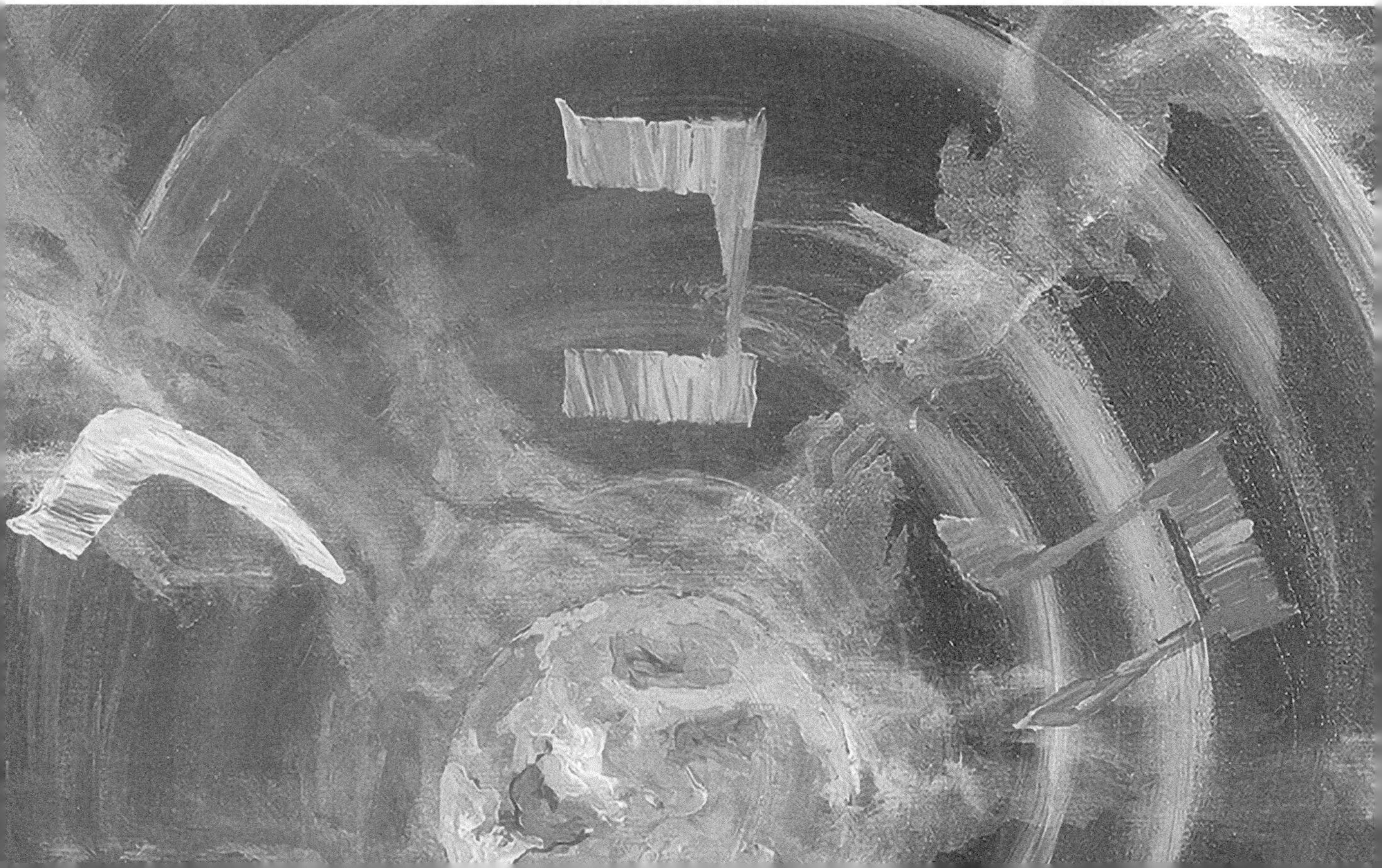

TEXT 3b

RABBI MENACHEM MENDEL OF LUBAVITCH, IBID.

וְעַל זֶה אָמְרוּ רַבּוֹתֵינוּ זַ"ל (ראש השנה טז, א) "אָדָם נִדּוֹן בְּכָל יוֹם", שֶׁבְּכָל יוֹם יֵשׁ דִּין הַאִם כְּדַאי וְרָאוּי הוּא הָאָדָם שֶׁיּוּמְשַׁךְ אֵלָיו מִן הַחֶסֶד הַנִּקְצָב לוֹ בְּיוֹם הַכִּיפּוּרִים טוֹבוֹת גַשְׁמִיִּים, דְהַיְינוּ שֶׁיֵּרֵד אוֹתוֹ הַחֶסֶד מִמַּדְרֵיגָה לְמַדְרֵיגָה עַד שֶׁיִּתְלַבֵּשׁ בָּעוֹלָם הַזֶּה. וּמְעַיְּינִין בְּמַעֲשָׂיו אִם הוּא רָאוּי לָזֶה, וְאִם לֹא, אָז יִשָּׁאֵר הַחֶסֶד לְמַעֲלָה, וְיִתּוֹסְפוּ לוֹ עֲבוּרוֹ טוֹב רוּחְנִי בָּעוֹלָם הָעֶלְיוֹן.

This is why the Talmud says (ROSH HASHANAH 16A), "A person is judged each day." Each day, there is a judgment to determine whether we are worthy on that day of having the kindness that was allotted to us converted into physical goodness by descending level after level until it reaches our world. If we are not worthy, the kindness that has been allotted to us remains in the spiritual realms, where we will experience it in the afterlife.

TEXT 3C

RABBI MENACHEM MENDEL OF LUBAVITCH, IBID.

וְזֶהוּ שֶׁמְּבַקְשִׁים "רְפָאֵינוּ", "בָּרֵךְ עָלֵינוּ" - רוֹצֶה לוֹמַר, שֶׁיּוּמְשַׁךְ מִן חֶסֶד הַנִּזְכָּר לְעֵיל טוֹב גַּשְׁמִי בָּעוֹלָם הַזֶּה מַה שֶּׁהָאָדָם צָרִיךְ, וְלֹא יִשָּׁאֵר לְמַעְלָה לְגַמְרֵי. כִּי אִם יִשָּׁאֵר לְמַעְלָה, לֹא יִהְיֶה לוֹ טוֹב בָּעוֹלָם הַזֶּה כְּלוּם.

This is why we pray for healing and for financial success. We are essentially asking that the kindness allotted to us be converted into the physical realm to meet our needs and that it should not remain in the spiritual realm, where it will have no relevance to us while we reside here in this world.

Grabbing goodness from Heaven's shelves? ***Rabbi David Aaron*** *explores:*

MYJLI.COM/PRAYER

Page corner detail from a 1475 N.E. Italy edition of *Arbaah Turim* (Jacob ben Asher, "Baal Haturim"), Florentine artists; Hayyim Barbut, scribe. Pen and ink on parchment, Sefardi semi-cursive script, unpunctuated. (London, British Library Collection of Illuminated Manuscripts)

TEXT 4

TALMUD, CHULIN 60B

כְּתִיב (בְּרֵאשִׁית א, יב) "וַתּוֹצֵא הָאָרֶץ דֶּשֶׁא" בִּתְלָת בְּשַׁבַּתָּא. וּכְתִיב (שָׁם, ב, ה) "וְכֹל שִׂיחַ הַשָּׂדֶה טֶרֶם יִהְיֶה בָאָרֶץ" בְּמַעֲלֵי שַׁבַּתָּא.

מְלַמֵּד, שֶׁיָּצְאוּ דְשָׁאִים וְעָמְדוּ עַל פֶּתַח קַרְקַע, עַד שֶׁבָּא אָדָם הָרִאשׁוֹן וּבִקֵּשׁ עֲלֵיהֶם רַחֲמִים וְיָרְדוּ גְשָׁמִים וְצָמְחוּ.

לְלַמֶּדְךָ, שֶׁהַקָּדוֹשׁ בָּרוּךְ הוּא מִתְאַוֶּה לִתְפִלָּתָן שֶׁל צַדִּיקִים.

Regarding the third day of Creation, the Torah states (GENESIS 1:12), "The earth sprouted forth vegetation." However, the opposite is implied in the Torah's description of the sixth day of Creation: "No shrub of the field had yet grown on the land" (IBID. 2:5).

This informs us that on the third day, the vegetation only grew slightly, remaining this way until Adam arrived [on the sixth day] and prayed for G-d's mercy—as a result of which, rain fell and the vegetation grew.

This teaches us that G-d greatly desires the prayers of the righteous.

QUESTION FOR DISCUSSION

Text 4 indicates that prayers of petition are uniquely desired by G-d (more than other forms of prayer). Why might that be the case?

TEXT 5

RABBI SHNE'UR ZALMAN OF LIADI, *LIKUTEI TORAH,* KORACH, P. 55D

הַשְׁפָּעַת חֶסֶד זֶה הוּא מִתְעַכֵּב וְשׁוֹהֶה עַד שֶׁנִּמְשַׁךְ וּבָא לְמַטָּה, שֶׁהֲרֵי בְּכָל הִשְׁתַּלְשְׁלוּת מֵהֵיכָל לְהֵיכָל הוּא עַל יְדֵי מִשְׁפָּט אִם רָאוּי הוּא שֶׁיּוּמְשַׁךְ הַהַשְׁפָּעָה לְמַטָּה . . .

וְעַיֵּין בְּרַבּוֹת פָּרָשָׁה וָאֶתְחַנַּן (ב, יז): יֵשׁ תְּפִלָּה שֶׁנַּעֲנֵית לְאַרְבָּעִים יוֹם כּוּלִי, וְיֵשׁ תְּפִלָּה שֶׁנַּעֲנֵית לְעֶשְׂרִים יוֹם כּוּלִי, וְיֵשׁ תְּפִלָּה שֶׁנַּעֲנֵית לְיוֹם אֶחָד כּוּלִי.

The transmission of this kindness is often obstructed and delayed until it finally reaches our physical world. This is due to the judgments—repeated at each heavenly juncture—that determine whether the person is worthy for the flow to be permitted to descend to the next level. . . .

Indeed, the Midrash says (*DEVARIM RABAH* 2:17), "Some prayers are answered after forty days, some after twenty days, and others on that same day."

RABBI SHNE'UR ZALMAN OF LIADI (ALTER REBBE) 1745–1812

Chasidic rebbe, halachic authority, and founder of the Chabad movement. The Alter Rebbe was born in Liozna, Belarus, and was among the principal students of the Magid of Mezeritch. His numerous works include the *Tanya*, an early classic containing the fundamentals of Chabad Chasidism, and *Shulchan Aruch HaRav*, an expanded and reworked code of Jewish law.

TEXT 6a

II KINGS 20:1

בַּיָּמִים הָהֵם, חָלָה חִזְקִיָּהוּ לָמוּת. וַיָּבֹא אֵלָיו יְשַׁעְיָהוּ בֶן אָמוֹץ הַנָּבִיא,
וַיֹּאמֶר אֵלָיו: כֹּה אָמַר ה', צַו לְבֵיתֶךָ, כִּי מֵת אַתָּה וְלֹא תִחְיֶה.

In those days, Hezekiah fell terminally ill. Isaiah the prophet, son of Amoz, came to him and said, "This is what G-d says, 'Set your house in order, for you are going to die; you will not live.'"

Prayer at the Western Wall (detail), Tal Paz-Fridman, C-type photograph.

TEXT 6b

TALMUD, BERACHOT 10A

> אָמַר לֵיהּ: כְּבַר נִגְזְרָה עָלֶיךָ גְּזֵירָה.
>
> אָמַר לֵיהּ: בֶּן אָמוֹץ, כַּלֵה נְבוּאָתְךָ וְצֵא! כָּךְ מְקוּבְּלַנִי מִבֵּית אֲבִי אַבָּא: אֲפִילוּ חֶרֶב חַדָּה מוּנַּחַת עַל צַוָּארוֹ שֶׁל אָדָם, אַל יִמְנַע עַצְמוֹ מִן הָרַחֲמִים.

Isaiah responded, “The decree against you has already been issued.”

Said Hezekiah, “Son of Amoz, cease prophesying and leave! I have received the following tradition from my ancestors: ‘Even if a sharp sword is held against a person’s neck, do not refrain from praying for mercy!’”

TEXT 6C

II KINGS 20:2–6

> וַיַּסֵּב אֶת פָּנָיו אֶל הַקִּיר וַיִּתְפַּלֵּל אֶל ה' לֵאמֹר: אָנָּה ה'! זְכָר נָא אֵת אֲשֶׁר הִתְהַלַּכְתִּי לְפָנֶיךָ בֶּאֱמֶת וּבְלֵבָב שָׁלֵם, וְהַטּוֹב בְּעֵינֶיךָ עָשִׂיתִי. וַיֵּבְךְּ חִזְקִיָּהוּ בְּכִי גָדוֹל.
>
> וַיְהִי יְשַׁעְיָהוּ לֹא יָצָא חָצֵר הַתִּיכֹנָה, וּדְבַר ה' הָיָה אֵלָיו לֵאמֹר: שׁוּב וְאָמַרְתָּ אֶל חִזְקִיָּהוּ נְגִיד עַמִּי: כֹּה אָמַר ה' אֱלֹקֵי דָּוִד אָבִיךָ, שָׁמַעְתִּי אֶת תְּפִלָּתֶךָ, רָאִיתִי אֶת דִּמְעָתֶךָ, הִנְנִי רֹפֵא לָךְ . . .

Hezekiah turned to face the wall, and he prayed to G-d.

“Please, oh G-d! Remember now how I have walked before you truthfully and sincerely, and I did that which is good in your eyes.” And Hezekiah wept profusely.

Even before Isaiah was able to leave the middle courtyard [of Hezekiah’s palace], G-d told him to go back and tell Hezekiah, “So says G-d, the G-d of your ancestor David, ‘I have heard your prayers, and I have seen your tears; I will heal you. . . .’”

TEXT 7

THE REBBE, RABBI MENACHEM MENDEL SCHNEERSON, *SEFER HAMAAMARIM MELUKAT* (*TORAT MENACHEM* EDITION), 2, PP. 271–272

וְעִנְיַן הַתְּפִלָּה הוּא בַּקָּשָׁה מֵהַקָּדוֹשׁ בָּרוּךְ הוּא שֶׁגַּם בְּאִם לֹא יֶשְׁנָהּ חַס וְשָׁלוֹם הַהַשְׁפָּעָה גַּם בְּהַמָּקוֹר, וְלֹא עוֹד אֶלָּא שֶׁנִּגְזַר עָלָיו שֶׁיִּהְיֶה חוֹלֶה חַס וְשָׁלוֹם וְכַיּוֹצֵא בָּזֶה, מִכָּל מָקוֹם, תּוּמְשַׁךְ לוֹ הַשְׁפָּעָה חֲדָשָׁה מֵאוֹר אֵין סוֹף שֶׁלְּמַעְלָה מֵהִשְׁתַּלְשְׁלוּת.

דְּזֶהוּ שֶׁאוֹמְרִים בְּכַמָּה תְּפִלּוֹת יְהִי רָצוֹן, דְּפֵירוּשׁ יְהִי רָצוֹן הוּא שֶׁיִּהְיֶה רָצוֹן חָדָשׁ.

Even if no blessing has been allotted to us in the spiritual source of blessing—or worse yet, even if it has been determined in Heaven that something negative will occur, such as an illness, G-d forbid—our prayers serve as appeals to G-d to change our reality through generating an entirely new bestowal of Divine energy from His infinite self that transcends the entire spiritual system.

This explains the terminology included in many of our prayers, "May it be Your will." The implication of "may it *be*" is that we are asking for a completely new will to be issued.

RABBI MENACHEM MENDEL SCHNEERSON 1902–1994

The towering Jewish leader of the 20th century, known as "the Lubavitcher Rebbe," or simply as "the Rebbe." Born in southern Ukraine, the Rebbe escaped Nazi-occupied Europe, arriving in the U.S. in June 1941. The Rebbe inspired and guided the revival of traditional Judaism after the European devastation, impacting virtually every Jewish community the world over. The Rebbe often emphasized that the performance of just one additional good deed could usher in the era of Mashiach. The Rebbe's scholarly talks and writings have been printed in more than 200 volumes.

TEXT 8

RABBI SHNE'UR ZALMAN OF LIADI, *TORAH OR,* MIKETS 42B

הַתְּפִלָּה הִיא בַּקָּשַׁת יְהִי רָצוֹן - שֶׁיִּתְהַוֶּוה בְּחִינַת רָצוֹן, שֶׁכְּמוֹ שֶׁכְּבָר נִמְשַׁךְ רָצוֹן הָעֶלְיוֹן בְּחָכְמָה, הִנֵּה הַחָכְמָה מְחַיֶּיבֶת עַל פִּי הַתּוֹרָה . . . שֶׁהֶעָוֹן גּוֹרֵם יִסּוּרִים חַס וְשָׁלוֹם. אֲבָל עַל יְדֵי הַתְּפִלָּה יְהִי רָצוֹן, נִמְשַׁךְ רָצוֹן הָעֶלְיוֹן שֶׁלְּמַעְלָה מִבְּחִינַת חָכְמָה, וְשָׁם הוּא רַחֲמִים פְּשׁוּטִים, וְרַבּוּ פְשָׁעֶיךָ כוּלֵי.

Prayer is a request that a new divine will come into being, as we say, "May it be Your will." This is necessary because the current will that has already descended into the spiritual system of bestowal . . . corresponds to our merits and can therefore produce an outcome that we would wish to avoid. Our prayers, however, elicit a fresh divine will that transcends this spiritual system; they tap into a sublime source in which undiscriminating mercy prevails and where blessing is not contingent upon our actions.

My Old Village (detail), Leon Zernitsky, oil on canvas, Toronto, 2012.

TEXT 9

THE REBBE, RABBI MENACHEM MENDEL SCHNEERSON, *LIKUTEI SICHOT* 29, P. 187

בַּיי תְּפִלָּה, אַף עַל פִּי אַז תַּכְלִיתָה אִיז עֶס זָאל אוֹיפְגֶעטָאן וֶוערְן אַ שִׁינוּי בְּגַשְׁמִיּוּת, "שֶׁיִּתְרַפֵּא הַחוֹלֶה וְיֵרֵד הַגֶּשֶׁם מִשָּׁמַיִם לָאָרֶץ וְיוֹלִידָהּ וְיַצְמִיחָהּ", אִיז דָאס אָבֶּער אַ תּוֹצָאָה דֶערְפוּן וָואס מֶען פּוֹעֶל'ט אַ רָצוֹן חָדָשׁ כִּבְיָכוֹל בַּיי הַקָּדוֹשׁ בָּרוּךְ הוּא, אוּן **דָאס** קוּמְט בְּעִיקָּר דוּרְךְ כַּוָּונַת הַלֵּב פוּן מִתְפַּלֵּל, "שֶׁיְּפַנֶּה אֶת לִבּוֹ מִכָּל הַמַּחֲשָׁבוֹת וְיִרְאֶה עַצְמוֹ כְּאִילּוּ הוּא עוֹמֵד לִפְנֵי הַשְּׁכִינָה" (מִשְׁנֶה תּוֹרָה, הִלְכוֹת תְּפִלָּה ד, טז).

בְּשַׁעַת אַ אִיד אִיז מְפַנֶּה לִבּוֹ פוּן אַלֶע זַיינֶע מַחֲשָׁבוֹת וּרְצוֹנוֹת אוּן אִיז זִיךְ מְבַטֵּל כְּעַבְדָּא קַמֵּיהּ מָרֵיהּ צוּם אוֹיבֶּערְשְׁטֶען אִיז דָאס פּוֹעֵל, אוֹיךְ לְמַעֲלָה כִּבְיָכוֹל (כַּמַּיִם הַפָּנִים לְפָנִים) אַז עֶס זָאל זַיין אַ רָצוֹן חָדָשׁ, וָועלְכֶע אִיז נִיט לוֹיט דִי הַגְבָּלוֹת פוּן סֵדֶר הָעוֹלָם, בִּיז אֲפִילוּ נִיט לוֹיט דֶעם סֵדֶר וְהַגְבָּלָה פוּן תּוֹרָה, עֲשִׂיַּית רָצוֹן חָדָשׁ.

The point of petitioning G-d in prayer is to effect a change in the physical world—that the sick be healed, that rain fall and cause the crops to grow, and so forth. Such changes are the result of our eliciting a new divine will. We precipitate this fresh divine will primarily through our state of mind during prayer by "freeing the mind from all other concerns and seeing ourselves as though we are standing before G-d" (MAIMONIDES, *MISHNEH TORAH*, LAWS OF PRAYER 4:16).

When we free ourselves from all of our personal thoughts and interests and completely surrender ourselves to G-d, this moves G-d to respond in kind with a freshly minted will that disregards the limitations of nature as well as the limitations set out by the Torah.

TEXT 10

TALMUD, BERACHOT 34B

מַעֲשֶׂה בְּרַבִּי חֲנִינָא בֶּן דוֹסָא, שֶׁהָלַךְ לִלְמוֹד תּוֹרָה אֵצֶל רַבִּי יוֹחָנָן בֶּן זַכַּאי, וְחָלָה בְּנוֹ שֶׁל רַבִּי יוֹחָנָן בֶּן זַכַּאי.

אָמַר לוֹ: חֲנִינָא בְּנִי, בַּקֵּשׁ עָלָיו רַחֲמִים וְיִחְיֶה!

הִנִּיחַ רֹאשׁוֹ בֵּין בִּרְכָּיו, וּבִקֵּשׁ עָלָיו רַחֲמִים, וְחָיָה.

אָמַר רַבִּי יוֹחָנָן בֶּן זַכַּאי: אִלְמָלֵי הֵטִיחַ בֶּן זַכַּאי אֶת רֹאשׁוֹ בֵּין בִּרְכָּיו כָּל הַיּוֹם כּוּלוֹ, לֹא הָיוּ מַשְׁגִּיחִים עָלָיו . . . הוּא דוֹמֶה כְּעֶבֶד לִפְנֵי הַמֶּלֶךְ, וַאֲנִי דוֹמֶה כְּשַׂר לִפְנֵי הַמֶּלֶךְ.

Rabbi Chanina ben Dosa went to study Torah under the tutelage of Rabbi Yochanan ben Zakai.

Rabbi Yochanan's child fell ill. Rabbi Yochanan turned to his student and said, "Chanina! Pray for my son that he should survive!"

Chanina buried his head in his lap and prayed for G-d's mercy. The child recovered.

Said Rabbi Yochanan, "Had I placed my head in my lap and prayed all day long, I would not have been answered. . . . For I am like a minister before the king, whereas Chanina is like a servant before the king."

TEXT 11

RABBI SHNE'UR ZALMAN OF LIADI, *LIKUTEI TORAH,* BALAK, P. 70D

שֶׁעִיקַר הַמְכֻוָּון בִּתְפִלָּה הוּא שֶׁמְּבַקְשִׁים שֶׁיִּהְיֶה אוֹר אֵין סוֹף בָּרוּךְ הוּא שֶׁלְּמַעֲלָה מֵהִשְׁתַּלְשְׁלוּת בָּרוּךְ וְנִמְשַׁךְ לְמַטָּה . . . וְרוֹפֵא חוֹלֵי עַמּוֹ יִשְׂרָאֵל וּמְבָרֵךְ הַשָּׁנִים עַל דֶּרֶךְ מָשָׁל הוּא הַכְּלִי שֶׁבּוֹ מִתְגַּלֶּה אֱלֹקוּתוֹ יִתְבָּרֵךְ לְמַטָּה בְּגַשְׁמִיּוּת כְּשֶׁנּוֹתֵן חַיִּים וּבְרִיאוּת לְחוֹלִים וּבְרָכָה עַל פְּנֵי הָאֲדָמָה . . . נִמְצָא שֶׁכָּל בַּקָּשׁוֹת שֶׁבִּשְׁמוֹנֶה עֶשְׂרֵה הֵם כֵּלִים לְגִילּוּי אֱלֹקוּתוֹ יִתְבָּרֵךְ מַמָּשׁ לְמַטָּה.

The ultimate objective of prayer is that the infinite divine energy that transcends the spiritual system should descend into our world. . . . When we pray for the healing of the sick or for a good agricultural year, these requested outcomes are the vehicles through which this G-dliness becomes revealed to us in a physical way. . . . Likewise, all of our requests in prayer are essentially requests that we be able to experience G-d in our physical lives.

Dawid Hamelech (King David), Ludwig Meidner, charcoal and watercolor drawing, London, 1949–1952. (Jüdisches Museum Frankfurt, Germany)

Exercise for the Week

Tangible Relationship. This week, make a brief prayer in which you request something from G-d. Be mindful that your goal is not simply to have a particular wish granted, but that you strongly desire to witness G-d's hand in your life for the sake of forging a deeper, more personal relationship with G-d. Hopefully, your prayer will indeed be granted, and when that occurs, take a moment to reflect not only on the blessing you received, but on the ultimate gift of the Creator's overt presence in your life.

We'll discuss how it went during the next lesson.

KEY POINTS

1 On the Jewish New Year, G-d allots a specific measure of kindness for each person. This kindness, in its raw divine state, remains excessively distant from the kind of goodness we appreciate in this world. It must pass through a long chain-like series of descents and contractions to be converted into material goodness.

2 G-d designed prayer to be a tool that stimulates this conversion process.

3 There are various forms of prayer, but there is something special about our prayers of petition. These are fundamental to building a relationship with G-d, similar to the special closeness that emerges after a friend aids us in a crisis. Moreover, the act of reaching out to a friend for assistance is itself a powerful demonstration of an important bond. And when we turn to G-d for help, as opposed to any other purported power, we make a strong statement about our belief and connection with Him.

4 Prayer can also trigger a new divine will by bypassing the spiritual system to reach G-d Himself, Who transcends the spiritual order. Whereas Heaven's default decisions are largely merit-based, undiscriminating mercy prevails in G-d Himself as He transcends His spiritual system.

5 Overriding the spiritual merit-based system is possible because G-d mimics our actions. Brushing aside our natural instincts and desires to focus profoundly on relating to G-d—surrendering ourselves to His will and internalizing our dependence on Him—causes G-d to respond in kind: He brushes aside His default merit-based system of granting blessings and focuses on relating directly with us from His transcendent self.

6 A prayer for a material blessing is a request for G-d to reveal Himself within the context of our human experience. Actively seeking to experience G-d in our lives deepens our relationship with Him.

Additional Readings

WHY PRAY?

BY CHANI WEINROTH

A good friend of mine, whose lifestyle differs from my own, once asked me whether she could pose a frank question.

"Tell me, Chani, why do you still pray? You've been ill for eight years now, which means that you have been praying for eight years straight. Don't you see that it doesn't help? Besides, you've told me many times that no one has recovered from such an advanced stage of the disease. What's the point of praying when you don't believe it can help you?"

It must admit that she posed an excellent question.

Let me rewind to the earliest dawn of my prayer for recovery. It was born after that fateful meeting with a doctor who informed me I had no more than six months to live.

"This figure is based on statistics," he intoned, "but statistics are occasionally at odds with reality. In other words, I cannot guarantee that you will last even six months."

Those were his final words on the matter. With that, our meeting ended, but not my life. I began praying, and I am still here. So who can claim that it does not help?

Of course, what I prayed for has not exactly emerged. I prayed for health and I remain ill.

However, prayer is not a shopping list, where you compare your list with your purchases and mark off what you did or did not find in the store that day. Prayer provides something different altogether that is not necessarily measured by answers to our requests.

CHANI WEINROTH, 1983–2017

Mother, author, and lecturer. Throughout her eight-year battle with cancer, she wrote inspirational letters to her children in which she shared her life, wisdom, and faith. She published these letters under the title *B'Eretz Hachayim* and went on to publish two more books.

The Purpose of Prayer

What prompts us to pray in the first place? In the majority of cases, it is some kind of lack. He needs money? He prays. She needs a husband? She prays. They have no children? They pray. Health, shelter, and even pressure over a critical exam—these are the kind of matters that compel us to open our hearts in prayer. We pray that our wishes be granted.

If matters such as the above are indeed our motivation for praying, then what happens if our prayers are apparently not accepted—at least in relation to the contents of our prayers? We have set ourselves up for disappointment or even despair. It then becomes all too easy to view our prayer as a disintegrated illusion or like childish naiveté that has passed and been disproven. But this approach to prayer is a grave error.

I will not deny that to request something repeatedly for eight long years, only to have the request flatly rejected, is unquestionably disappointing. However, I would like to describe what prayer has indeed given me over these past eight years:

For me, prayer is not a means to achieving an end. True, I desire good health, and I certainly introduce this deepest desire into my prayers, but I view prayer as a goal in itself. I pray for the sake of praying. Requests for good health and so many other things for which we plead in prayer serve to invigorate our prayer experience, but they are not there for the sake of testing the reliability of prayer in terms of fulfilling someone's shopping list.

We do not always pay attention to the fact that our prayers are not formulated to read like a shopping list or the like. Take for example the prayer for healing. It begins, *refa'enu . . . ve-nerafe,* "Heal us, G-d, and we will be cured; rescue us and we will be saved. . . ." The blessing, however, is not yet complete. It continues, *ki . . . melech rofe ne'eman ve-rachaman atah*, "For You, Almighty King, are a faithful and merciful healer." I stand before G-d in prayer, but not merely for the sake of lodging a request. Rather, a prayer for something I lack is an opportunity to remind myself of G-d's sheer awesomeness.

If you have ever experienced the mitzvah of *hafrashat challah*, which involves separating a piece of raw dough before baking bread, you can relate to the kind of experience I am describing. But this experience is not restricted to the performance of a mitzvah. Anyone who has burst into tears due to pain or grief can testify to experiencing some sort of relief once the tears subside. Why is that? Has the issue been resolved? Did the problem disappear at the first sight of tears? Certainly not. But internally, something has been unloaded. There is a sense that someone higher is listening, and that the tears were not in vain. That feeling is more or less what I am delighted to experience after a good prayer.

Don't End!

I remind myself of two things before launching into prayer. First, G-d is not some kind of Santa Claus who we might ask for a present and he'll tuck it under a tree for us. In addition, G-d does not need our prayers. The prayers were designed to serve as gifts for us, not gifts for G-d. He wants us to pray, but He does not need our prayers. We are the ones who need our prayers.

If you have ever experienced a truly powerful prayer that caused you to feel exceptionally close to G-d, you know that in that blissful moment a tremendous fear creeps in, when you wonder, "What will happen when this prayer is over? I'm soaring and desperately wish to avoid landing. I want to stay close to Him for just a little longer."

Healthy Soul

Our prayer for healing lumps two concepts together: *refu'at ha-nefesh u'refu'at ha-guf*, "healing of the body and healing of the soul." I often wonder if it is indeed possible to differentiate between the two.

I used to volunteer at a service that provides healing for the soul. I remember the day I arrived at the center shortly after giving birth to my daughter Shirah. I was not feeling well, and it was difficult for me to rise from my seat. I noticed a sturdy, muscular young man who was being treated at the center. If asked to guess his profession, I would suggest boxing. I turned to him with a small request for assistance.

"Please do a favor and pass me that cup."

He stared at me with dull eyes, and without the faintest hint of cynicism, he replied, "I don't have the strength."

Believe me, I believed him. Despite my low hemoglobin following the birth I am convinced that I had greater strengths than the bulging muscles threatening to rip through this strapping young man's shirt.

If we encounter a person whose legs have been amputated, we do not tell him, "What are you waiting for? Try to walk! Don't panic, you can do it. . . ." By contrast, when we meet someone suffering from such severe depression that they cannot remove their noses from their blankets, we approach them illogically with a rational sounding demand, "Get up! Let's go! What is this nonsense? With a little bit of will, you can be up on your feet."

As for me, I focus ever stronger on my prayers for health of body and health of soul.

To my friend who asked, "Chani, why on earth do you still pray?" I respond:

I need to feel close to G-d. And this need is fully met through prayer. As for your inquiry, "Don't you see that it doesn't help?" I place my hand on my heart and declare in full sincerity that there are moments of prayer in which I feel so very close to G-d that I feel fully well and healthy. That is the honest truth. It is difficult for me to put it precisely into words, just as it is difficult to describe the precise taste of coffee to someone who has never tasted coffee in their lives. But one who tasted, knows.

Translated from *Olam Hafuch Ra'iti* (Weinroth Books 2016), pp. 46–49
Reprinted with permission of the author's family

DIVINE PROVIDENCE

BY RABBI JACOB IMMANUEL SCHOCHET

It is quite apparent that the acts of man will not necessarily prove successful. Man may do all that is necessary, and do so in a proper way, and still fail to realize his goals. It is likewise with prayer: one may pray properly, at the right time and with the right devotion, yet his request is not fulfilled.

Now the reason may be that G-d refuses to assent as a form of punishment or trial, or because the petitioner is not yet fully prepared and ready. Then, again, there may be some other, external impediment.

Another, and possibly most frequent reason, is that "No" may also be an answer, and in fact the best possible answer. The request may not have been assented to by Divine Providence for a good reason: Omniscient G-d knows that the favour requested is ultimately not in the best interest of the petitioner. For many of man's prayers are inappropriate and unreasonable. They are mere personal desires which we, thinking in terms of 'here and now,' imagine to be needs or essential for our welfare and happiness. Of this it has been said, "'The needs of Your people are many and their wit is scant': because their wit is scant, that is why their needs are many."

In this context we must consider two things. On the one hand, a man must always retain faith and trust in G-d, and hope that his requests (insofar that they are proper, reasonable, and suitable) will be fulfilled. This trust in G-d must be strong and sincere, to the extent that "even when a sharp sword is already on your neck, do not refrain from asking for G-d's mercy."

On the other hand, one must be careful not to fall prey to the sin of presumptuous calculation on prayer (*iyun tefilah*), that is, to expect that G-d will definitely accept and grant the request as compensation due for praying. To be sure, one ought to hope, wait patiently, "Hope in G-d, be strong . . . and hope in G-d" (Psalms 27:14). Nonetheless, one must also keep in mind and consider that (as stated) there are various reasons why requests may be refused. Thus there is no reason to despair. On the contrary: contemplation on this principle should lead man to "examine his deeds, as it is written, (Lamentations 3:40), 'Let us search our ways and investigate'" (Berachot 5a).

The proper attitude to prayer, and its most suitable content, therefore, would be some form of the prayer of R. Eliezer: "L-rd of the Universe! Do Your will in heaven above, and give repose of spirit to those that fear you below; and do what is good in your eyes. Blessed are You, G-d, who hears prayer." This means: "Do not attend to my words or to my requests to do what *my heart* desires or what *I* ask; for oftentimes I pray for something which is bad for me, because I imagine and think that it is good. You, however, know better than I whether it is good for me or bad. Therefore: *You* decide, and not I; do what *You* know is good—'do what is good in Your eyes.'"

"Salvation belongs to G-d" (Psalms 3:9). G-d alone, and not man, knows the way of salvation. Thus "Cast your burden upon G-d and He will sustain you" (Psalms 55:23). "Commit your way unto G-d and trust in Him, and He will act" (Psalms 37:5) to provide what is good and beneficial for you.

All Prayers Answered

It would seem that some prayers are not answered. This does not mean, however, that they were in vain or not effective.

First of all, the principal objective of prayer is not that it be answered according to wish. Thus we are

RABBI JACOB IMMANUEL SCHOCHET, PHD, 1935–2013

Torah scholar and philosopher. Rabbi Schochet was born in Switzerland. Rabbi Schochet was a renowned authority on kabbalah and Jewish law and authored more than 30 books on Jewish philosophy and mysticism. He also served as professor of philosophy at Humber College in Toronto, Canada. Rabbi Schochet was a member of the executive committee of the Rabbinical Alliance of America and of the Central Committee of Chabad-Lubavitch Rabbis, and served as the halachic guide for the Rohr Jewish Learning Institute.

taught that he who sets his mind in prayer on the anticipation of seeing it fulfilled (*iyun tefilah*), will suffer heartache, as it is written, "Hope deferred makes the heart ache" (Proverbs 13:12). The ultimate goal, therefore, is not the actual fulfillment of the request submitted, but the awareness "that in the whole universe there is none to whom it is fitting to pray other than G-d," and the recognition that man is altogether deficient "and only G-d can provide whatever he lacks."

The mental, emotional and spiritual results of prayer, as defined above, are more than sufficient to render *tefilah* worthwhile and effective.

To be sure, this does not mean that one should ignore the literal or common meaning of prayer, to petition G-d for all and any needs. On the contrary: when one sees that he prayed and was not answered, he should pray again and again, as it is said, "Hope in G-d, be strong and let your heart be valiant, and hope in G-d." Nonetheless, one must not lose sight of the essence and underlying premises of the principle of *tefilah*.

Secondly: Some objectives, as, for example, the Messianic redemption, require multiple prayers—both in terms of the prayers articulated as well as in terms of petitioners. Though the literal results of these prayers are not perceived at the time, each of them is and remains significant: each of these prayers is effective, albeit partially, insofar that each contributes to the necessary sum-total, the ultimate whole.

Moreover, these individual prayers are not only part of a whole, which takes time to complete, but they effect partial or 'miniature' responses of the very genus of the request submitted to G-d. For throughout the period of the *galut* there are many forms of 'miniature' salvations and redemptions.

Thirdly, and most importantly: Every single prayer is effective and answered, though not necessarily on the level of the petitioner. In the words of the Baal Shem Tov:

> *One must believe that as soon as the prayer has been uttered, one is answered for what has been requested. It may be asked, that at times the fulfillment of the request is not perceived. In fact, however, (the prayer has been answered, except that) it is in a manner hidden from the petitioner. For example, one may have prayed specifically for the removal of his distress, and this request was granted in terms of the world in general. (The petitioner's personal anguish may remain, but) that itself is actually for his own good, or to expiate some sin, and the like. When man's mind is set on awaiting the actual fulfillment on the specific, personal level, he brings materialism into the prayer, which in fact should be completely spiritual, for the sake of the* Shechinah *and not for the sake of the mundane. (The ulterior motive, therefore,) becomes a separating barrier.*

In another version, recorded by the Baal Shem Tov's grandson and disciple R. Mosheh Chaim Ephrayim of Sudylkov:

My master and grandfather said that all prayers are effective in the upper worlds, and sometimes in other parts of the earth. (Sometimes one may ask for one thing, and he is given something else; and sometimes the prayer's effects are limited to the upper worlds.) He based this on the verse, "When the exalted things are debased among the children of man" (Psalms 12:9)—i.e., "the things that stand in the pinnacle of the universe, yet people debase them." This refers to prayer which effects awesome things in the highest places of the worlds, yet people think that their prayers are not accepted and therefore treat them lightly.

For sometimes the effect of prayer is in the upper realms of the universe, and not below, and people, therefore, think that their prayer was, Heaven forbid, in vain. In truth, however, this is not the case. All prayers are accepted, but their effect is according to what omniscient G-d determines to be for the best interests of man and the world.

> *Excessive self-deprecation on the part of man, thinking his prayers to be of no avail, is in effect false humility, and may lead him astray. False humility causes man to think that his service of G-d, his prayers and Torah, is of no consequence. In truth, however, he must realize that he is a 'ladder set on the earth, and its top reaches into heaven': all his motions, his speech, his conduct and*

> *involvements, leave impressions in the uppermost realms. By thinking to himself, 'Who am I that I could blemish or correct anything above or below, that my doings will leave a mark,' he will be led to follow the inclinations of his heart, imagining that he has nothing to worry about.*

Thus we are taught, '*Da mah lema'alah mimach*'—know, that whatever is Above—it is all *from and through you yourself*! All of man's actions are of cosmic significance. All of man's actions elicit commensurate reactions.

Deep Calling Unto Deep (Brooklyn: Kehot Publication Society, 1990), pp. 89–96
Reprinted with permission of the publisher

"FOR YOU LISTEN TO THE PRAYERS OF EVERY MOUTH"

BY RABBI SHMUEL KAPLAN

The *Gemara* relates the following episode:[1] Rava observed Rav Hamnuna *davenen* for an extended period of time and said, "*Chayei olam*, everlasting life [earned by Torah study], is being forsaken for *chayei shaah*, momentary life [earned through *tefillah*]." The *Gemara* continues that Rav Hamnuna's conduct can be justified because there is a distinct time for prayer and a distinct time for Torah study.

The defense that the *Gemara* offers for Rav Hamnuna's prolonged *davenen* seems lacking. The essence of Rava's objection was that Rav Hamnuna was taking time away from Torah study and using it for *tefillah*. How, then, does the fact that *tefillah* "has its [own] distinct time" justify taking time away from the study of Torah, everlasting life, for the sake of *tefillah*, momentary life?

We must say that the notion of *tefillah* possessing "its distinct time" means not only time in the literal sense, but also that *tefillah* possesses its own intrinsic value, in addition to it being *chayei shaah*. This distinguishing aspect of *tefillah*—that *tefillah* has a distinct value of its own—places it on equal footing with Torah study, even though *tefillah* concerns itself with matters of *chayei shaah*, momentary life.

In *Hilchos Talmud Torah*,[2] the Alter Rebbe explains why the pious men of the earlier generations would spend nine hours a day in prayer:

> *They were not concerned with the fact that their Torah study would be neglected, for though Torah study is equivalent to [the observance of] all [the mitzvos], they were bonding their minds [during prayer] to the Master of All, blessed be He, with awe and with powerful love, cleaving to Him so genuinely that they would transcend their consciousness of the material world around them. And the mitzvah of genuinely cleaving [to G-d] with awe and love surpasses the mitzvah of Torah study and takes precedence over it, as it is written,[3] "The primary element [and starting point] of wisdom is the awe of G-d."*

This is what the *Gemara* means, that the time of *tefillah* is "distinct," i.e., that it has its own unique value.

RABBI SHMUEL KAPLAN

Chabad *shliach*. Rabbi Kaplan is the director of Chabad-Lubavitch of Maryland, overseeing its institutions and activities in more than 20 cities. A Torah scholar and a renowned orator, he is on the executive committee of Merkos L'Inyonei Chinuch, the education and outreach arm of the Chabad-Lubavitch Movement; a member of JLI's executive committee; and the chairman of JLI's advisory board.

An Interactive Relationship

The Torah is Divine intellect presented to us in G-d's words, and *mitzvos* are the Divine will presented to us through His commandments. In both these instances, the person involved in either Torah study or the performance of *mitzvos* is engaged in a Divinely initiated activity. *Tefillah*, on the other hand, although it, too, utilizes G-d's words, is not primarily a Divine matter. Rather, it originates as a human act: human intent, human emotion and human thought are being directed toward G-d. The fact that *tefillah* originates within man is indeed why it is termed "momentary life." In this respect, *tefillah* differs radically from other elements of Jewish observance, particularly the study of Torah. Hence, people might think that it possesses a lesser spiritual quality.

True, the Torah indeed originates in G-d's wisdom, while *tefillah* originates in man's thought. Nevertheless, *tefillah* is not merely man's words. G-d Himself is an integral participant in the act of *tefillah*. In the study of Torah and the observance of *mitzvos*, the individual is the main focus of the activity; it is he who is studying the Torah or performing the *mitzvah*. *Tefillah*, on the other hand, focuses not only on the individual doing the *davenen*, but equally—in actuality, even more than equally—on G-d Himself, Who is actively engaged in a person's *tefillah* by listening intently to the words of *tefillah* recited by the individual. Thus, we declare during the *Shemoneh Esreh*, *Ki Atah shomei'a tefillas kol peh*—"For You hear the prayers of every mouth."

Questions That Beg Answers

The idea that G-d, the Creator of all existence, listens to the words, thoughts and feelings that emanate from a lowly, physical being is nothing short of astonishing. Moreover, it is seemingly completely incomprehensible. Why should G-d listen to individual prayers? How is it befitting for Him to do so?

The questions are legitimate. Nevertheless, the fact remains that G-d chose to do so; *tefillah* is indeed a joint project between the individual and G-d. In order for the act of *tefillah* to take place, two things have to happen: Man has to pray and G-d has to listen. *Tefillah* is an act of partnership between man and G-d. If man alone is praying and G-d is not listening, then prayer has not occurred, no matter how sincere the *davener* may be. Only when a person prays and G-d hearkens to man's prayer is the act of prayer accomplished.[4]

A Different Set of Scales

In order to fully understand and appreciate this notion—that G-d is actively and intimately participating in our *tefillah* by listening to every single word we utter—it is necessary to examine the very beginning of Creation and existence and to understand how it came about. In *Parshas Bereishis*, the account of the origin of existence begins with the words, *Bereishis bara Elokim* . . .—"In the beginning, when G-d created. . ."

The understanding that Creation consists of G-d creating something entirely new—something that did not exist prior to its being created—leads to an entirely different understanding of G-d and His relationship to the world and all the beings that He created.

Viewing G-d as the Creator of all establishes that the relationship between G-d and His creations is one of *ein aroch*: a state in which no comparison can be made between Creator and created. Creation, by definition, involves bringing something into being from absolute nothingness. There can be no point of commonality or equation between the Creator and the created, since there can be no intersecting point between something and nothing—it can be only one or the other. Thus, everything we consider to be something, based on our definition of what it means to be or exist (i.e., confined to the limitations and defining factors of time and space), is in reality nothing when viewed through the infinite perspective of the Creator. What we perceive as "nothing," on the other hand, lacking as it does the dimensions by which we define being, is in actuality the ultimate being—the ultimate "something."

The implication of this, as regards Creation, is that nothing in Creation, however significant it may seem (and even the entirety of existence as a whole), has any value at all in comparison to the Creator. Thus, all of Creation combined or any individual entity is equally nothing before Him. Since the very measurements of time and space are utterly insignificant to G-d, anything that exists within these parameters cannot have any significance to Him either. It follows then that when G-d chooses to value something in Creation, it is not because of any value that the thing might intrinsically possess (because on His scales, it has no such value), but rather its value lies strictly in the fact that G-d chooses to give it value. Hence, whatever G-d chooses to value, however incomprehensible it may be why He made this choice, once He chooses to do so, His very choice—and His choice alone—provides it with value.

The classic example used to illustrate this concept is the relationship of numbers to infinity. In relation to one billion, one is but a billionth of a billion. Although minute in comparison to one billion, however, it still bears some degree of comparison, for if one were to be considered as nothing in comparison to one billion, then billions of ones would also amount to nothing, since a billion is composed of a billion ones. On the other hand, in relation to infinity, even a billion to the billionth power is absolute nothing. Moreover, one and a billion to the billionth power have exactly the same value in relationship to infinity: Both are equally nothing in relation to it. Therefore if an infinite being, for whatever purpose or reason, chooses to assign value either to one or to a billion to the billionth power, then it is that infinite being's choice, and his choice alone, that gives the number any value.

So, too, regarding the matter at hand: G-d's choosing to value the *tefillah* of an individual, or even one word of that *tefillah*, is what makes it valuable, even if we fail to see its value. The reason we don't see the value of a single word of *tefillah* is that we are viewing it from our limited perspective, and from that perspective, one lone word of *tefillah* doesn't amount to much. But from the perspective of G-d, one word, or an entire *tefillah*, or for that matter the entire universe, is equally removed from Him. When He decides that one word is indeed valuable, it truly becomes so.

A Wake-Up Call

The above explanation should bring about a radical change in our approach to our daily recitation of the words of *tefillah*. When we learn to appreciate how G-d listens intently to each and every word of prayer that we utter, that He cherishes and values each and every one of our words, we will never remain indifferent to the words we recite in prayer, words that G-d, Himself, values and cherishes.

This is best illustrated by a well-known story of the Baal Shem Tov:[5]

Once on Yom Kippur, the Baal Shem Tov perceived that there was a harsh decree in Heaven against a particular community. He exerted himself strenuously in *tefillah* on behalf of this community. When the time for *Neilah* arrived, the Baal Shem Tov's disciples realized the gravity of the situation and joined with their master in fervent prayer.

Hearing the anguished cries and intense prayer of the Baal Shem Tov and his disciples, the congregation was stirred to offer their own heartfelt cries for mercy. The time for the *Maariv* service had already arrived, and still the Baal Shem Tov continued his fervent *Neilah* prayer. The atmosphere in the *shul* reached new heights of intensity.

For several years, a young shepherd lad had been attending the *Yamim Nora'im tefillos* at the Baal Shem Tov's *shul*. He was completely illiterate. Throughout the services, he would stand and gaze at the face of the chazzan without uttering a single word.

As a simple shepherd, he was only familiar with various animal sounds, and the sound he most favored was the cry of a rooster. Sensing the intensity of the atmosphere, he too desired to pray. Crying out with the crow of a rooster, he then exclaimed, "G-d have mercy!"

Some of the congregants were angered at his crowing and demanded that he be silent. The lad replied, "I am also a Jew and your G-d is also my G-d." The old *shamesh* of the *shul*, Reb Yoseph Yuzpeh, calmed the angry congregants and told the lad to stay put.

A few moments later, the Baal Shem Tov and his holy disciples quickly concluded their *Neilah* prayer and the Baal Shem Tov's face was radiant with joy.

The Baal Shem Tov later explained in detail the decree that he saw in Heaven and how all his efforts and prayers were ineffective in averting the decree. And then, suddenly the penetrating sound of a rooster uttered by the young shepherd was heard on High and everything changed dramatically. The harsh decree was instantly abolished.

It is G-d Who chooses to listen to the words of prayer, and it is His choice that makes the words of *tefillah* so precious—even if they are just an imitation of a rooster's crow.

The Siddur Illuminated by Chassidus (Brooklyn, N.Y.: Kehot Publication Society, 2013), pp. 287–291
Reprinted with permission of the author

Endnotes:

1 *Shabbos* 10a.

2 The Alter Rebbe's *Shulchan Aruch, Hilchos Talmud Torah* 4:5.

3 *Tehillim* 111:10.

4 To be sure, this partnership is not a factor in determining the revealed *response* that *tefillah* elicits. This, of course, is entirely within G-d's domain. Even the most sincere prayers, to which G-d has surely listened, may not—in a revealed state—accomplish their objective; for example, a person may pray for the recovery of a loved one and the person for whom he is praying may not—Heaven forbid—recover.

5 *Igros Kodesh* of the Rebbe Rayatz, Vol. 4, Letter no. 1020.

Lesson 3

IT'S ALL HEBREW TO ME

MAKING SENSE OF LITURGY, ONE STEP AT A TIME

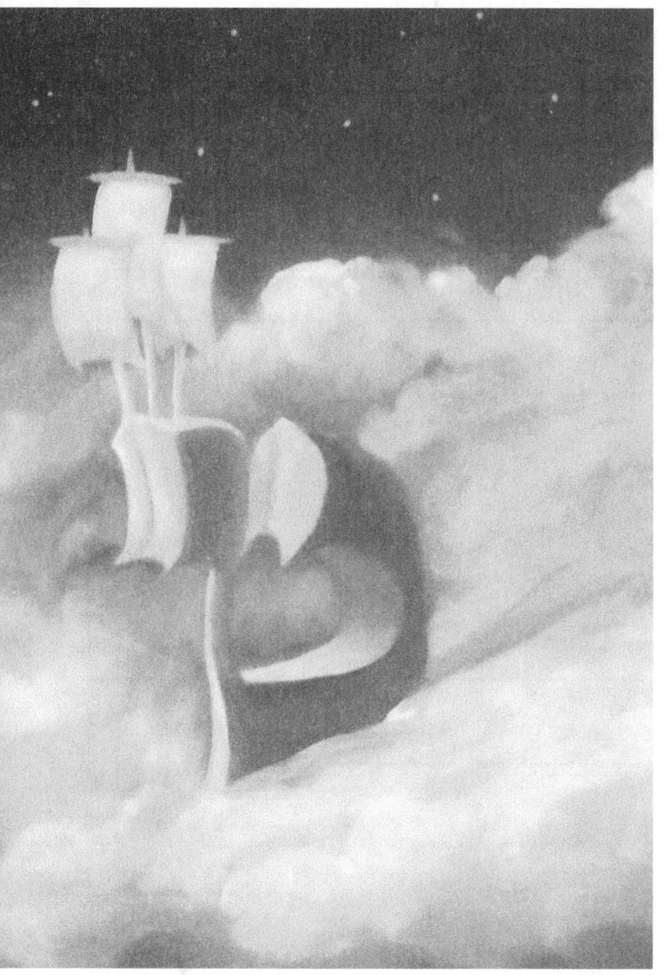

Purity, David Louis, Israel, oil on canvas.

Confusing. Random. Repetitive. To the uninitiated in the deeper dynamics of powerful prayer, the Jewish prayer book is bewildering. This lesson bares the brilliance and strategy buried in the sequence of its many verses and prayers. It sheds light on the structure critical for genuine and intimate human-to-G-d dialogue, resulting in a step-by-step guide to our divine relationship.

Exercise 3.1

Caption each of the five illustrations below.

TEXT 1

THE REBBE, RABBI MENACHEM MENDEL SCHNEERSON, *SEFER HAMAAMARIM MELUKAT* (TORAT MENACHEM EDITION), 2, PP. 266–267

הַהֶפְרֵשׁ בֵּין עוֹלָמוֹת הָעֶלְיוֹנִים לְעוֹלָם הַזֶּה: דְּבָעוֹלָם הַזֶּה נִרְגָּשׁ שֶׁמְּצִיאוּתוֹ מֵעַצְמוּתוֹ.

וּכְמְבוּאָר . . . הַהֶפְרֵשׁ בֵּין נִבְרָא וְאוֹר.

דְּאוֹר הוּא רַאְיָה עַל הַמָּאוֹר, דִּכְשֶׁאָנוּ רוֹאִים אוֹר, הָאוֹר עַצְמוֹ מַרְאֶה וּמְגַלֶּה שֶׁיֵּשׁ מָאוֹר, מַה שֶּׁאֵין כֵּן יֵשׁ הַנִּבְרָא הִנֵּה לֹא זוּ בִּלְבַד שֶׁאֵינוֹ מְגַלֶּה בּוֹרֵא, אֶלָּא עוֹד זֹאת שֶׁהוּא מַעֲלִים וּמַסְתִּיר עַל זֶה, וְאַדְּרַבָּה נִרְגָּשׁ שֶׁמְּצִיאוּתוֹ מֵעַצְמוּתוֹ (אֶלָּא שֶׁמִּצַּד הַשֵּׂכֶל מוּכְרָח שֶׁאֵינוֹ כֵּן).

The unique quality of our physical world, which distinguishes it from all spiritual worlds, is that the beings of this world feel as though they exist independently.

This can be explained . . . by analyzing the difference between "light" and "creations."

Light is a reflection of a luminary. The very existence of light demonstrates to the onlooker that there is a luminary.

Creations, however, are different. Not only do they not reflect their Creator; they conceal Him. Creations feel as though they exist independently. Only through logic can they realize this isn't so.

RABBI MENACHEM MENDEL SCHNEERSON 1902–1994

The towering Jewish leader of the 20th century, known as "the Lubavitcher Rebbe," or simply as "the Rebbe." Born in southern Ukraine, the Rebbe escaped Nazi-occupied Europe, arriving in the U.S. in June 1941. The Rebbe inspired and guided the revival of traditional Judaism after the European devastation, impacting virtually every Jewish community the world over. The Rebbe often emphasized that the performance of just one additional good deed could usher in the era of Mashiach. The Rebbe's scholarly talks and writings have been printed in more than 200 volumes.

TEXT 2

THE REBBE, RABBI MENACHEM MENDEL SCHNEERSON,
TORAT MENACHEM 5715:2, PP. 268–269

דְהִנֵה תְּפִלָּה הִיא בַּעֲלִיָה מִלְמַטָה לְמַעֲלָה, דְהַסֵדֶר בַּעֲבוֹדַת הַתְּפִלָּה הוּא שֶׁהַהַתְחָלָה הוּא מִמַּדְרֵיגוֹת נְמוּכוֹת בְּיוֹתֵר, וְאַחַר כָּךְ עוֹלֶה בְּעִילוּי אַחַר עִילוּי, עַד שֶׁבָּא לְמַדְרֵיגוֹת הַנַעֲלוֹת בְּיוֹתֵר. וּכְמוֹ שֶׁכָּתוּב (בראשית כח, יב), "סוּלָם מוּצָב אַרְצָה וְרֹאשׁוֹ מַגִיעַ הַשָּׁמָיְמָה", שֶׁהַתְחָלַת הַתְּפִלָּה הוּא מֵעִנְיָנִים נְמוּכִים שֶׁמוּצָבִים אַרְצָה, וְכָךְ הוּא עוֹלֶה בְּעִילוּי אַחַר עִילוּי בְּסֵדֶר וְהַדְרָגָה, עַד שֶׁבָּא לְעִנְיָנִים הַנַעֲלִים בְּיוֹתֵר, וְעַד שֶׁמַגִיעַ הַשָּׁמָיְמָה.

Prayer is a process of ascent. It starts from the lowest spiritual point and ascends, step by step, to the pinnacle of spirituality. This is like the ladder in Jacob's dream, "A ladder planted in the earth that reaches up to Heaven" (GENESIS 28:12). So, too, prayer begins in a lowly "earthlike" state and ascends gradually until it reaches the spiritual pinnacle, reaching "up to Heaven."

Figure 3.1

The Ladder of Prayer

STEP	STATE	SECTION OF PRAYER-BOOK
1	Unawareness	Before prayer
2	Acknowledgment	Modeh Ani – *Hodu*
3	Admiration	Verses of Song (*Pesukei Dezimrah)*
4	Association	
5	Intimacy	The Shema and its blessings
6	Beyond Self-Awareness	Amidah

Baffled by the structure and meaning of the prayers? A 6-part series by ***Mrs. Malkie Bitton:***

MYJLI.COM//PRAYER

TEXT 3

RABBI CHAIM ELIEZER BICHOVSKY, *GINZEI NISTAROT, OR NE'ERAV,* P. 21

הָרַב הַמַּגִּיד הָיָה שׁוֹהֶה בִּתְפִלָּתוֹ כַּמָּה שָׁעוֹת, וְהָיָה בִּסְבִיבָה שֶׁלּוֹ אִישׁ אֶחָד לַמְדָן וִירֵא שָׁמַיִם וּמִתְפַּלֵּל עַל פִּי כַּוָּנַת אֲרִי זַ"ל, וְלֹא הָיָה מַאֲרִיךְ כָּל כַּךְ וְהָיָה לוֹ לְפֶלֶא.

הָאִישׁ הַנִּזְכָּר לְעֵיל הָיָה עָשִׁיר, וְהָיָה נוֹסֵעַ פַּעַם בַּשָּׁנָה לְלַייפְּצִיג, וְשׁוֹהֶה כְּדֵי מִסְחָרוֹ וְחוֹזֵר לְבֵיתוֹ, וְיוֹשֵׁב כָּל הַשָּׁנָה עַל הַתּוֹרָה וַעֲבוֹדָה.

פַּעַם אַחַת, עָבַר לְרֶגֶל מִסְחָרוֹ דֶּרֶךְ מֶעזְרִיטְשׁ וְנִשְׁאַר שָׁם לִרְאוֹת הַתְּפִלָּה שֶׁל הַמַּגִּיד. וְנִכְנַס אֵלָיו וְשָׁאַל מִמֶּנּוּ, שֶׁהוּא מִתְפַּלֵּל גַּם כֵּן עַל פִּי כַּוָּנַת הָאֲרִי זַ"ל וְאֵינוֹ מוּכְרָח לְהַאֲרִיךְ כָּל כַּךְ?

שָׁאַל לוֹ הַמַּגִּיד, מִמַּה הוּא מִתְפַּרְנֵס?

וְאָמַר לוֹ, שֶׁיֵּשׁ לוֹ מְעַט סְלָעִים, וְנוֹסֵעַ פַּעַם בַּשָּׁנָה עַל יְרִיד וּמֵבִיא סְחוֹרוֹת הַיְדוּעִים לוֹ, וּמוֹכֵר אוֹתָם בְּעִירוֹ תֵּיכֶף, וּמֵהָרֶיוַח מִתְפַּרְנֵס.

שָׁאַל לוֹ [הָרַב הַמַּגִּיד], "וּמֵהֵיכָן תֵּדַע שֶׁהִרְוַוחְתָּ?"

אָמַר לוֹ, "אֲנִי כּוֹתֵב הַסַּךְ שֶׁהוֹצֵאתִי עַל הַסְּחוֹרָה וְהַהוֹצָאוֹת, וְכַאֲשֶׁר אֲנִי מוֹכֵר אֲנִי כּוֹתֵב כַּמָּה פָּדִיתִי, וַאֲנִי מְנַכֶּה הַקֶּרֶן וְהַהוֹצָאוֹת מִסַּךְ הַנִּפְדֶּה, וּמַה שֶּׁנִּשְׁאַר הוּא הָרֶיוַח".

אָמַר לוֹ הָרַב הַמַּגִּיד, "וְלָמָּה לְךָ לְבַלּוֹת זְמַן לִנְסוֹעַ עַל הַיְרִיד וְלָבוֹא? תִּכְתּוֹב עַל הַנְּיָיר הַקֶּרֶן וְהַהוֹצָאוֹת, וְתִכְתּוֹב הַפִּדְיוֹן, וּתְנַכֶּה הַקֶּרֶן וְהַהוֹצָאוֹת מִן הַפִּדְיוֹן!"

וְהִתְחִיל הַסּוֹחֵר לִצְחֹק, "וְכִי מִן הַכְּתִיבָה יָבוֹא הָרֶיוַח בְּלֹא נְסִיעָה וּקְנִיָּה? וּבְהֶכְרֵחַ צָרִיךְ לִנְסוֹעַ וְלִקְנוֹת וּלְבַלּוֹת זְמַן וְלִמְכּוֹר, וְאָז יוּכַל לִהְיוֹת רֶיוַח".

אָמַר לוֹ הַמַּגִּיד, "הַכַּוָּנוֹת הֵם גַּם כֵּן כְּמוֹ הַסְּחוֹרָה: אִם לֹא תִּהְיֶה קָשׁוּר בְּדַעְתְּךָ כְּאִלּוּ אַתָּה שָׁם, הוּא כְּאִלּוּ כּוֹתֵב הַקֶּרֶן וְהָרֶיוַח, אֲשֶׁר מִזֶּה לֹא יֵשׁ שׁוּם תּוֹעֶלֶת. אֲבָל, אִם תִּקְשׁוֹר נַפְשְׁךָ שָׁמָּה, וְיִהְיֶה שְׁהוּת לִקְנוֹת דָּבָר חֵפֶץ, אָז תַּרְוִיחַ בְּהַכַּוָּנוֹת. וְעַל כֵּן צָרִיךְ עַל זֶה שְׁהוּת זְמַן בְּעֵת הַתְּפִלָּה".

RABBI CHAIM ELIEZER BICHOVSKY
D. 1924

Chasidic philosopher and publisher. Rabbi Bichovsky lived in the Ukraine and moved to Israel toward the end of his life. He was a student of Rabbi Shemariah Noach of Babruysk and is noted for publishing many manuscripts of Chabad Chasidic philosophy. He served as bookkeeper and chairman of Colel Chabad, a charity in Israel established by Rabbi Shne'ur Zalman of Liadi in 1788.

The Magid of Mezeritch would pray for many hours, meditating on the kabbalistic themes explained by the Arizal. Nearby, there lived another learned and G-d-fearing man who also prayed with the Arizal's kabbalistic meditations. But this man's prayers didn't take nearly as long as the Magid's, making him wonder why the Magid prayed so slowly.

This man was a wealthy businessman. Once a year, he would travel to Leipzig to take care of his business affairs. Once finished, he would return home and spend the rest of the year engrossed in study and divine service.

On one of his trips to Leipzig, this man stopped in Mezeritch to observe the Magid praying. After the Magid finished praying, the man entered the Magid's room and asked him, "Why does it take you so long to pray? I also pray with the Arizal's meditations, but it doesn't take me nearly as long!"

The Magid asked the man, "What is your source of income?"

"Why Repeat the Same Prayers?" ***Rabbi Manis Friedman*** *responds:*

MYJLI.COM/PRAYER

Jewish Cart, Eduard Gurevich, Israel, painting.

"Every year, I travel to the business fair in Leipzig and buy merchandise. When I get back home, I sell it immediately and make a profit from the sales," he replied.

What's the function of our prayer book? Analysis by ***Rabbi Even-Israel Steinsaltz:***

MYJLI.COM/PRAYER

"And how do you know that you've made a profit?" asked the Magid.

"I document the prices that I buy and sell the merchandise for," the man explained. "I then subtract the buying price and my other business expenses from the sales price. The remaining sum is profit."

"But why do you waste so much time traveling to and from Leipzig?" the Magid then asked. "Why don't you just document the buying and selling prices and subtract the former from the latter?"

The businessman began to laugh. "Will documentation itself really make any money? You need actual merchandise! I need to travel to Leipzig and take the time to actually buy and sell the merchandise. Only then can I make a profit."

The Magid responded, "The meditations of prayer are just like merchandise. If you don't actually experience the meditation, it is like only documenting buying and selling prices. This is ineffective. You need to apply yourself to the meditation and take the time to actually 'buy something.' Only then will the meditations be effective. This is why it takes me so long to pray."

TEXT 4

MODEH ANI, PRAYER UPON WAKING

מוֹדֶה אֲנִי לְפָנֶיךָ מֶלֶךְ חַי וְקַיָּם, שֶׁהֶחֱזַרְתָּ בִּי נִשְׁמָתִי בְּחֶמְלָה. רַבָּה אֱמוּנָתֶךָ.

I offer thanks to You, living and enduring King, for You have mercifully restored my soul within me; Your faithfulness is great.

The secrets of Modeh Ani, by ***Rabbi Simon Jacobson*** *and* ***Mrs. Shaindy Jacobson:***

MYJLI.COM/PRAYER

Forest Hope, Yehoshua Wiseman, acrylic on canvas, Jerusalem.

our soul is taken every night [78]
and returns it in the Am.

THE REBBE, RABBI MENACHEM MENDEL SCHNEERSON,
TORAT MENACHEM 5715:2, PP. 232–233

וּלְהָבִין מַהוּ עִנְיַן הַהוֹדָאָה שֶׁמּוֹדִים לוֹ יִתְבָּרֵךְ, וַהֲרֵי אֵינוֹ שַׁיָּךְ מַחֲלוֹקֶת נֶגְדּוֹ יִתְבָּרֵךְ, עַד שֶׁיִּצְטָרְכוּ לְהוֹדוֹת לוֹ.

אַךְ הָעִנְיָן בָּזֶה הוּא, שֶׁאֵין זוֹ מַחֲלוֹקֶת בְּגוּף הָעִנְיָן, כִּי אִם, שֶׁהֶרְגֵּשׁ הַנִּבְרָאִים הוּא שֶׁלְּמַטָּה יֵשׁ וּלְמַעְלָה אַיִן, וְלָכֵן אִי אֶפְשָׁר לִהְיוֹת בְּהַשָּׂגָתָם הַדֵּיעָה הָעֶלְיוֹנָה שֶׁלְּמַעְלָה יֵשׁ וּלְמַטָּה אַיִן . . .

אָמְנָם אַף שֶׁעִנְיָן זֶה אֵינוֹ בְּהַשָּׂגַת הַתַּחְתּוֹן, מִכָּל מָקוֹם מוֹדִים אֲנַחְנוּ לָךְ, שֶׁאָנוּ מוֹדִים שֶׁהָאֱמֶת הוּא כְּמוֹ שֶׁהוּא בְּהַדֵּיעָה הָעֶלְיוֹנָה, שֶׁלְּמַעְלָה יֵשׁ וּלְמַטָּה אַיִן.

The theme of conceding to G-d requires explanation: How is it possible to argue with G-d, making it necessary to concede to Him?

The "argument" we are discussing isn't over objective reality. It is a difference in feeling. We and G-d differ in how we feel about the world: while G-d experiences Himself as a genuine entity and the world as a created entity, we experience the world as a genuine entity and G-d's existence as theoretical. We simply aren't capable of experiencing the world the same way G-d does. . . .

And yet, despite our innate feeling, we concede to G-d's experience of reality. We concede that His existence is genuine and ours is only created.

TEXT 6

RABBI YOSEF YITSCHAK SCHNEERSOHN, *LIKUTEI DIBURIM* 1, P. 75B

אוּן דָאס אִיז דֶער זִין פוּן דֶעם וָוארְט "תְּהִלָּה" דִי לוֹיב אוּן דֶערְצֵיילוּנְג וֶועלְכֶע פַארְבִּינְדְט דֶעם לוֹיבֶער אוּן דֶערְצֵיילֶער מִיט דֶעם וֶועמֶען עֶר לוֹיבְּט, אַז בְּשַׁעַת עֶר זָאגְט דִי לוֹיבּ וֶוערְטֶער פִּילְט עֶר זִיךְ אִין אַ נָאהֶענְטֶער בַּאצִיהוּנְג מִיט דֶעם וֶועמֶען עֶר לוֹיבְּט.

ווִי מִיר זֶעהֶען בְּמוּחָשׁ, וֶוען אֵיינֶער דֶערְצֵיילְט ווִי אִים אִיז אוֹיסְגֶעקוּמֶען צוּ זֶעהֶען דֶעם גְרוֹיסֶען כָּבוֹד וָואס אַ מְדִינָה הָאט גֶעגֶעבֶּען אִיר מוֹשֵׁל אִין אֵיינֶעם פוּן דִי פַּייֶערְטֶעג וֶועלְכֶע וֶוערֶען גֶעפַייֶערְט אִין יֶענֶער מְדִינָה, אוּן עֶר דֶערְצֵיילְט דָאס מִיט אַלֶע פְּרָטִים – דִי רַייכְקַייט אוּן שֵׁיינְקַייט אוּן דִי גְרוֹיסֶע מֶענְשֶׁען וֶועלְכֶע עֶר הָאט אִין יֶענֶעם טָאג גֶעזֶעהֶען–אִיז בְּשַׁעַת עֶר דֶערְצֵיילְט, שְׁטֵייט עֶר אִין אַ גֶעהוֹיבֶּענֶעם שְׁטִימוּנְגְס - גֶעפִיהל וָואס מִיט דֶעם אַלֵיין גֵייט עֶר אַרוֹיס פוּן זַיין וָואכֶעדִיגֶען לֶעבֶּען אוּן שְׁטֵייט הֶעכֶער אוּן אֵיידֶעלֶער.

דֶערְפַאר וֶוערְט תְּפִלָּה אָנְגֶערוּפֶען בְּשֵׁם סוּלָם, ווִי עֶס שְׁטֵייט, "וְהִנֵּה סֻלָּם מֻצָּב אַרְצָה וְרֹאשׁוֹ מַגִּיעַ הַשָּׁמָיְמָה". תְּפִלָּה אִיז דֶער סוּלָם וֶועלְכֶער פַארְבִּינְדְט דֶעם מִתְפַּלֵל עִם הַקָּדוֹשׁ בָּרוּךְ הוּא, וָואס דוּרְךְ דִי שִׁירוֹת וְתִשְׁבָּחוֹת שֶׁבִּתְפִלָּה וֶוערְט דִי הִתְקַשְּׁרוּת הַמִּתְפַּלֵּל עִם הַקָּדוֹשׁ בָּרוּךְ הוּא.

RABBI YOSEF YITSCHAK SCHNEERSOHN (RAYATS, FRIERDIKER REBBE, PREVIOUS REBBE) 1880–1950

Chasidic rebbe, prolific writer, and Jewish activist. Rabbi Yosef Yitschak, the sixth leader of the Chabad movement, actively promoted Jewish religious practice in Soviet Russia and was arrested for these activities. After his release from prison and exile, he settled in Warsaw, Poland, from where he fled Nazi occupation and arrived in New York in 1940. Settling in Brooklyn, Rabbi Schneersohn worked to revitalize American Jewish life. His son-in-law, Rabbi Menachem Mendel Schneerson, succeeded him as the leader of the Chabad movement.

Praising another creates a connection between the person giving the praise and the person they are praising. When one praises another, the person praising feels a closeness with the subject of the praise.

For example, a person had the opportunity to witness the great honor that a country bestowed upon its ruler during a national celebration. When that person later recounts the spectacle to others with all its detail—the wealth, grandeur, and powerful people who were present—he or she becomes inspired. The person relating the praise is transported from the mundanities of day-to-day life and feels uplifted.

This is why prayer is called a ladder: it connects the individual with G-d, as the verse says, "A ladder planted in the earth that reaches up to Heaven." This connection between the individual and G-d is formed through the songs and praises of prayer.

discover an interest in god.

Does G-d need our praise? Jewish theologians explain:

MYJLI.COM/PRAYER

Service of the Heart (detail), Chenoch Lieberman, 1950.

Figure 3.2

The Structure of the Verses of Song

PRAYER(S)	FUNCTION/THEME	ORIGIN
Baruch She'amar, p. 30*	Introductory blessing	Men of the Great Assembly
Ashrei–Halelukah, pp. 31–35	G-d's creation and involvement in His magnificent world.	King David (Psalms 146–150)
Vayevarech–Vecharot, pp. 35–36	Various praises of G-d	King David (Chronicles 29)
	Early history of the Jewish people	Nehemiah (Nehemiah 9)
Vayosha–Az Yashir, pp. 36–37	Splitting of the Sea	Exodus 14–15
Yishtabach, p. 38	Concluding blessing	Men of the Great Assembly (Some say, King Solomon)

* The page number references are to the *Siddur Tehilat Hashem* prayer book (New York: Merkos L'Inyonei Chinuch, 2004).

Exercise 3.2

Each of the four quotes on the following page express different themes. Indicate which Quote(s) conveys each of the themes.

QUOTE(S)	THEME
	G-d's control over the universe
	G-d's kindness toward His creations
	The vastness of the universe
	The multitudes within the universe
	The ingenious design of the universe

Quote A

BARUCH SHE'AMAR, VERSES OF SONG, MORNING PRAYERS

Blessed is He who spoke and the world came into being; Blessed is He. Blessed is He who says and does. Blessed is He who decrees and fulfills.

Quote B

ASHREI, VERSES OF SONG, MORNING PRAYERS

You open Your hand and satisfy the desire of every living thing.

Quote C

PSALMS 147, VERSES OF SONG, MORNING PRAYERS

He counts the number of the stars; he gives a name to each of them. Great is our Master and abounding in might; His understanding is beyond reckoning.

Quote D

VAYEVARECH DAVID, VERSES OF SONG, MORNING PRAYERS

You have made the heavens, the heavens of heavens, and all their hosts, the earth and all thereon, the seas and all therein.

TEXT 7

MAIMONIDES, *MISHNEH TORAH,* LAWS OF THE FOUNDATIONS OF THE TORAH 2:2

בְּשָׁעָה שֶׁיִּתְבּוֹנֵן הָאָדָם בְּמַעֲשָׂיו וּבְרוּאָיו הַנִּפְלָאִים הַגְּדוֹלִים, וְיִרְאֶה מֵהֶם חָכְמָתוֹ שֶׁאֵין לָהּ עֶרֶךְ וְלֹא קֵץ, מִיָּד הוּא אוֹהֵב, וּמְשַׁבֵּחַ, וּמְפָאֵר, וּמִתְאַוֶּה תַּאֲוָה גְדוֹלָה לֵידַע הַשֵּׁם הַגָּדוֹל.

When one meditates on G-d's great and wondrous creations and sees how they reflect G-d's infinite genius, one will immediately be aroused to love, praise, and glorify Him and yearn with a tremendous desire to know His great name.

RABBI MOSHE BEN MAIMON (MAIMONIDES, RAMBAM) 1135–1204

Halachist, philosopher, author, and physician. Maimonides was born in Córdoba, Spain. After the conquest of Córdoba by the Almohads, he fled Spain and eventually settled in Cairo, Egypt. There, he became the leader of the Jewish community and served as court physician to the vizier of Egypt. He is most noted for authoring the *Mishneh Torah,* an encyclopedic arrangement of Jewish law, and for his philosophical work, *Guide for the Perplexed.* His rulings on Jewish law are integral to the formation of halachic consensus.

Horseshoe Falls from Below the High Bank, Gustav Grunewald, oil on canvas, United States, 1832. (Fine Arts Museums of San Francisco)

TEXT 8

BARUCH SHE'AMAR, VERSES OF SONG

בָּרוּךְ שֶׁאָמַר וְהָיָה הָעוֹלָם.

Blessed is He who spoke and the world came into being.

TEXT 9

RABBI SHNE'UR ZALMAN OF LIADI, *SHAAR HAYICHUD VEHA'EMUNAH*, CHAPTER 11

מִדּוֹתָיו שֶׁל הַקָּדוֹשׁ בָּרוּךְ הוּא, כְּשֶׁבָּאוֹת לִבְחִינַת הִתְגַּלּוּת פְּעוּלָּתָן בַּתַּחְתּוֹנִים, נִקְרָא גִילּוּי זֶה וְהַמְשָׁכַת פְּעוּלָּה זוֹ בְּשֵׁם "מַאֲמָר" וְ"צֵירוּף אוֹתִיּוֹת"...

כְּמוֹ אוֹתִיּוֹת הַדִּבּוּר בָּאָדָם עַל דֶּרֶךְ מָשָׁל, שֶׁהֵן מְגַלּוֹת לַשּׁוֹמְעִים מַה שֶּׁהָיָה צָפוּן וְסָתוּם בְּלִבּוֹ.

The tools G-d uses to reveal Himself in the act of Creation are referred to as "speech" and "combinations of letters" . . . .

Their function is similar to that of human speech: to reveal to others that which was originally hidden in the heart.

RABBI SHNE'UR ZALMAN OF LIADI (ALTER REBBE) 1745–1812

Chasidic rebbe, halachic authority, and founder of the Chabad movement. The Alter Rebbe was born in Liozna, Belarus, and was among the principal students of the Magid of Mezeritch. His numerous works include the *Tanya*, an early classic containing the fundamentals of Chabad Chasidism, and *Shulchan Aruch HaRav*, an expanded and reworked code of Jewish law.

TEXT 10

RABBI SHALOM DOVBER SCHNEERSOHN, *SEFER HAMAAMARIM* 5659, P. 35

הַדִּיבּוּר וְהָאוֹתִיוֹת דְּמַלְכוּת דַּאֲצִילוּת הֵם מַעֲלִימִים וּמַצְפִּינִים עַל הַחָכְמָה בִּינָה דַּעַת וְהַמִּדּוֹת הַמִּתְלַבְּשִׁים בְּדִיבּוּר, שֶׁלֹּא יִתְגַּלֶּה כְּלַל בַּבְּרִיאָה, כִּי אִם אֵיזֶה הֶאָרָה מוּעֶטֶת מְאֹד.

The content contained in the "speech" of G-d—be it intellectual or emotional—is concealed from the entities it creates. The created entities therefore perceive only a minute amount of the content they hold.

RABBI SHALOM DOVBER SCHNEERSOHN (RASHAB) 1860–1920

Chasidic rebbe. Rabbi Shalom Dovber became the fifth leader of the Chabad movement upon the passing of his father, Rabbi Shmuel of Lubavitch. He established the Lubavitch network of *yeshivot* called Tomchei Temimim. He authored many volumes of Chasidic discourses and is renowned for his lucid and thorough explanations of kabbalistic concepts.

"I will sing of the mercies of the L-RD forever; to all generations will I make known Thy faithfulness with my mouth." [Psalms 89:2], Rivka Gruzman, oil painting.

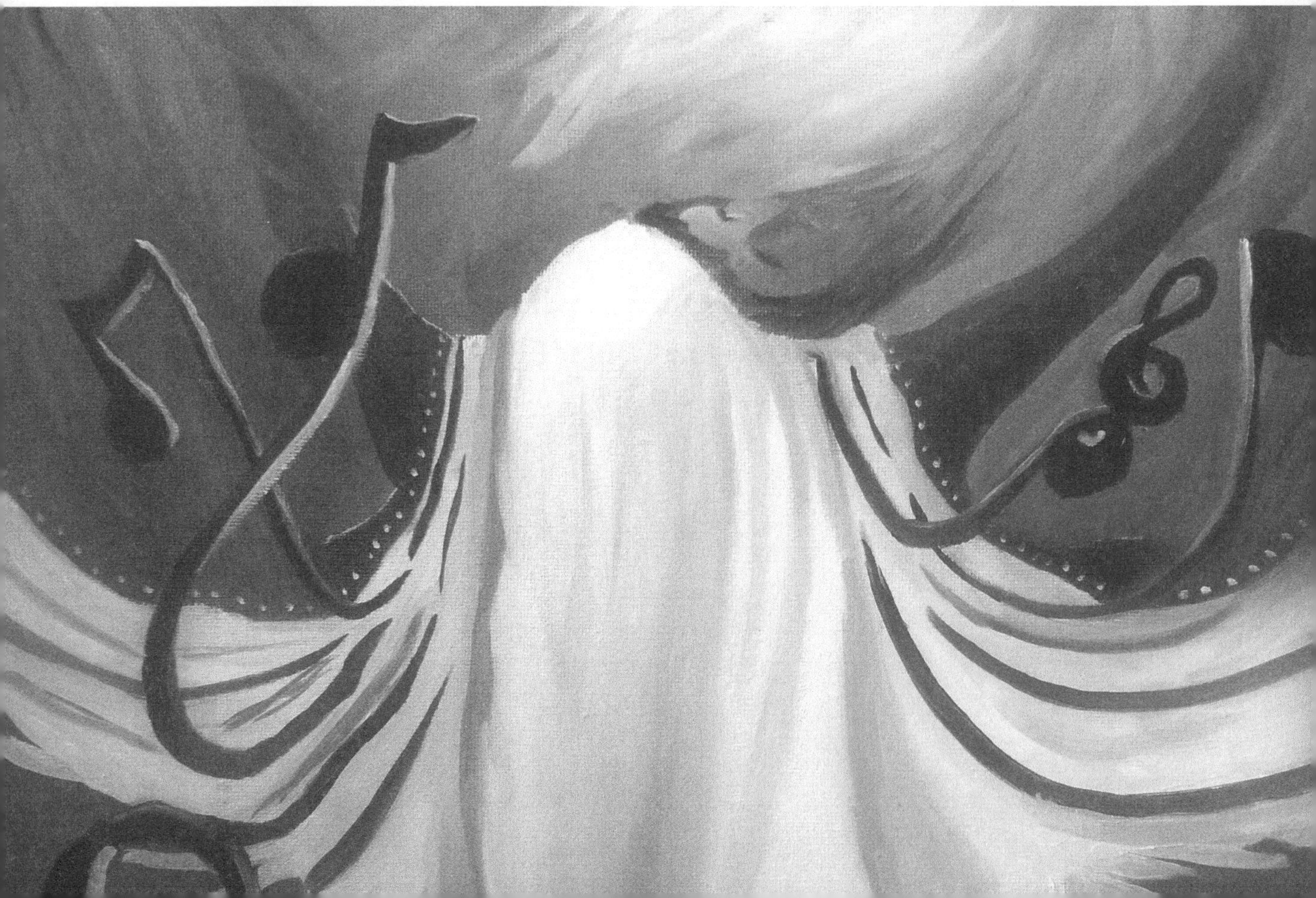

Exercise 3.3

The left column of the chart names four worldly features. The middle column asks you to describe its practical function. The third column asks you to imagine a spiritual function it may serve.

ITEM	PRACTICAL FUNCTION	SPIRITUAL FUNCTION
Body		
Sun		
Career		
Family		

TEXT 11

RABBI SIMON JACOBSON, *TOWARD A MEANINGFUL LIFE* (NEW YORK: WILLIAM MORROW AND CO., 1995), P. 234

By opening our mind to a new possibility—that our human reality is really but a small part of an all-encompassing reality—we are able to move beyond the boundaries of human existence. We begin learning to think like G-d Himself. . . .

Your very perspective of the world begins to change; you begin to glimpse the "light" within the "container." You recognize G-d in everything around you. When you eat, you understand that you are nourishing yourself for constructive and G-dly purposes. You realize that every object has a divine purpose greater than the mere fulfillment of your own needs. Your table is meant for study, your living room for meaningful conversations. Your job is no longer just a means to earn a living, but an opportunity to behave more morally and ethically, and to introduce G-d in to our world. A doctor recognizes the divine wonder within the human body and an engineer sees in his work a reflection of divine design and unity.

And finally, you learn to be sensitive to divine providence. You recognize that everything from the fluttering of a leaf in the wind to the movement of the galaxies is driven by G-d's hand. Instead of looking at life from the outside in, you learn to look from the inside out.

RABBI SIMON JACOBSON

Author of the best-selling *Toward a Meaningful Life* (New York: William Morrow, 1995), which has been translated into 12 languages, and founder of the Meaningful Life Center, which seeks to bridge the secular and the spiritual. For over 14 years, Rabbi Jacobson headed a team of scholars responsible for publishing the public talks of Rabbi Menachem M. Schneerson, the Lubavitcher Rebbe. He is also the publisher of *The Algemeiner* (formerly *Der Algemeiner Journal*), a New York-based newspaper covering American and international Jewish and Israel-related news.

TEXT 12

YISHTABACH, VERSES OF SONG, MORNING PRAYERS

> ... בּוֹרֵא כָּל הַנְשָׁמוֹת, רִבּוֹן כָּל הַמַּעֲשִׂים, הַבּוֹחֵר בְּשִׁירֵי זִמְרָה, מֶלֶךְ יָחִיד חֵי הָעוֹלָמִים.

. . . Creator of all souls, Ruler of all creatures, Who takes pleasure in songs of praise; You are the only King, the Life of all the worlds.

Page from *machzor* (festival prayer book) (detail), author: Joseph Zaddik, early-mid-15th century, Spain, pen and ink on parchment. (London, British Library Collection of Illuminated Manuscripts)

TEXT 13

RABBI YOSEF YITSCHAK SCHNEERSOHN, *SEFER HAMAAMARIM* 5689, P. 59

> וּכְמוֹ עַל דֶרֶךְ מָשָׁל בְּאִילָן, שֶׁכּוֹרְתִים הָעֲנָפִים הַיְבֵשִׁים וְהַמְקוּלְקָלִים בִּכְדֵי שֶׁהָעֲנָפִים הַחַיִּים יִצְמְחוּ בְּטוֹב יוֹתֵר . . .
>
> כְּמוֹ כֵּן הוּא בְּהָאָדָם שֶׁנִקְרָא עֵץ הַשָּׂדֶה, צְרִיכִים לְהַכְרִית הַחוֹחִים וְהַקוֹצִים הַמוֹנְעִים וּמְעַכְּבִים, בִּכְדֵי שֶׁיִהְיֶה צְמִיחַת הָאִילָן, שֶׁיַּעֲלֶה לְמַעֲלָה . . .
>
> דְלִהְיוֹת שֶׁבְּטִבְעוֹ הוּא חוּמְרִי וְעַל כֵּן מְקוֹמוֹ הוּא בְּחוּמְרִיּוּת הָעוֹלָם . . . וּצְרִיכִים לְהוֹצִיאוֹ (אֶת הַנֶפֶשׁ הַבַּהֲמִית) מִמְקוֹמוֹ וּמֵרְשׁוּתוֹ.
>
> וְהוּא עַל יְדֵי הַהִתְבּוֹנְנוּת דִפְסוּקֵי דְזִמְרָה.

A gardener cuts off the dried-out and dead branches of a tree so that the living branches can thrive. . . .

The same is true of the human being, who the Torah calls a "tree of the field." The thorns that impede and hinder growth need to be cut off so that the "tree" can continue to grow higher and higher. . . .

Since the animal soul is by nature materially oriented, "planted" in the materiality of the world . . . one needs to remove the animal soul from its familiar habitat.

This is achieved through the meditation of *Pesukei Dezimrah* (the Verses of Song).

TEXT 14

PSALMS 148, VERSES OF SONG, MORNING PRAYERS

הַלְלוּיָ-ה,

הַלְלוּ אֶת ה' מִן הַשָּׁמַיִם, הַלְלוּהוּ בַּמְּרוֹמִים.

הַלְלוּהוּ כָל מַלְאָכָיו, הַלְלוּהוּ כָּל צְבָאָיו. הַלְלוּהוּ שֶׁמֶשׁ וְיָרֵחַ, הַלְלוּהוּ כָּל כּוֹכְבֵי אוֹר. הַלְלוּהוּ שְׁמֵי הַשָּׁמָיִם, וְהַמַּיִם אֲשֶׁר מֵעַל הַשָּׁמָיִם.

יְהַלְלוּ אֶת שֵׁם ה', כִּי הוּא צִוָּה וְנִבְרָאוּ. וַיַּעֲמִידֵם לָעַד לְעוֹלָם, חָק נָתַן וְלֹא יַעֲבוֹר.

הַלְלוּ אֶת ה' מִן הָאָרֶץ,

תַּנִּינִים וְכָל תְּהֹמוֹת. אֵשׁ וּבָרָד, שֶׁלֶג וְקִיטוֹר, רוּחַ סְעָרָה עֹשָׂה דְבָרוֹ. הֶהָרִים וְכָל גְּבָעוֹת, עֵץ פְּרִי וְכָל אֲרָזִים. הַחַיָּה וְכָל בְּהֵמָה, רֶמֶשׂ, וְצִפּוֹר כָּנָף. מַלְכֵי אֶרֶץ וְכָל לְאֻמִּים, שָׂרִים וְכָל שֹׁפְטֵי אָרֶץ. בַּחוּרִים וְגַם בְּתוּלֹת, זְקֵנִים עִם נְעָרִים. יְהַלְלוּ אֶת שֵׁם ה' כִּי נִשְׂגָּב שְׁמוֹ לְבַדּוֹ,

הוֹדוֹ עַל אֶרֶץ וְשָׁמָיִם.

Praise G-d!

Praise G-d from the heavens; praise Him in the celestial heights.

Praise Him, all His angels; praise Him, all His hosts. Praise Him, sun and moon; praise Him, all the shining stars. Praise Him, heavens of heavens and the waters that are above the heavens.

Let them praise the name of G-d, for He commanded, and they were created. He has established them forever, for all time; He issued a decree, and it shall not be transgressed.

Praise G-d from the earth, sea monsters and all that dwell in the depths; fire and hail, snow and vapor, stormy wind carrying out His command; the mountains, all hills, fruit-bearing trees, and all cedars; the beasts and all cattle, creeping things, insects, and winged fowl; kings of the earth and all nations, rulers and all judges of the land; young men as well as maidens, elders together with young lads. Let them praise the name of G-d, for His name is sublimely transcendent. It is unto Himself; only its radiance is upon the earth and heavens.

TEXT 15a

RABBI ZALMAN GOPIN, *LILMOD EICH LEHITPALEL*, 3, P. 129

וְנִשְׁאֶלֶת הַשְּׁאֵלָה: כֵּיצַד יְכוֹלִים הַבְּהֵמוֹת וְהַחַיּוֹת אוֹ עֲצֵי הַפְּרִי וְהָאֲרָזִים, לְשַׁבֵּחַ אֶת הַקָּדוֹשׁ בָּרוּךְ הוּא? יֶתֶר עַל כֵּן: כֵּיצַד יְכוֹלִים הַנִּבְרָאִים הַדּוֹמְמִים, כְּמוֹ שֶׁלֶג וְקִיטוֹר אוֹ הָרִים וּבְקָעוֹת, לְשַׁבֵּחַ אֶת הַקָּדוֹשׁ בָּרוּךְ הוּא?

Can beasts and animals, trees and cedars, really praise G-d? The question is even more pronounced when it comes to entirely inanimate beings like snow and vapor, mountains and hills. How can they praise G-d?

RABBI ZALMAN GOPIN
1945–

Chasidic mentor, lecturer, and author. Rabbi Gopin serves as lead Chasidic mentor at the Chabad yeshiva of Kfar Chabad, Israel. He also serves as senior educator at Mayanei Yisrael, an adult education institute for Chasidic teachings. He has authored a number of books on Chasidic philosophy and is a frequent lecturer on the subject.

TEXT 15b

RABBI ZALMAN GOPIN, IBID., 3, PP. 109–110

אֶלָּא הַכַּוָּונָה לַחַיּוּת הָאֱלֹקִית הַמְחַיֶּה אֶת הַנִּבְרָאִים וְהִיא הַמְשַׁבַּחַת וּמְהַלֶּלֶת אֶת ה'...

וְכֵיוָן שֶׁהַשֶּׁבַח הוּא עִנְיָין פְּנִימִי וְנַפְשִׁי, לָכֵן הַחַיּוּת שֶׁל כָּל נִבְרָא מְשַׁבַּחַת אֶת הַקָּדוֹשׁ בָּרוּךְ הוּא בְּהֶתְאֵם לְדַרְגָּתָהּ: הַשָּׁמַיִם חֲפֵצִים לְהִתְקָרֵב לַה' כְּפִי שֶׁהֵם מַשִּׂיגִים אֶת הַקָּדוֹשׁ בָּרוּךְ הוּא, וְהַחַיּוּת שֶׁל הַגְּבָעוֹת, מִשְׁתּוֹקֶקֶת לַחֲזוֹר לִמְקוֹרָהּ כְּפִי שֶׁהִיא מַרְגִּישָׁה אוֹתוֹ, וְכָךְ גַּם כָּל נִבְרָא וְנִבְרָא.

The psalm isn't referring to the physical bodies of these beings. It is referring to the G-dly energies that enliven them; they praise G-d. . . .

Praise is personal and soulful. Thus, the G-dly energy within each being praises G-d in its own way. The energies within the skies and the hills each desire to become closer to G-d in a different way, according to how they identify with Him. The same is true of the G-dly energy within each creature.

Exercise for the Week

Creation and Creator. This week, take two or three minutes to meditate on the magnificence and brilliance of G-d's creation, and the ways in which creation reflects on its Creator. Follow this up immediately with an out-loud recital of Psalm 148.

We'll discuss how it went during the next lesson.

KEY POINTS

1 Like a ladder, prayer has many rungs. Each rung is a deeper way of connecting with G-d. The prayer book guides us up this prayer ladder.

2 In order to establish a connection with G-d, we first need to accept His perspective on reality: that the world is created and exists for a purpose.

3 Praising G-d helps us learn about G-d and become inspired by Him. This is the function of the Verses of Song.

4 Everything in creation is invested with spiritual content and exists for a purpose. The meditations of the Verses of Song help us train ourselves to see the world this way.

Appendix

TEXT 16

MIDRASH TEHILIM 19

"הַשָּׁמַיִם מְסַפְּרִים כְּבוֹד אֵ-ל" (תְּהִילִים יט, ב).

מָשָׁל לְגִבּוֹר שֶׁנִּכְנַס בַּמְּדִינָה וְלֹא הָיוּ יוֹדְעִין מַה כֹּחוֹ. אָמַר לָהֶן פִּקֵּחַ אֶחָד:
מֵאַבְנָא דַהֲוָא מִתְעַשֵּׁשׁ אַתּוּן יוֹדְעִין מַה כֹּחוֹ.

כַּךְ מֵהַשָּׁמַיִם אָנוּ לְמֵידִין כֹּחוֹ שֶׁל הַקָּדוֹשׁ בָּרוּךְ הוּא.

"The skies recount the praise of G-d" (PSALMS 19:2).

This can be understood through the following analogy: A mighty man was a newcomer in town, and the townsmen sought a way to gauge the extent of his strength. A wise person told them, "From the rock that this man raises, you will be able to determine his strength."

Similarly, we can determine the strength of G-d from the skies.

MIDRASH TEHILIM

A rabbinic commentary on the Book of Psalms. Midrash is the designation of a particular genre of rabbinic literature usually forming a running commentary on specific books of the Bible. This particular Midrash provides textual exegeses and develops and illustrates the principles of the Book of Psalms.

Additional Readings

IS G-D A HE?

BY TAMAR FRANKIEL, PHD

Over the past few decades, a new and distinctive movement has emerged among Jews who are attempting to reclaim some kind of spiritual meaning for their lives. The question has been: If we are recovering our connection to the Divine, can we find that connection in traditional Judaism?

The question has been particularly difficult for many Jewish women because of the picture of G-d we inherited. The G-d we learned about as youngsters, that distant, kingly figure who watched over us seemed, for women discovering their feminine consciousness, too blatantly male. In popular feminism, the G-d of the Hebrew Bible, of Jewish, Christian, and Muslim tradition, has gotten a bad reputation as the patriarchal G-d of Western culture. Some turned to other religions in search of a G-d beyond gender or a philosophy that did not require a belief in G-d at all.

Is it true that G-d in Jewish teachings is patriarchal, that is, thoroughly imbued with male characteristics and values? On first glance, it would seem so. After all, G-d appears to be male. The siddur (prayer book) and the Bible refer to G-d only as He. Traditional Jewish teachings point out that G-d is really beyond all attributes, including those of gender. But, feminist writers have argued, while that is a nice theory, we as human beings need to use symbols and words to express our experience of the Divine. Can we not call G-d She? Further, the words we have inherited for G-d—Father, judge, Creator, L-rd—seem to spring from male experience, not female. Can a woman have an authentic relation to a G-d named only by male titles? Feminists have suggested that the titles reflect deeper levels of experience and perception that are also thoroughly male. The feminine experience of the Divine, whatever that might be, is simply not available in the tradition.

This longing for something authentically feminine is deep and significant. From it has come the desire to create new women's rituals and new feminine interpretations of the Bible. But how can these be also authentically Jewish? As serious Jewish feminists have recognized, we cannot create a new Judaism out of whole cloth. It might be possible in some other religion to create something new and still call it by the name of that religion, but not in Judaism: we are connected, intimately and deeply, to Torah itself, the Torah that was given at Sinai and has been passed down faithfully among our people through the ages. New creations lack depth unless they are connected to the tradition we have received, to our history, even if that history seems thoroughly male.

Two responses to this issue have emerged. One is a radical rereading of the Torah from a modernist historical perspective, suggesting that Jewish women in ancient times had religious resources which were not acknowledged by the men who handed down the Torah. Some feminists argue that we can resurrect the goddess-symbols of the ancient Near East. They suggest that the matriarchs themselves may have worshipped goddesses, and that Israelite women are known certainly to have done so. (We know of these practices from the criticisms heaped on goddess-worship by the prophets, but feminists dismiss those criticisms as mere propaganda of the zealous male followers of the patriarchal G-d.) Therefore, they say, we can borrow from goddess worship its rich feminine

DR. TAMAR FRANKIEL, PHD, 1946–

Dean of Academic Affairs and Professor of Comparative Religion at the Academy for Jewish Religion in Los Angeles, California. Her areas of interest include Jewish women, spirituality, and prayer. She has authored several books on these subjects, including *Loving Prayer*.

imagery; we can speak of the Queen of Heaven rather than just the King; we can use images of birth and fertility as well as of creation and conquest.

A second, more moderate view suggests that we do not need to return to goddesses. But, since G-d is neither male nor female, we can use feminine language and symbols to express uniquely feminine aspects of G-d. We can creatively retranslate Hebrew words, giving them a different nuance that is either beyond gender or has a feminine flavor. We can say Ruler of the universe rather than King, for example, to give a more neutral description. We can speak of G-d as our Father and Mother; we can mention the matriarchs as well as the patriarchs in our prayers and stories. Thus, the remembering and retelling of the tradition can come to have a less masculine cast, while remaining true to the words of the tradition as we have received it, and without passing over into idolatry.

Imaginative as these might seem, there are certain problems with such proposals. First, on ancient goddesses: these figures are not as beneficent as they might seem. We might like to fantasize a goddess as an all-beneficent mother in contrast to a harsh, legalistic father figure. But this is not true to what we know of ancient religions. Goddesses were not always sweet and beneficent. Some of the ritual practices connected to the goddesses were violent and, by modern standards, inhumane. In some cases the rituals involved sexual practices unacceptable to Jewish sensibilities.

Moreover, goddesses were not forbidden merely because they were feminine. Male gods were forbidden also, the Baals as well as the Asherahs. The prophets, from Moses onward, were struggling to unify the worship of G-d in order to ensure that the Jewish people remained connected to their unique historical experience of G-d, the G-d who brought them out of Egypt. We cannot forget that, no sooner had the newly freed slaves received the Torah, they began worshipping the golden calf, a favorite image of a Canaanite male god, even though they said, "This is the god that brought us out of Egypt." It would have been easy to extend the confusion, to become involved in the worship practiced by the Canaanite inhabitants of the land of Israel, and ultimately to forget our own history. In fact, that is exactly what we did; that is why the prophets repeatedly had to call the people to stop worshipping idols. They were reminding us that the Jewish perception of the Divine was connected with history, with purpose and direction that transcended any given place. The G-d who brought us out of Egypt had something bigger in mind, something more than sustaining our life, bringing us success and prosperity, or even life after death.

That sense of larger vision, of greater purpose, has sustained the Jewish people through the ages; and that larger vision assures us also that our G-d is ultimately beyond gender. To borrow from other religious experiences just because they are female can, and in our history almost always did, dilute the reality of our unique Jewish experience.

Women are attracted to goddess figures because it is possible to see in them characteristics women can imitate: strength, creativity, compassion. But this has been for centuries a major emphasis of Jewish thought about G-d: Recognizing that we cannot know G-d's essence, we focus on the Divine attributes or characteristics in order to learn the *derech Hashem*, the way of G-d, the things we can imitate and bring into our own lives. When we ask whether G-d is patriarchal or matriarchal, male or female, we are asking about these characteristics. How indeed has G-d revealed Himself/Herself, that aspect of the Divine that we can understand, to our people?

One would think, from feminist criticisms, that the Jewish view of G-d's attributes would list predominantly negative male characteristics: strength, warlikeness, imperialistic control, jealousy. But what in fact are the attributes which our sages have found in G-d? We can take them from the Kabbalah of Isaac Luria: wisdom, knowledge, lovingkindness, strength, harmony, perseverance, beauty, generativity, presence in earthly life. We can take them from the thirteen attributes: merciful, compassionate, slow to anger, abundant in kindness and truth, preserving kindness for thousands of generations, ever-forgiving. Indeed, our tradition finds a multitude of ways—more than we can easily translate into English—to describe the love and compassion of G-d for human beings. In any case, there is clearly no justification for criticizing the Jewish view of G-d as full of undesirable male characteristics.

Yet the gender-specific language remains. If G-d's characteristics really transcend gender, why do we speak of G-d only as He?

Actually, there is nothing wrong with an individual using feminine words for G-d to address her as mother or imagine oneself talking to an intimate female friend. For some individuals, this helps to develop a richer and more intimate relationship to G-d. We can also write and share our own interpretations of G-d's compassion, G-d's judgment, G-d's creative work in the world in feminine terms. This may help us to come to experience the fullness of G-d in our lives.

But this is not a full answer, for there is still the arena of public prayer, where tradition insists that we should adhere to the established text of the siddur. Here many feminists are eager for changes in language and substance. Some Jewish organizations have rushed ahead to revise translations of the prayer book, eliminating gender references, sometimes eliminating portions of the prayers themselves.

We must say, first of all, that this does injustice to the Hebrew language itself, not to mention the centuries of prayer of the Jewish people, who cherished these words as the channels by which we might address G-d. The issue is not merely introducing some feminine language for our personal enrichment, but our relation to the whole of Jewish tradition and the whole Jewish people.

Nor is it only a matter of dutifully respecting the communal tradition. We are easily led astray here because of our cultural disposition to value individual self-expression. We tend to honor the tradition only so long as it feels authentic to us. But what this really means is that we do not well understand communal expression, so we tend to brush it aside.

We must ask: are there not some powerful reasons why our sages have, through the centuries, kept a certain kind of language for our address to G-d, and have been very careful about what comes to be included in our siddur? Indeed there are.

The mystics tell us, following images used by the prophets, that our relation to G-d, as a people, can be conceived in sexual terms. G-d is male, the Jewish people is female. The Shir HaShirim, Song of Songs, which accompanies the celebration of Pesach and which, in some communities, is sung every Friday night, represents G-d and Israel as two lovers. The holidays can be mystically conceived as representing seasons in the relationship between Israel and G-d: Pesach is the first commitment of the two lovers, the engagement, so to speak; Shavuot is G-d's giving us his ketubah or wedding contract; and Sukkot is the consummation of the marriage. In a related set of images, all souls of Israel together is the Shabbat Queen, who is also the Shechinah (feminine aspect of the Divine), who unites with her husband, G-d, on Shabbat.

These images are a way to convey to us that the relation between G-d and human beings is a dynamic model, of which our best understanding is the relation between male and female. If our imagination fails at this point, it is partly a failure of our society, particularly of the widespread weakening of marriage and family in our times. Our grasp of the true meaning of the marriage relationship is dim and vague. We tend either to idealize it as romance (the teenagers Romeo and Juliet), or we criticize it as an instrument of patriarchal oppression, where the husband owns and dominates the wife.

Thus, some feminist writers have severely criticized the Jewish image of the Divine/human marriage. For example, Rosemary Reuther attacks the images found in some of the prophetic writings which accuse Israel of being the harlot while G-d acts like a petty, jealous husband.

This criticism totally fails to understand the depth and richness of the husband/wife experience in Judaism and, in particular, the notion of fidelity as part of marriage. Most of us today can barely grasp this, so we miss how the symbol of G-d as the husband and the Jewish people as the wife is the deepest imaginable relationship. Yet this image, this metaphor for G-d and the Jewish people, holds the secret of the apparently patriarchal language of Bible and siddur, the masculine terms we use for G-d.

In our days of new feminine consciousness, when we are asking what it means to be female or male, this language turns us back to our fundamental relationship to G-d. A woman discovering herself as woman first questions G-d: Why do you appear as male? Or she questions the rabbis: Why did you write about

Him as like you and not like us? But we must push the question to a deeper level: what do masculine and feminine, male and female, really mean? How are they unique and how do they come together?

We must certainly reject the interpretation that the male (G-d) has all the power and the female (Israel) is his instrument. That would be thoroughly un-Jewish. We need only recall the famous Talmudic story of Rabbi Eliezer, who was intent on having G-d put his personal seal on a certain halachic decision. The sages, however, decided the matter another way. G-d's response was, "Thus my children have decided." G-d might well have said, in the above anecdote, "Thus my wife has decided." For, in another context, G-d tells Abraham, "In all that Sarah tells you, listen to her voice." The feminine has power, influence, and impact on the world just as does the masculine. They are in continuous interaction, an ongoing dance, in which each elevates and enriches the other.

This metaphor of G-d and Israel as husband and wife helps us understand that when we address G-d as a community, we address Him as male. When we pray in the traditional ways, we are not merely doing our duty by honoring what has been passed down. We are entering into a relationship with G-d by our speech, helping to create a relationship that has its own dynamic, the dynamic of the people, Israel, speaking, in love and intimacy, to her Divine partner. And, as with a marriage, it is only with years of practice that the full richness of this communication becomes a reality for us.

The so-called patriarchal G-d thus turns out to be only one face of G-d. The question once was asked why, in our prayers, we address G-d as G-d of Abraham, G-d of Isaac, and G-d of Jacob rather than more simply as G-d of Abraham, Isaac, and Jacob. The sages answered: Because G-d showed a different face to each one. So also with us. We live in a time when many are speaking of the feminine faces of G-d; this brings to our awareness dimensions of G-d that we might have forgotten. We may also see Him in more traditional terms as Creator, Ruler, Redeemer, Giver of the Torah. We need not reject any of these, male or female, but only use them to deepen our understanding of ourselves as individuals, of our people, and of G-d. Learning to live with and think deeply into our words for G-d is part of our spiritual growth, part of the deepening of consciousness we see in our times.

"G-d and Patriarchy," published in *Feeding Among the Lilies: The Wellsprings Reader*, by Baila Olidort (editor) (Brooklyn, NY: Wellsprings Journal, 1999), pp. 245–253

AN APPROACH TO CHASSIDIC *DAVENING*

BY RABBI SHMUEL KAPLAN

Our Bond with G-d—Rational and Suprarational
The essence of the act of *tefillah* is a person's direct encounter with G-d and acknowledging His ultimate truth: *Hashem Elokeichem Emes*—"G-d, your L-rd, is Truth."

This truth was first brought to light to man in the initial encounter between Moshe *Rabbeinu* and G-d at the Burning Bush. Moshe *Rabbeinu* asked G-d: "When *Bnei Yisrael* will ask me, 'What is His name?' what shall I answer them?"[1] G-d answered: אהי-ה אשר אהי-ה, "I will Be what I will Be."[2] Commentators point out that the numerical value of the word אהי-ה is 21; אהי-ה אשר אהי-ה is thus 441, the numerical square of the word אהי-ה (21 x 21), which is also the numerical value of the word emes (אמת)—"truth." In effect, when Moshe *Rabbeinu* encountered G-d, he was encountering the ultimate truth of His being. As our Sages tell us:[3] *Chossamo shel HaKadosh Baruch Hu Emes*—"The seal of the Holy One, Blessed be He, is Truth."

Now, G-d Himself spoke to Moshe. Thus, the meaning of "the truth of His being" could not simply refer to the fact of His existence. Since He was actively communicating with Moshe, obviously He exists. The "truth of His being" must therefore imply something much more profound.

Moshe was being shown a higher truth, and his experience serves as a lesson for all of us. By and large, people who believe in a Divine Being operate under the mindset that they and the world around them exist. They see, feel and experience life with all their senses, and that determines their reality. They also believe that G-d exists—and that He also controls, to whatever degree, the world's events—even though they do not experience Him with their senses. But Who G-d truly is, the truth of His being, is entirely beyond them.

While this may be a valid approach for man, it cannot be G-d's perspective, nor can it be *His* truth. He existed before the world was created and will continue to be after existence as we know it ceases. Thus, the truth of His being is of an entirely different nature than our existence. His being is ultimate truth, permanent, immutable and unaffected by any other event, even that of Creation itself. As the verse states:[4] *Ani Hashem lo shanisi*—"I, G-d, have not changed." This verse expresses the ultimate truth that not only does He exist, but that He is the only true Being in existence; only He possesses entirely independent existence. The fact that we see ourselves as having independent existence has no bearing on the fact that the truth of G-d's oneness precludes any other independent existence but His.

Tefillah is the process by which we attempt to encounter G-d by recognizing the truth of His being. The structure of *tefillah* as formulated by the Men of the Great Assembly provides a means to gain this awareness. In a step-by-step manner, *tefillah* enables us to ascend from the consciousness of materiality to an appreciation of G-d and His truth.

In this vein, the *Zohar*[5] describes *tefillah* as a ladder that stands on the ground and reaches the heavens, for *tefillah* is a systematic pattern of growth that enables man to progress in his awareness of G-d and to bond with Him.

The Process Begins
When a person awakens in the morning, the first thing he becomes aware of is his consciousness; i.e., he is aware that he is, that he exists. At this initial stage, all he can do is acknowledge that in addition to himself, G-d also exists. By reciting the *Modeh Ani* prayer, he acknowledges that he shares a relationship

RABBI SHMUEL KAPLAN

Chabad *shliach*. Rabbi Kaplan is the director of Chabad-Lubavitch of Maryland, overseeing its institutions and activities in more than 20 cities. A Torah scholar and a renowned orator, he is on the executive committee of Merkos L'Inyonei Chinuch, the education and outreach arm of the Chabad-Lubavitch Movement; a member of JLI's executive committee; and the chairman of JLI's advisory board.

with G-d; G-d has granted him life by returning his soul to him.

This is essentially what the *Modeh Ani* prayer states: *Modeh ani lefanecha*—"I thankfully acknowledge You, [i.e., Your existence] . . . for You have compassionately restored my soul within me." This is the first and lowest level of acknowledgment of G-d's truth.

This same concept—that G-d exists and is the One who grants us life—is further amplified by *Birchos HaShachar* (the Morning Blessings), where we acknowledge that every specific function, talent and ability that we possess has been granted to us by G-d. At this point, we are still operating from the fundamental perspective that our existence is true, while G-d is seen as the force that facilitates our existence.

Growing in Awareness

The next phase of recognition begins with *Pesukei DeZimrah* (Verses of Praise). Here we seek to expand our awareness beyond our own being and understand the relationship between G-d and the entire world. G-d is not only the Creator of the world, He is also intimately involved in its day-to-day functioning and operation. We appreciate that G-d is the Force behind nature; it is He "Who covers the Heavens with clouds, Who prepares rain for the earth, Who causes grass to grow on the mountains, Who gives animals their food, to the offspring of the raven that call out."[6]

As we recite these verses, we start to change our conception of the world. Instead of seeing it as an independently functioning entity, we appreciate that its existence and functioning is wholly dependent on a higher reality—G-d. Moreover, not only is the world dependent on G-d for its very existence; its every function is constantly dependent on G-d's guidance and will.

On a Higher Plane of Reality

After reaching the awareness that we ourselves and the world around us are all subordinate to the higher truth of G-d's ultimate existence, in *Birchos Kerias Shema* (the blessings before the *Shema*) we focus on the spiritual counterpart of our physical existence: the higher realms above, and the celestial beings, the angels, who abide within them. In our material world, G-dliness is not apparent; we see physicality. In the spiritual worlds, the opposite is true. The angels' awareness of G-d is as cogent as our awareness of physicality.

In the realm of angels, there are two basic categories: the *Ofanim* and the *Chayos HaKodesh*, who primarily abide in the World of *Yetzirah*; and the *Seraphim*, who abide in the World of *Beriah*. As described in the blessing of the *Shema*, the *Ofanim* and the *Chayos HaKodesh* respond to the declaration of the loftier *Seraphim*, doing so with a mighty clamor.

Often, one shouts loudly when taken by surprise. So too, the *Ofanim* and *Chayos HaKodesh* operate from their natural, innate perspective—they are beings that possess self-awareness, although totally dependent on G-d, the Ultimate Being. Upon hearing the declaration of the *Seraphim*, they become aware of a much higher level of existence and, in consternation, they shout out with a mighty clamor. In contrast, the *Seraphim* become totally subsumed[7] in their very source, losing all independent consciousness and self-awareness. As a result, they are not even able to raise a clamor.

So fully do the *Seraphim* identify with the ultimate reality of G-d's oneness—that there is no other being but Him and that He is the source of all—that they become completely subsumed in G-d, their Divine source. As a result of this total nullification, the *Seraphim* cease to be. (For this reason, we describe G-d as *Yotzer Mesharsim*, "Who creates ministering angels," using the present tense, for these angels are truly brought into being anew every day.)

When the *Ofanim* and *Chayos HaKodesh* realize that their preconceived view of their own reality[8] is not the true reality, they react with a loud cry of surprise (*Gevald, s'iz doch nisht azoy!*—"Oh, my! It isn't at all as I thought!"). While the *Ofanim* and *Chayos HaKodesh* aren't able to achieve the lofty level of *bittul*, self-transcendence, achieved by the *Seraphim*, their exposure to the service of the *Seraphim* humbles them, enabling them to gain awareness of G-d's oneness and yearn for a connection with Him.

A Jew's Uniqueness

After appreciating that the entire creation, both the physical and spiritual realms, are expressions of G-d's oneness, the *davener* turns the focus back to himself.

Doing so requires making a distinction between an angel and a Jew. An angel is programmed by its Creator to carry out its service and is assured that, as a result, it will attain lofty levels of self-nullification. A Jew, on the other hand, has been granted free choice and thus operates under his *own* decision-making capacity.

This is the focus of the next blessing in *Birchos Kerias Shema, Ahavas Olam*. The *berachah* states: *Chemlah gedolah viyeseirah chamalta aleinu*—"You have bestowed upon us an abundant and exceeding measure of compassion." This "exceeding measure of compassion" consists of the ability to freely choose to acknowledge G-d and recognize His oneness. However, because this task is an extremely difficult one, flying as it does in the face of our own senses, the *berachah* includes a plea for G-d to have mercy upon us and assist us in achieving this goal: *Avinu, Av HaRachaman, hamerachem rachem na aleinu, vesein libeinu binah lehavin u'lehaskil . . . be'ahavah*— "Our Father, merciful Father, Who shows mercy, have mercy upon us and implant understanding in our hearts so that we may lovingly comprehend. . . ."

After highlighting the potentials we have been given, we state the purpose for which we have been granted these gifts. Thus we conclude the blessing: "You, our King, have lovingly brought us close to Your great name, so that we may . . . proclaim Your oneness."

The Statement of Our Inner Self

The next stage is the recitation of the verse *Shema Yisrael*. It is a call to our inner *Yisrael*, the soul's G-dly spark.[9]

The conclusion of the first verse of *Shema* is its most critical part: *Hashem Echad*—"[not only is G-d One but also] there is only G-d"—nothing else besides Him truly exists, despite the evidence of our own senses to the contrary.

With this statement, a person—like the *Seraphim* above—understands and experiences the ultimate truth of G-d's oneness—that there is no other true existence outside of Him. The *Seraphim*, however, are wholly consumed by their understanding and are therefore subsumed in their source, losing their ability to exist independently. A Jew, by contrast, can reach this understanding and experience while he exists in this material world.

Becoming More Than Ourselves

Up to this point, the entire process of *tefillah* has been built on progressive levels of intellectual understanding and contemplation—stemming from the soul's internal faculties—with correspondingly greater degrees of emotional feeling, until ultimately arriving at the intellectual pinnacle of the truth of G-d's oneness. The next step in *tefillah*, the *Shemoneh Esreh*, introduces the suprarational level of *tefillah*.

We experience events and situations on two levels: those that influence us because we understand them, and others that influence our psyche and state of mind though we do not necessarily comprehend them; indeed, we may not even be aware of them. The soul also functions on these two distinct levels: a level where the soul integrates its experience, and a supraconscious level, where the experience is beyond such integration.

Until now we have been addressing the cognitive levels that can be integrated and how they lead to recognizing the ultimate truth of G-d. In the *Shemoneh Esreh*, the supraconscious faculties (*kochos makifim*) of the soul, the dimensions of our being that transcend reason, are given expression.

The outward physical posture of *Shemoneh Esreh*—standing at attention, feet together and bowing as prescribed—reflects this higher, transcendent level. Standing itself indicates a subservient position as opposed to comfortably sitting; the head—the location of one's intellect—lowered and bowed, serves as further acknowledgment that there are realms beyond intellect.

This is the function of the *Shemoneh Esreh*: We humbly acknowledge G-d's perspective—that He is the only true Being and nothing else exists, whether we understand this or not. Our soul's superconscious experiences this state of total submission, and in turn conveys its impact to the conscious levels of our being.

In this, man steps beyond his individual identity and subsumes himself to G-d, identifying with Him to the fullest extent humanly possible.

Pesukei DeZimrah: An Overview of Its Internal Structure

The *Anshei Knesses HaGedolah* ("Men of the Great Assembly") instituted the recitation of Pesukei DeZimrah, Verses of Praise, in our daily *tefillah* "so that we first recite G-d's praises and only then make requests of Him."[10] The *Gemara* relates[11] that this sequence has its source in Moshe *Rabbeinu's* prayer to enter *Eretz Yisrael.* There, he begins with G-d's praise: "G-d, You have begun to show Your servant Your greatness and Your strong hand," and only afterwards continues with his request:[12] "Permit me to cross [the Jordan] and see the land."

Pesukei DeZimrah begins with the blessing of *Baruch SheAmar* and ends with the blessing *Yishtabach.* The main body of this section of prayer is the final six chapters of the Book of *Tehillim* (145-150). *Tehillah LeDavid,*[13] the first of these psalms, was chosen by our Sages in light of the teaching:[14] "Whoever recites *Tehillah LeDavid* three times a day is guaranteed a portion in the World to come." Since *Tehillah LeDavid* is followed in the Book of *Tehillim* by five additional psalms that praise G-d[15] (concluding the entire Book of *Tehillim),* these chapters were also added to our daily prayers by our Sages.

Enabling the Heart to Sing

The literal translation of the term *Pesukei DeZimrah,* "Verses of Song," provides us with insights into the role this section of prayer plays in our inner Divine service. That title implies that in these prayers, we are not merely reciting G-d's praises, our hearts are singing with heartfelt feeling.[16] This emotional expression is fundamental to the purpose of prayer because it engages the animal soul. Just as an animal is dominated by its instinctive drives, our animal souls are primarily emotionally oriented. The songs of *Pesukei DeZimrah* introduce the animal soul to an emotional experience that revolves around spiritual awareness.

This is an important preliminary step as one ascends the ladder of prayer. The peak of our spiritual experience in prayer is the *Shemoneh Esreh* where a person stands before G-d in transcendent self-nullification, giving expression to his G-dly soul. Nevertheless, such a spiritual state must be attained through a process of gradual ascent.

Our Sages teach[17] that a person is obligated to feed his animals before he himself eats. The counterpart to that law in our Divine service is that before proceeding to the higher rungs of prayer, where the G-dly soul is given expression, one must "feed the animal," by praying with vibrant feelings of love and fear which nourish the spiritual potential of the animal soul.[18]

> *"Every man's innermost parts shall sing to Your name, as it is written,*[19] *'My entire being shall declare. . . .'"*[20]

Our emotions involve the heart, the organ which produces vitality and energy to the entire body. Similarly, our emotional arousal in prayer naturally overflows and affects our other organs and limbs. As a result, we sway back and forth in prayer, and when inspired, will break out in song. *Pesukei DeZimrah* highlights G-d's immanence in creation, how He permeates its every aspect. Similarly, the awareness it generates permeates not only our minds and hearts, but our entire being.

The connection of G-d's immanence with emotions is further underscored by the kabbalistic concept that the world was created through G-d's seven emotive attributes, which in turn, are reflected in the seven-day cycle of time.[21] Thus the portion of prayer which emphasizes emotional expression makes us aware of the manner in which G-d's emotions are expressed in Creation.

As evident from the explanations below, all the different facets of this section of prayer come together as an integral whole, each contributing to the heightened emotional expression that characterizes *Pesukei DeZimrah.*

Baruch SheAmar

The opening blessing, *Baruch SheAmar,* is composed of two parts: an introduction followed by a blessing. The introduction begins, "Blessed be He Who spoke, and the world came into being," focusing on the fact that G-d created the world from absolute nothingness through the medium of speech via the Ten Utterances of Creation found in the first chapter of the Torah.

Now, since the fundamental state of the world is nothingness, G-d's speech must continuously serve as an active force to bring the world into being. In that vein, the Baal Shem Tov[22] interprets the verse:[23] "Forever, G-d, Your word stands firm in the heavens" to mean that were the creative power of G-d's Ten Utterances to cease, all existence would return to non-being. Thus the statement "Blessed be He Who spoke, and the world came into being" teaches that all creation is a continuous manifestation of G-d's creative power.

By using the metaphor of speech, the Torah—and this prayer—is explaining how it is possible for the Creation to appear separate and independent from G-d. Just as humans use speech to communicate to others, Divine speech is the medium through which a realm of existence that appears separate can come into being. Nevertheless, that separation is only a function of our perception. In truth, all existence is one with its Divine source.

The blessing at the conclusion of this prayer continues this theme, praising G-d as "unique, granting life to the worlds." The term "unique," *Yachid*, refers to G-d's singular oneness, as He exists for Himself, as it were, before the Creation, independent of all other existence.[24] From that level, He emanates light that "grant[s] life to the worlds" continuously bringing them into being.

Mizmor LeSodah, the *Todah*-Offering

Baruch SheAmar is followed by Psalm 100, *Mizmor lesodah*, the psalm associated with the *todah*, thanksgiving, offering brought in the *Beis HaMikdash*. Our Sages teach[25] that in the times of *Mashiach*, although all other offerings shall cease, the *todah*-offering will endure. For all other sacrifices, even the *olah*-offerings, are associated in some way with sin and seeking forgiveness. The *todah*-offering, by contrast, is purely an offering of thanksgiving to G-d.

The word *todah* shares the root of the Hebrew term *hodaah*, which means acknowledging an opposing point of view and conceding that it is correct although one does not fully understand why. There are levels of G-dliness—for example, the G-dliness that pervades the natural order—whose existence can be comprehended intellectually. With regard to these levels, there is no need to acknowledge G-d's Presence; it can be recognized by our minds.

There are, however, aspects of G-dliness that transcend nature. These, man cannot comprehend but can merely acknowledge. In the times of the *Beis HaMikdash*, a thanksgiving-offering accompanied by the recitation of this psalm was brought when a person was saved through Divine providence beyond what is usually revealed in the natural order.[26] By and large, we conceive of G-d working His providence through and within the bounds of nature. When we are in a dangerous situation and come through unscathed, we are able to capture a glimpse of something much loftier.[27] This awareness is emphasized by the verse in this psalm: "Know that G-d (using G-d's transcendent name *Havayah*) is the L-rd (the Divine name *Elokim*, indicating G-d as the Master of nature)." This understanding enables us to perceive that ultimately, the miraculous and transcendent are the very reality of nature itself.

Yehi Chevod

Yehi Chevod is a collection of verses from *Tehillim* that were chosen to be included because they summarize the core messages of the entire Book of *Tehillim* up to the 145th psalm of *Ashrei*.[28] The beginning phrase of this prayer can be translated as a request: "May the glory of G-d be extended into the world," asking that His glory permeate the world entirely so that the world itself will reveal how it is G-d's dwelling.[29] It is also a command, compelling, as it were, His glory to descend.

To explain the above: In a mystical sense, extending G-d's glory to the world means conveying influence from *Z'eir Anpin*, where G-d's attributes are revealed ("His glory"), to *Malchus* ("the world").[30] *Malchus* is the realm of speech. On this basis, we can understand the connection between *Yehi Chevod* and the *Ashrei* prayer that follows it. The verses of *Ashrei* are alphabetic, referring to the repository of speech and letters associated with *Malchus*. As mentioned, our world is created through G-d's speech. When the higher attributes represented by *Yehi Chevod* descend into the realm of *Malchus*, the creation is permeated by G-d's glory. To further emphasize this pattern of descent, the verses of *Yehi Chevod* mention G-d's name nineteen times, which—similar to the nineteen blessings of the *Shemoneh Esreh*—indicates a downward flow of spiritual influence.[31]

Psalm 145:
***Ashrei*—In Praise of the Divine Attributes**

Psalm 145, *Ashrei*, is the primary focus of the entire *Pesukei DeZimrah*. The *Gemara*[32] provides two reasons for this: a) its verses of praise are structured according to the order of the *alef-beis* and include all its letters (with the exception of the letter *nun*); and b) it includes the most significant verse of the entire *Pesukei DeZimrah*: "You open Your hand and satiate the desire of every living being."

This psalm is introduced with two preliminary verses, imported from other psalms,[33] that begin with the word *ashrei*. The word *ashrei* is an amalgamation of the words "fortunate," "rich," and "praiseworthy," all of which allude to the concept of pleasure. The pursuit of pleasure is generally acknowledged to be the highest and primary driving force behind all the varied functions, faculties and pursuits of a human being, including the attributes of intelligence and emotion. This is why the kabbalistic symbol for pleasure is a crown (*kesser*), because a crown rests upon the head, the highest part of a person's body, encompassing all that is contained in one's head as well as the entire body beneath it. For this reason, a king, who is above the populace, wears a crown to symbolize his exalted position.

Speech, which is composed of the letters of the *alef-beis* and is identified with the attribute of *Malchus*, is also directly rooted in *Kesser*. Thus, a king, who wears a crown (*kesser*), expresses his sovereignty through his speech (*Malchus*), as is known, "A king rules through his words."[34]

The facility of speech is not a consequence of intelligence (though the subject of a person's speech might well be). Instead, it is rooted in the transcendent core of the human soul, which is identified with the attribute of *Kesser*. Evidence for this is the fact that children, possessing as they do some level of intelligence, may still not be able to talk. [35]

Since human beings were created in G-d's image, we can thus extrapolate that the Divine attributes also follow the above structure. Beginning the key psalm of *Pesukei DeZimrah* with the word *Ashrei* (repeated three times in these two verses) indicates that although we are about to recognize and praise G-d's Divine attributes which have joined together to produce the magnificence of Creation, ultimately all His power and might, as well as all of His beneficence that flows into the world through the medium of these attributes including speech, originates from the one transcendent Divine attribute: *Kesser*.[36]

The body of the *Ashrei* text begins with the words *Tehillah LeDavid*— "A psalm of praise by David." King David, the personification of Jewish kingship (*Malchus*), composed the psalms, which praise G-d through the medium of speech. To further allude to the significance of kingship in this psalm, three of its twenty-two verses address the idea of *Malchus*.

As mentioned above, the distinguishing feature of this psalm is that the verses are structured according to the *alef-beis*, and each praises one of G-d's specific attributes or qualities. The significance of this alphabetical form can be understood as follows: The Torah informs us that the world was created with G-d's words, using *Lashon HaKodesh*, the Holy Tongue. The letters of the *alef-beis* constitute the foundation for the words that make up the statements of Creation recorded in the Torah. These letters are thus the instruments with which G-d actually created the world, each letter representing a different creative force. Each distinct combination of *alef-beis* letters determines the uniqueness of each creation and becomes the singular name by which each created entity is identified. By using these *alef-beis* letters for an individual verse of praise in this psalm,[37] we are utilizing these core instruments of creation and transforming them into our praise of G-d. In addition, we also acknowledge that G-d, through these distinct letters, is uniquely invested in each individual creation.

■■■

Up until this point, *Pesukei DeZimrah* has focused on G-d's intimate involvement with the creation of every living being by emphasizing how the letters of Creation and the array of His attributes are involved in this process. As stated above, the sixteenth verse of the psalm, "You open Your hand and satiate the desire of every living being," is considered the core of *Pesukei DeZimrah*. This verse acknowledges that G-d not only creates every individual entity and being, but is also intimately involved in the function and survival of each entity.

The survival of any living organism is dependent on proper nourishment. Most living beings, human beings included, spend a substantial portion of their waking time and energy obtaining and ingesting the nourishment needed for their survival. Acknowledging that our sustenance is actually supplied to us by the Creator radically changes our most basic and customary perception of ourselves. Instead of thinking of ourselves as wholly independent beings, we come to the realization that we are totally dependent on G-d for our daily bread. Achieving this awareness is a fundamental objective of our entire Divine service.

Moreover, as every parent can testify, the constant awareness of the needs of one's children, and providing them with these needs, requires an inordinate amount of involvement and attention to detail. This parallels closely what G-d does for each one of us on a daily basis. Because this verse instills this awareness within us, it is considered the pivotal point and the primary purpose of the entire *Pesukei DeZimrah*.

Psalm 146: Personal Praise

After having extolled G-d in the previous psalm for unceasingly providing for our needs, our focus in this psalm turns to the individual who is praising G-d. The psalm is divided into two sections. The first emphasizes how both the body and soul of a person join in praise of G-d, each with its own emphasis. The soul's praise is termed *hillul*, while the praise offered by the body is termed *zemer*. As indicated by the phrase,[38] ". . . when His lamp shone forth (*behilo*)," *hillul*, translated as "praise," means shining forth. The soul is a medium through which the light of *Havayah*, the name associated with G-d's transcendence, shines forth. In contrast, the body offers *zemer*, praise in the form of an emotional song: "I will praise *Elokai* (using a derivative of the name of G-d associated with nature, *Elokim*) with my body."[39]

The second part of the psalm focuses on G-d's overall design for creation, with body and soul each fulfilling its destined role. This is primarily expressed in the verse, "He executes judgment on behalf of the oppressed." The intent of the word "oppressed" includes not only the physically oppressed, but also the "oppressed" sparks of holiness,[40] termed as such because in the process of creation, they fell and became scattered throughout the various spiritual and physical worlds. Elevating and redeeming these "holy sparks" underlies G-d's entire plan for the world's existence and serves as the common objective of each human life. Each individual is required to praise G-d for the specific role in this process that He has determined for him, utilizing his entirely unique body and soul to do so.[41]

Psalm 147:
Praise for G-d as He Is Manifest in Nature

This psalm expresses our praise for G-d's activities throughout the entire universe through the exquisite function and harmony that exists within the natural world. As the psalm states: "He counts the sum of the stars, naming them all." Each star is counted and named because each is unique and has a distinct role and purpose. In turn, each star exerts its influence on a particular worldly entity.

The psalm continues: "Our L-rd is great and abundant in power; His understanding is beyond calculation." Since each of these stars (as well as every other created being) is unique, it must have a distinct source that conceived it and a distinct creative force that brings it into being. This overall source is the Divine attribute of *Binah*—understanding—for it is this attribute that brings out the individual potentials that exist within the all-encompassing Divine life force. [42]

In the human realm, the faculty of understanding points out the dissimilarities that exist between different entities and highlights their individuality. In the spiritual realms above, the Divine attribute of *Binah* actually produces and brings about these differences.

This is why the psalm describes the attribute of understanding as being beyond calculation, a term usually associated with numbers and not intellect. Since each individual creation is distinct and has a unique source in *Binah*, the phrase "beyond calculation" is employed to emphasize how numerically vast are the workings of this attribute.

The theme that all of nature is a manifestation of G-d's handiwork, and each created being is specifically designed to fulfill a specific and precise purpose, is further amplified with the words: ". . . Who covers the heavens with clouds, Who prepares rain for the earth." Our world exists in a wondrous environment of continual self-renewal, displaying an exquisite balance between all the various forces of nature, all orchestrated to provide creatures with their needs. Thus the psalm continues, ". . . Who causes grass to grow on the mountains; Who gives animals their food." All the above points to G-d's individual providence over all of creation and His unremitting attentiveness to fulfilling the needs of every being.

Psalm 148: All of Creation Joins in Praise

Having described G-d's immanence and His providence over all creatures, our focus in this psalm turns to the loftier forms of creation. Thus the first verse states: "Praise G-d from the heavens," followed by the "lofty heights," "all His angels" and "all His hosts."

These four categories follow the order of the four spiritual worlds in descending order: The "heavens" refers to the most sublime level, the world of *Atzilus*; the "lofty heights"—the beginning point of independent self-awareness and *yeshus*—refers to the world of *Beriah*; "angels" refers to the world of *Yetzirah*, the primary abode of the angels; and finally, "hosts," referring to the spiritual realm of the world of *Asiyah*. Continuing with the descent into our physical world, the verse goes on to state: "Praise Him, sun and moon; praise Him all the stars that shine. He established them forever, for all time; He laid down the statute and it shall not be contravened." This demonstrates that it is G-d alone Who established the laws of nature, and it is these laws that govern the entire universe and the heavenly bodies within it. Moreover, only G-d, Who is truly infinite, can create entities that are unchanging and last forever, as the verse states: "He establishes them (the stars) forever, for all time."

In contrast to the downward direction of the first six verses of the psalm, the second segment reverses this order and ascends from the lower levels of creation to the higher ones. This begins in verse seven, which mentions the four elements that comprise the material world (earth, water, air and fire), and then travels from the inanimate to the animate in the higher categories of existence: plant, animal and human.

Thus, the sum total of G-d's entire creation—the symphony of all its different parts—and each individual song of praise for Him, serves as our acknowledgment that G-d's providence extends to all of creation. Because of His individual providence over every created being, each one is obligated to sing His praises.[43]

Psalm 149: The Future

The opening words of this psalm, "Sing to G-d a new song," turns our attention from the past and present to the future, the era of *Mashiach*. Recognizing G-d in nature, as well as seeing nature as the medium through which G-d's ongoing creative force expresses itself, will become the commonplace reality during the time of *Mashiach*. Indeed, achieving this reality is the objective and aim of all our efforts from the onset of human history. The era of *Mashiach* is a time when G-d's mastery over nature will become abundantly clear to all, bringing about the setting in which "*Yisrael* will rejoice in his Maker; let the children of Zion delight in their King," as the verse goes on to state.

Psalm 150: Praise G-d in His Transcendence

With this psalm, we attain the pinnacle of our praise of Him as we say, "Praise Him in His holy place; praise Him in the firmament where His power [is manifest]."

Having concluded the praise and recognition of G-d as He is immanent within creation, we now focus our praise of Him as He exists for Himself, infinitely beyond the parameters of creation. Moreover, not only do we personally engage in this process, we proceed to call upon all living things and all souls—including all ten soul attributes and each of the five different levels of each soul—to join in this process. All these aspects are inferred in the words, "All of the [individual] souls shall praise G-d"; that is, all the components of each soul, (its five levels,) and the entirety of every soul, (its ten soul powers,) shall praise Him.

After concluding this glorious recitation of praise, we recite four verses from the Book of Psalms, each beginning with the word *baruch*, emphasizing that the objective of all the above praises is to accomplish the revelation of "*baruch*"—drawing down Divine light into this world.

Additions to *Pesukei DeZimrah*

The above represents the conclusion of *Pesukei DeZimrah* as instituted by the *Anshei Knesses HaGedolah*. However, subsequently, the *Geonim* made several additions which have become universally accepted as part of the daily liturgy.

The first, *Vayevarech David*, "And David blessed [G-d]" is an excerpt from *Divrei HaYamim*,[44] referring to the preparations for the building of the First *Beis HaMikdash* in Jerusalem.[45] King David uttered these words of praise after he had transferred all the materials necessary for the construction of the *Beis Hamikdash* to his son, Shlomo, the one destined to build it.

The purpose of the *Beis Hamikdash* was to provide a physical space within the world where G-d's Presence would be revealed. This mirrors the intent of the recitation of *Pesukei DeZimrah* and *tefillah* in general: to recognize and draw down G-d's Divine power and light within creation.

In addition, the opening word of this passage consists of a blessing: "And David blessed (*Vayevarech*) G-d." As explained several times, "blessing" in Hebrew also means "to draw down." Drawing down G-dliness is thus part of the intent of this passage as well. Following his statement of blessing, David lists all of the Divine emotive attributes, while also acknowledging that although these attributes are an expression of, and are completely unified with, G-d, G-d Himself is truly beyond any and all of these attributes.

The second addition is from the book of *Nechemiah* and begins *Vivarchu Shem Kevodecha*— "Let [*Yisrael*] bless Your glorious Name."[46] It was recited at the time of the fortification of Jerusalem and the building of the Second *Beis HaMikdash*.

The final insertion in *Pesukei DeZimrah* is the Song of the Sea.[47] This song was sung by the Jewish people when they crossed the Sea of Reeds, when G-d provided them with a view of nature from His perspective. Thus the song states, "And *Yisrael* saw"—for this was the first time they were truly able to see matters from G-d's perspective. Furthermore, each of them pointed with a finger and declared, "*This* is my G-d."[48] For while it is necessary to understand that nature is but an additional expression of G-dliness, it is also necessary to recognize that nature itself is not bound by nature—it is just as much an expression of G-d's transcendence as it is a miracle. This is what the people saw at that awesome event.

Yishtabach

Yishtabach, the concluding blessing of *Pesukei DeZimrah*, includes the thirteen basic terms of praise for G-d used throughout our *tefillah* (*shir, u'shvachah, hallel, v'zimrah, oz, u'memshalah, netzach, gedulah u'gevurah, tehillah, v'siferes, kedushah, u'malchus*). It thereby serves as a summary of all the preceding Verses of Praise contained in this section of prayer. Finally, it closes with the words, "The King, Who is alone, gives life to the worlds."[49]

Because *Pesukei DeZimrah* emphasizes G-d as He is invested in creation and nature, it is also necessary for us to state explicitly that ultimately, G-d is not defined by His act of Creation in any way. He is beyond anything within our conception. Moreover, even as He actively creates all beings, He essentially remains totally alone and transcendent.

The Siddur Illuminated by Chassidus (Brooklyn, N.Y.: Kehot Publication Society, 2013), pp. 297–301, 311–320
Reprinted with permission of the author

Endnotes

1 *Shmos* 13:13.
2 Ibid.: 14.
3 *Shabbos* 55a.
4 *Malachi* 3:6.
5 Vol. III, p. 306b.
6 *Tehillim* 147:8–9, included in the *Pesukei DeZimrah* prayers.
7 Consumed, or burned up, hence the name *Seraphim*, which means "burning up."

[8] They believe that they exist, but they believe that their existence depends on something else.
[9] This is the spark that gives man the potential for free choice, his superiority over even the loftiest angels, as described above.
[10] *Berachos* 32a, as interpreted by *Eliyahu Rabbah* 1:14; *Likkutei Torah, Bamidbar*, p. 28b, et al.
[11] *Berachos*, op. cit.
[12] *Devarim* 3:24.
[13] Known more familiarly as Ashrei.
[14] *Berachos* 4b.
[15] In total, the word *Hallelukah* (lit., "Praise G-d") is mentioned ten times in the final five psalms, corresponding to the ten structural forms used in the composition of the various chapters of *Tehillim*: *shir*, *shevach*, *hallel*, etc.
[16] This notion is also reflected in the fact that in the kabbalistic structure of prayer, *Pesukei DeZimrah* corresponds to the world of *Yetzirah*, the realm of emotion.
[17] *Berachos* 40a.
[18] *Likkutei Torah, Vayikra*, p. 49b.
[19] *Tehillim* 35:10.
[20] The *Nishmas* prayer in the *Shabbos* liturgy.
[21] See *Ramban*, commentary to *Bereishis* 2:2.
[22] As quoted in *Tanya, Shaar HaYichud VehaEmunah*, ch. 1.
[23] *Tehillim* 119:89.
[24] *Torah Or*, p. 90c.
[25] *Midrash Tanchuma, Parshas Emor*, Sec. 14.
[26] More particularly, as stated in *Berachos* 54b, the todah-offering must be brought after being saved from one of four life-threatening situations.
[27] *Peirush HaMilos*, p. 92b.
[28] As noted, this is more formally referred to as *Tehillah LeDavid*, the beginning words of Psalm 145.
[29] *Or HaTorah, Bamidbar*. Vol. 2, p. 514.
[30] I.e., the realm of spiritual existence that brings our world into being.
[31] *Peirush HaMilos*, p. 101d ff.
[32] *Berachos* 4b.
[33] From Psalms 84 and 144.
[34] *Koheles* 8:4.
[35] *Tanya, Iggeres HaKodesh*, Epistle 4.
[36] *Siddur im Dach; Peirush HaMilos*, p. 107b ff.
[37] The omitted *nun* was included in the word *hanoflim* in the following verse that begins with the letter *samach*.
[38] *Iyov* 29:3.
[39] *Tanya, Shaar HaYichud VehaEmunah*, ch. 6.
[40] *Siddur im Dach*.
[41] More particularly, the soul's role is to elevate the body and the sustenance that the body consumes, as this sustenance contains the fallen sparks of creation.
[42] Since our expression of *Pesukei DeZimrah* has its source in the world of emotions, this aspect of *Binah* refers to the interinclusion of Binah in the world of emotions, which is *Yetzirah*.
[43] *Toras Shmuel* 5627, p. 169.
[44] I *Divrei HaYamim* 29:10–13.
[45] King David's blessing of G-d included here is the culmination of his final charge to the nation of Israel to entrust his son Shlomo with the building of the First *Beis HaMikdash*.
[46] *Nechemiah* 9:5–8, 9:8–11.
[47] *Shmos* 14:30–31, 15:1–19.
[48] *Shmos Rabbah* 23:15.
[49] To illustrate the meaning behind this verse, an alternate translation was used.

Lesson 4

HEAR O ISRAEL

ACHIEVING TRUE TRANSCENDENCE IN PRAYER

The Hands, Miro Pogran, Czech Republic, lithograph, 2005.

G-d created a complex universe bursting with wonder, beauty, and awe. But G-d is far beyond all that. Although we exist within the confines of nature, we can reach into the infinite presence of G-d beyond creation. This lesson explores the mysticism and meaning of the Shema prayer, Judaism's ultimate declaration of faith and our portal to a relationship with a G-d who is both transcendent and intimate.

TEXT 1

VIKTOR FRANKL, *MAN'S SEARCH FOR MEANING* (BOSTON: BEACON PRESS, 2014), PP. 107–108

Let me recall that which was perhaps the deepest experience I had in the concentration camp. The odds of surviving the camp were no more than one in twenty-eight, as can easily be verified by exact statistics. It did not even seem possible, let alone probable, that the manuscript of my first book, which I had hidden in my coat when I arrived at Auschwitz, would ever be rescued. Thus, I had to undergo and to overcome the loss of my mental child. And now it seemed as if nothing and no one would survive me; neither a physical nor a mental child of my own! So I found myself confronted with the question whether under such circumstances my life was ultimately void of any meaning.

Not yet did I notice that an answer to this question with which I was wrestling so passionately was already in store for me, and that soon thereafter this answer would be given to me. This was the case when I had to surrender my clothes and in turn inherited the worn-out rags of an inmate who had already been sent to the gas chamber immediately after his arrival at the Auschwitz railway station. Instead of the many pages of my manuscript, I found in a pocket of the newly acquired coat one single page torn out of a Hebrew prayer book, containing the most important Jewish prayer, *Shema Yisrael*. How

VIKTOR EMIL FRANKL, M.D., PHD
1905–1997

Founder of logotherapy. Frankl was a professor of neurology and psychiatry at the University of Vienna Medical School. During World War II he spent 3 years in various concentration camps, including Theresienstadt, Auschwitz, and Dachau. Frankl was the founder of the psychotherapeutic school called logotherapy. Frankl authored 39 books, which have been published in 38 languages. His most famous book, *Man's Search for Meaning*, has sold over 9 million copies in the U.S. alone.

should I have interpreted such a "coincidence" other than as a challenge to live my thoughts instead of merely putting them on paper?

A bit later, I remember, it seemed to me that I would die in the near future. In this critical situation, however, my concern was different from that of most of my comrades. Their question was, "Will we survive the camp? For, if not, all this suffering has no meaning." The question which beset me was, "Has all this suffering, this dying around us, a meaning? For, if not, then ultimately there is no meaning to survival; for a life whose meaning depends upon such a happenstance—as whether one escapes or not —ultimately would not be worth living at all."

The Flames Will Not Consume You [Isaiah 43:2], Leon Zernitsky, Canada, acrylic and gesso on canvas.

QUESTIONS FOR DISCUSSION

1 In your opinion, what is the underlying difference between Frankl's conception of meaning and that of his comrades?

2 Do you think the "association" rung of the prayer ladder, depicted in Illustration Four, Excercise 3.1, Lesson Three, has the ability to inspire Frankl-like thinking?

Association: Illustration Four, Excercise 3.1, Lesson Three

Figure 4.1

Shema and Its Blessings

SECTIONS	PARAGRAPHS	THEME	ORIGINS
First blessing, pp. 39–41*	*Yotser or,* *Hame'ir la'arets,* *Titbarech,* *Et Shem Hakel,* *Kadosh,* *Lakel baruch*	Creation of light and darkness Angels' praise of G-d	Men of the Great Assembly
Second blessing, pp. 41–42	*Ahavat olam*	G-d's love of the Jewish people	Men of the Great Assembly
Shema, pp. 42–44	Shema, *Baruch Shem,* *Ve'ahavta,* *Vehayah im shamoa,* *Vayomer*	Belief in G-d Commitment to the Torah Exodus	Deuteronomy 6:4–9 Deuteronomy 11:13–21 Numbers 15:37–41
Third blessing, pp. 44–45	*Emet veyatsiv,* *Ezrat avoteinu,* *Shirah chadashah*	G-d's faithfulness to the Jewish people Exodus	Men of the Great Assembly

* The page number references are to the *Siddur Tehilat Hashem* prayer book (New York: Merkos L'Inyonei Chinuch, 2004).

TEXT 2

FIRST BLESSING OF THE SHEMA, MORNING PRAYERS

> כּוּלָּם אֲהוּבִים, כֻּלָּם בְּרוּרִים, כֻּלָּם גִּבּוֹרִים ,כֻּלָּם קְדוֹשִׁים, וְכֻלָּם עֹשִׂים בְּאֵימָה וּבְיִרְאָה רְצוֹן קוֹנָם. וְכֻלָּם פּוֹתְחִים אֶת פִּיהֶם בִּקְדֻשָּׁה וּבְטָהֳרָה, בְּשִׁירָה וּבְזִמְרָה, וּמְבָרְכִים וּמְשַׁבְּחִים, וּמְפָאֲרִים וּמַעֲרִיצִים, וּמַקְדִּישִׁים וּמַמְלִיכִים.
>
> אֶת שֵׁם הָאֵ-ל, הַמֶּלֶךְ הַגָּדוֹל, הַגִּבּוֹר וְהַנּוֹרָא קָדוֹשׁ הוּא . . . כֻּלָּם כְּאֶחָד עוֹנִים בְּאֵימָה וְאוֹמְרִים בְּיִרְאָה:
>
> קָדוֹשׁ קָדוֹשׁ קָדוֹשׁ ה' צְבָאוֹת.

*A journey through the siddur with **Rabbi Shmuel Kaplan**:*

MYJLI.COM/PRAYER

All the angels are beloved, all are pure, all are mighty, all are holy, and all perform the will of their Maker with fear and awe. And all of them open their mouths in holiness and purity, with song and melody, and bless and adore, glorify and revere, hallow and ascribe sovereignty to—

The name of the Almighty G-d, the great, powerful, and awe-inspiring King; holy is He. . . . Together, all exclaiming in unison, with awe, and declaring in reverence:

"Holy, holy, holy is the L-rd of hosts."

TEXT 3

RABBI SHNE'UR ZALMAN OF LIADI, *LIKUTEI TORAH,* EMOR 32B

וְעִיקַר הַהַשָּׂגָה הוּא זֶה אֵיךְ שֶׁהוּא יִתְבָּרֵךְ קָדוֹשׁ וּמוּבְדָל בִּבְחִינַת אֵין עֲרוֹךְ אֵלָיו בָּרוּךְ הוּא, וּמָקוֹר הַמְשָׁכַת הַחַיּוּת מִמֶּנּוּ יִתְבָּרֵךְ לִהְיוֹת בִּחִינַת מְמַלֵּא כָּל עָלְמִין הוּא רַק עַל יְדֵי צִמְצוּם עָצוּם בִּבְחִינַת שַׂעֲרָה כְּנִזְכָּר לְעֵיל . . .

וְהִנֵּה עַל יְדֵי הִתְבּוֹנְנוּתָם וְהַשָּׂגָתָם בָּזֶה, אֲזַי הֵם מִתְלַהֲבִים וּמִתְלַהֲטִים בִּתְשׁוּקָה וְרִשְׁפֵּי אֵשׁ לְאִסְתַּכְּלָא בִּיקָרָא דְמַלְכָּא בִּבְחִינַת סוֹבֵב כָּל עָלְמִין שֶׁהוּא קָדוֹשׁ וּמוּבְדָל. וְלָכֵן נִקְרָאִים שְׂרָפִים, עַל שֵׁם הָרִשְׁפֵּי אֵשׁ וְהַתְּשׁוּקָה הַנִּפְלָאָה. וְזֶהוּ שֶׁאוֹמְרִים קָדוֹשׁ . . . שֶׁעִיקַר תְּשׁוּקָתָם לְהַשִּׂיג בְּחִינַת סוֹבֵב כָּל עָלְמִין הַנִּקְרָא קָדוֹשׁ.

The angels perceive the element of G-d that completely transcends them and the worlds in which they reside. For only a minimal amount of His energy, like the minimal amount of life-force found in a hair, is manifest in the worlds. . . .

Due to the angels' acute awareness of the transcendent aspect of G-d, they burn with a fiery desire to experience this element of G-d that is not manifest in the world. Indeed, one of the schools of angels is termed *seraphim* (those that burn), referring to their burning desire to experience G-d.

This is the meaning of the praise, *kadosh,* that the angels say. . . . They yearn to experience the element of G-d that is *kadosh*—that transcends the worlds.

RABBI SHNE'UR ZALMAN OF LIADI (ALTER REBBE) 1745–1812

Chasidic rebbe, halachic authority, and founder of the Chabad movement. The Alter Rebbe was born in Liozna, Belarus, and was among the principal students of the Magid of Mezeritch. His numerous works include the *Tanya*, an early classic containing the fundamentals of Chabad Chasidism, and *Shulchan Aruch HaRav,* an expanded and reworked code of Jewish law.

TEXT 4a

RABBI YOSEF YITSCHAK SCHNEERSOHN, *KUNTRES TORAT HACHASIDUT*, PP. 10–11

פַּעַם יָשְׁבוּ הַחֶבְרַיָּא קַדִּישָׁא – הֵן הֵמָּה כְּבוֹד קְדוּשַּׁת תַּלְמִידֵי הָרַב הַמַּגִּיד נִשְׁמָתוֹ בְּגִנְזֵי מְרוֹמִים זַ"ע – וְשׂוֹחֲחוּ בֵּינֵיהֶם בְּמַעֲלַת מַדְרֵיגוֹת מַלְאֲכֵי מָרוֹם, אוֹפַנִּים וְחַיּוֹת הַקֹּדֶשׁ בְּמֶרְכָּבָה הָעֶלְיוֹנָה אֲשֶׁר בְּכָל עוֹלָם וְעוֹלָם.

אֶחָד הַתַּלְמִידִים דִּבֵּר בְּמַעֲלַת הַמַּלְאָכִים שֶׁהֵם שִׂכְלִים נִבְדָּלִים, וְכָל חֲיוּתָם הוּא דְּבַר ה', וְהַשֵּׁנִי דִּבֵּר בְּמַעֲלָתָם שֶׁל הָאוֹפַנִּים וְחַיּוֹת הַקֹּדֶשׁ אֲשֶׁר הֵם תָּמִיד בְּאַהֲבָה וְיִרְאָה שֶׁהוּא רָצוֹא וָשׁוֹב . . . וְהַשְּׁלִישִׁי מֵהַחֲבֵרִים הַקְּדוֹשִׁים מְבַאֵר בְּמַעֲלָתָם שֶׁל הַשְּׂרָפִים שֶׁהֵם עוֹד לְמַעֲלָה בְּמַדְרֵיגָה לִהְיוֹת עֲמִידָתָם הוּא בְּעוֹלָם הַבְּרִיאָה.

וְהַחֶבְרַיָּא קַדִּישָׁא בְּקִנְאָתָם הַפְלָאַת מַעֲלַת רוֹמְמוּת נְעִימוֹת יְדִידוּת עֲבוֹדָתָם שֶׁל הַנֶּאֱצָלִים הָעֶלְיוֹנִים, הִתְלַהֲבוּ וְהִתְלַהֲטוּ בְּרִשְׁפֵּי אֵשׁ לַהֲבַת שַׁלְהֶבֶת גַּעֲגוּעֵי עֲבוֹדַת הַשֵּׁם יִתְבָּרֵךְ, הִנֵּה רוּבָּם כְּכוּלָּם מְרַחֲשִׁים בְּשִׂפְתוֹתֵיהֶם וְקוֹלָם לֹא יִשָּׁמַע, כּוּלָּם רוֹעֲדִים וְגוֹעִים בִּבְכִיָּה.

אֲחָדִים מֵהַחֶבְרַיָּא קַדִּישָׁא הָיוּ פְּנֵיהֶם לְהָבִים, עֵינֵיהֶם לְטוּשׁוֹת, וְכַפֵּיהֶם פְּרוּשׂוֹת מִבְּלִי תְּנוּעָה כַּהֲלוּמֵי רַעַם, וַאֲחָדִים נִגְּנוּ בְּנִיגּוּן חֲרִישִׁי, וְלִבָּם סוֹעֵר אֲשֶׁר עוֹד מְעַט וְנַפְשָׁם תִּשְׁתַּפֵּךְ בְּחֵיק בּוֹרֵא כָּל הַנְּשָׁמוֹת.

The students of the Magid of Mezeritch, "the holy group," once sat and discussed the exalted level of the angels—the *ophanim* and *chayot hakodesh* of the supernal *merkavah* (chariot)—that reside in the spiritual worlds.

One student described the angels as purely intellectual beings, acutely aware of the word of G-d that enlivens them. Another student extolled how the *ophanim* and *chayot hakodesh* are in a perpetual emotional cycle of love and awe, yearning and returning. Yet a third student explained the unique spiritual experience of the *seraphim,* who reside in the realm of *beriah.*

RABBI YOSEF YITSCHAK SCHNEERSOHN (RAYATS, FRIERDIKER REBBE, PREVIOUS REBBE) 1880–1950

Chasidic rebbe, prolific writer, and Jewish activist. Rabbi Yosef Yitschak, the sixth leader of the Chabad movement, actively promoted Jewish religious practice in Soviet Russia and was arrested for these activities. After his release from prison and exile, he settled in Warsaw, Poland, from where he fled Nazi occupation and arrived in New York in 1940. Settling in Brooklyn, Rabbi Schneersohn worked to revitalize American Jewish life. His son-in-law, Rabbi Menachem Mendel Schneerson, succeeded him as the leader of the Chabad movement.

Inspired by the tremendous spirituality of the heavenly angels, the members of the holy group burned with a great desire to become closer to G-d. They whispered with their lips, their voices inaudible; they trembled and wept.

Some of them sat there, their faces alight, eyes glowing, and their arms remaining outstretched as if thunderstruck. Others hummed soft melodies, their hearts astir—their souls yearning to be reunited with their Creator.

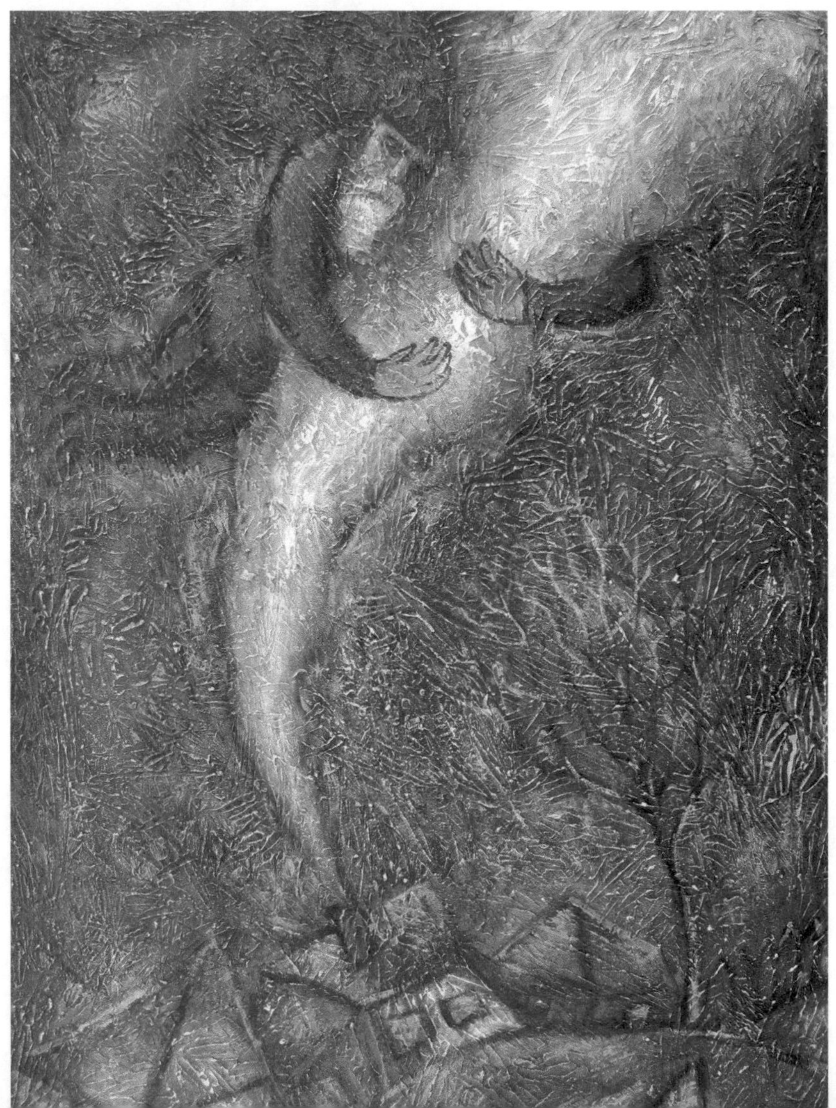

Connection to my Old Jewish Village, Leon Zernitsky, Canada, acrylic on canvas.

Figure 4.2

Association: Illustration Five, Excercise 3.1, Lesson Three

TEXT 4b

RABBI YOSEF YITSCHAK SCHNEERSOHN, IBID.

בְּלִי סָפֵק – אוֹמֵר כְּבוֹד קְדוּשַּׁת אָחִי – אֲשֶׁר בְּאִם לֹא הָיָה נִכְנַס כְּבוֹד קְדוּשַּׁת מוֹרֵנוּ וְרַבֵּנוּ הָרַב הַמַּגִּיד לְבֵית הַמִּדְרָשׁ בְּשָׁעָה הַהִיא, כִּי אֲחָדִים מֵהַחֲבֵרִים הַקְּדוֹשִׁים הָיוּ כָּלִים מַמָּשׁ בִּכְלוֹת הַנֶּפֶשׁ מִגּוֹדֶל תְּשׁוּקַת צִמְאוֹנָם לְהִכָּלֵל בְּחֶבְיוֹן עוּזּוֹ יִתְבָּרֵךְ וְיִתְעַלֶּה, אֲבָל מִכֵּיוָן שֶׁנִּשְׁמְעוּ צְעָדֵי מוֹרֵנוּ וְרַבֵּנוּ, הִנֵּה כְּרֶגַע נֵעוֹרוּ כָּל הַחֶבְרַיָּא קַדִּישָׁא מֵעוֹמֶק דְּבֵיקוּתָם הַנִּפְלָאָה וַיַּעַמְדוּ הָכֵן לְקַבֵּל פְּנֵי הַקֹּדֶשׁ.

כְּשֶׁנִּכְנַס מוֹרֵנוּ וְרַבֵּנוּ יָשַׁב בְּרֹאשׁ הַשּׁוּלְחָן וַיֹּאמַר תּוֹרָה:

"אָנֹכִי עָשִׂיתִי אֶרֶץ וְאָדָם עָלֶיהָ בָרָאתִי" (ישעיהו מה, יב), אָנֹכִי מִי שֶׁאָנֹכִי, שֶׁהוּא נֶעֱלָם וְנִסְתָּר גַּם מִנֶּאֱצָלִים הֶיוֹתֵר עֶלְיוֹנִים, הִלְבִּישׁ עַצְמוּתוֹ יִתְבָּרֵךְ בְּכַמָּה צִמְצוּמִים לְהַאֲצִיל הַנֶּאֱצָלִים וְלִבְרוֹא הַנִּבְרָאִים שְׂרָפִים חַיּוֹת וְאוֹפַנִּים מַלְאָכִים וְעוֹלָמוֹת עַד אֵין מִסְפָּר, וּבְצִמְצוּמִים עַד אֵין שִׁיעוּר, עָשִׂיתִי אֶרֶץ הַלָּזוּ הַגַּשְׁמִית, וְאָדָם עָלֶיהָ בָּרָאתִ"י, הָאָדָם הוּא תַּכְלִית הַהִתְהַוּוּת, וּבָרָאתִ"י בְּגִימַטְרִיָּא תַּרְיַ"ג הוּא תַּכְלִית הָאָדָם . . .

כְּשֶׁגָּמַר מוֹרֵנוּ וְרַבֵּנוּ אֶת הַתּוֹרָה חָזַר לְהֵיכַל קָדְשׁוֹ. וּבְתוֹרָה זוּ הִרְגִּיעַ רוּחַ קָדְשָׁם שֶׁל הַחֶבְרַיָּא.

Had the Magid not entered the study hall at that moment, some of the students would have certainly expired from their burning desire to be subsumed in G-d's vast greatness. But upon hearing the footsteps of the Magid, the students were instantly brought back to their senses as they stood to welcome their teacher.

When the Magid entered the room, he sat down at the head of the table and began to speak:

"The verse says, 'I created the world and placed humankind upon it' (ISAIAH 45:12). This verse can be interpreted as follows:

"'I'—referring to G-d's very essence, which is beyond even the most exalted of spiritual beings—concealed Myself in order to create *seraphim, chayot hakodesh, ophanim,* and countless other angels and spiritual worlds. 'Created the world,' that is, the physical world, 'and placed humankind upon it,' humankind being the purpose of all of creation, through their fulfillment of the Torah."

Upon finishing this teaching, the Magid returned to his room. This teaching settled the students' fiery spirits.

The Spoonful of Milk, Marc Chagall, oil on canvas, Paris, 1912.

TEXT 5a

SECOND BLESSING BEFORE SHEMA, MORNING PRAYERS

אַהֲבַת עוֹלָם אֲהַבְתָּנוּ ה' אֱלֹקֵינוּ. חֶמְלָה גְדוֹלָה וִיתֵרָה חָמַלְתָּ עָלֵינוּ.

L-rd our G-d, you have loved us with everlasting love (*ahavat olam*). You have bestowed upon us exceedingly abounding mercy.

TEXT 5b

RABBI SHNE'UR ZALMAN OF LIADI, *TANYA,* CHAPTER 49

"אַהֲבַת עוֹלָם אֲהַבְתָּנוּ ה' אֱלֹקֵינוּ".

כְּלוֹמַר, שֶׁהִנִּיחַ כָּל צְבָא מַעֲלָה הַקְּדוֹשִׁים, וְהִשְׁרָה שְׁכִינָתוֹ עָלֵינוּ... וְהַיְינוּ כִּי אַהֲבָה דוֹחֶקֶת הַבָּשָׂר. וְלָכֵן נִקְרָא "אַהֲבַת עוֹלָם", שֶׁהִיא בְּחִינַת צִמְצוּם אוֹרוֹ הַגָּדוֹל הַבִּלְתִּי תַּכְלִית, לְהִתְלַבֵּשׁ בִּבְחִינַת גְּבוּל הַנִּקְרָא "עוֹלָם", בַּעֲבוּר אַהֲבַת עַמּוֹ יִשְׂרָאֵל, כְּדֵי לְקָרְבָם אֵלָיו לִיכָּלֵל בְּיִחוּדוֹ וְאַחְדוּתוֹ יִתְבָּרֵךְ.

וְזֶהוּ שֶׁנֶּאֱמַר: "חֶמְלָה גְדוֹלָה וִיתֵרָה",

פֵּרוּשׁ, יְתֵרָה עַל קִרְבַת אֱלֹקִים שֶׁבְּכָל צְבָא מַעְלָה.

"L-rd our G-d, you have loved us with everlasting love (*ahavat olam*)."

[Aside from meaning *eternal*, the word *olam* can also be translated as *world*. Thus, *ahavat olam* can be translated as *worldly love*.]

The reason why G-d's love toward us is described as "worldly love" is as follows:

Due to G-d's great love of His nation, the Jewish people, He set aside the spiritual beings. Rather, G-d contracted His infinite expression in order to invest Himself in the confines of the world, and thus rest His presence on us and bring us close to His unity. Indeed, love inspires contraction.

"You have bestowed upon us exceedingly abounding mercy."

This refers to the distinct closeness G-d has granted us, which exceeds that of any of the spiritual beings.

Page from *machzor* (festival prayer book) (detail), decorated first-word panel, northern Italy, 1466, artist: probably Giorgio d'Alemagna, scribe: Leon ben Joshua de Rossi of Cesena, pen and ink. (London, British Library Collection of Illuminated Manuscripts)

TEXT 6

DEUTERONOMY 6:4, SHEMA, MORNING PRAYERS

שְׁמַע יִשְׂרָאֵל ה' אֱלֹקֵינוּ ה' אֶחָד.

Hear O Israel, the L-rd is our G-d, the L-rd is One.

*"Our G-d is One." What does that tell me? **Rabbi Simon Jacobson** explores:*

MYJLI.COM/PRAYER

TEXT 7a

ZOHAR 3:257B

דְּאִיהוּ הֲוָה קֹדֶם כָּל הֲוָיָין, וְאִיהוּ בְּתוֹךְ כָּל הֲוָיָה, וְאִיהוּ לְאַחַר כָּל הֲוָיָה.

The word *Havayah* shares the same letters as the Hebrew words that translate as "was," "is," and "will be." This represents how G-d precedes creation, exists currently, and remains the same after creation.

ZOHAR

The seminal work of kabbalah, Jewish mysticism. The *Zohar* is a mystical commentary on the Torah, written in Aramaic and Hebrew. According to the Arizal, the *Zohar* contains the teachings of Rabbi Shimon bar Yochai, who lived in the Land of Israel during the second century. The *Zohar* has become one of the indispensable texts of traditional Judaism, alongside and nearly equal in stature to the Mishnah and Talmud.

TEXT 7b

ADON OLAM, MORNING PRAYERS

אֲדוֹן עוֹלָם אֲשֶׁר מָלַךְ בְּטֶרֶם כָּל יְצוּר נִבְרָא. לְעֵת נַעֲשָׂה בְחֶפְצוֹ כֹּל, אֲזַי מֶלֶךְ שְׁמוֹ נִקְרָא. וְאַחֲרֵי כִּכְלוֹת הַכֹּל, לְבַדּוֹ יִמְלֹךְ נוֹרָא. וְהוּא הָיָה וְהוּא הֹוֶה, וְהוּא יִהְיֶה בְּתִפְאָרָה.

L-rd of the universe, Who reigned before anything was created—at the time when by His will all things were made, then was His name proclaimed King. And after all things shall cease to be, the Awesome One will reign alone. He was, He is, and He shall be in glory.

***Professor Lewis Glinert** explains the history and meaning of Adon Olam:*

MYJLI.COM/PRAYER

Morning prayers at 14,000 feet above sea level, Western Breach, Mt. Kilimanjaro, Tanzania, Africa, Yehoshua Halevi Photography.

TEXT 8

RABBI YAAKOV BEN ASHER, *ARBAAH TURIM, ORACH CHAYIM* 5

וּבְהַזְכִּירוֹ "אֱלֹקִים", יְכַוֵּין שֶׁהוּא תַּקִּיף, אַמִּיץ, אֲשֶׁר לוֹ הַיְכוֹלֶת בָּעֶלְיוֹנִים וּבַתַּחְתּוֹנִים. כִּי "אֵ-ל" לָשׁוֹן כֹּחַ וְחוֹזֶק הוּא, כְּמוֹ: "וְאֶת אֵילֵי הָאָרֶץ לָקָח" (יְחֶזְקֵאל יז, יג).

The word *Kel* [the first two letters of *Elokim*] means power, as in the verse, "He took away the powerful ones (*eilei*) of the land" (EZEKIEL 17:18).

Therefore, when saying the name *Elokim,* one should contemplate that G-d is mighty and powerful, ruling the higher and lower worlds.

RABBI YAAKOV BEN ASHER (*TUR*, BAAL HATURIM) C. 1269–1343

Halachic authority and codifier. Rabbi Yaakov was born in Germany and moved to Toledo, Spain, with his father, the noted halachist Rabbi Asher, to escape persecution. He wrote *Arbaah Turim ("Tur")*, an ingeniously organized and highly influential code of Jewish law. He is considered one of the greatest authorities of halachah.

QUESTION FOR DISCUSSION

How might the names *Havayah* and *Elokim* correlate to the manifest and transcendent aspects of G-d?

TEXT 9

RABBI SHNE'UR ZALMAN OF LIADI, CITED IN *HAYOM YOM*, 12 CHESHVAN

> שְׁמַע יִשְׂרָאֵל - אַ אִיד דֶערְהֶערְט - הֲוָיָ"ה אֱלֹקֵינוּ - אַז כּוֹחֵנוּ וְחַיּוּתֵינוּ אִיז דָאס לְמַעְלָה מִן הַטֶּבַע, אוּן - הֲוָיָ"ה אֶחָד.

Shema Yisrael—a Jew perceives that,

Havayah Elokeinu—our strength and life is beyond nature, and

Havayah Echad—that G-d is One.

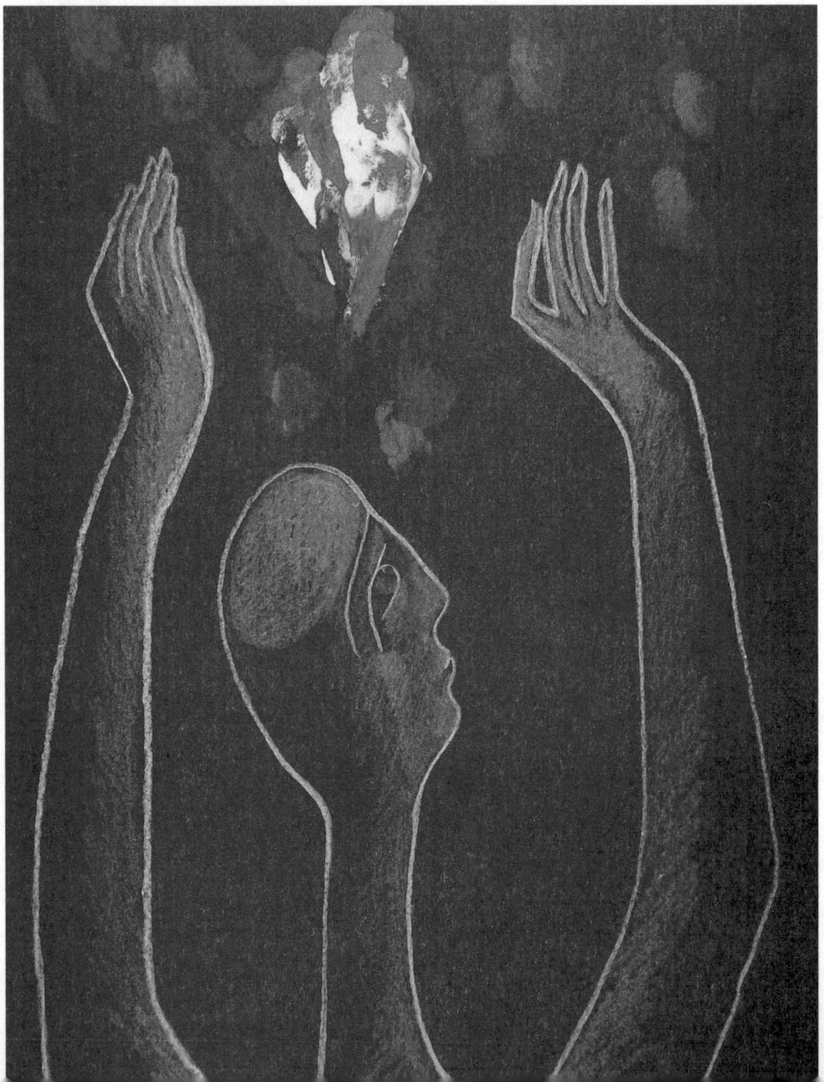

Dactyloscopic nocturnes. Shema Yisrael, drawing, Elisheva Nesis, Israel; pencil, colored pencils, acrylic, and fingers on paper.

TEXT 10a

DEUTERONOMY 6:5, SHEMA, MORNING PRAYERS

וְאָהַבְתָּ אֵת ה' אֱלֹקֶיךָ בְּכָל לְבָבְךָ, וּבְכָל נַפְשְׁךָ, וּבְכָל מְאֹדֶךָ.

You shall love the L-rd your G-d with all your heart, with all your soul, and with all your might.

TEXT 10b

MISHNAH, BERACHOT 9:5

בְּכָל לְבָבְךָ: בִּשְׁנֵי יְצָרֶיךָ, בְּיֵצֶר טוֹב וּבְיֵצֶר הָרָע.
וּבְכָל נַפְשְׁךָ: אֲפִלּוּ הוּא נוֹטֵל אֶת נַפְשְׁךָ.
וּבְכָל מְאֹדֶךָ: בְּכָל מָמוֹנֶךָ.

"With all your heart": with both your positive and negative inclinations.

"With all your soul": even if it costs your life.

"With all your might": with all your possessions.

MISHNAH

The first authoritative work of Jewish law that was codified in writing. The Mishnah contains the oral traditions that were passed down from teacher to student; it supplements, clarifies, and systematizes the commandments of the Torah. Due to the continual persecution of the Jewish people, it became increasingly difficult to guarantee that these traditions would not be forgotten. Rabbi Yehudah Hanassi therefore redacted the Mishnah at the end of the 2nd century. It serves as the foundation for the Talmud.

TEXT 11

DEUTERONOMY 11:13–14, SHEMA, MORNING PRAYERS

> וְהָיָה אִם שָׁמֹעַ תִּשְׁמְעוּ אֶל מִצְוֹתַי, אֲשֶׁר אָנֹכִי מְצַוֶּה אֶתְכֶם הַיּוֹם, לְאַהֲבָה אֶת ה' אֱלֹקֵיכֶם, וּלְעָבְדוֹ בְּכָל לְבַבְכֶם וּבְכָל נַפְשְׁכֶם. וְנָתַתִּי מְטַר אַרְצְכֶם בְּעִתּוֹ, יוֹרֶה, וּמַלְקוֹשׁ. וְאָסַפְתָּ דְגָנֶךָ, וְתִירֹשְׁךָ וְיִצְהָרֶךָ.

And it will be, if you will diligently obey my commandments which I enjoin upon you this day, to love the L-rd your G-d and to serve Him with all your heart and with all your soul: I will give rain for your land at the proper time.

TEXT 12

MISHNAH, BERACHOT 2:1

> אָמַר ר' יְהוֹשֻׁעַ בֶּן קָרְחָה: לָמָּה קָדְמָה פַּרְשַׁת שְׁמַע לִוְהָיָה אִם שָׁמֹעַ? כְּדֵי שֶׁיְּקַבֵּל עָלָיו עוֹל מַלְכוּת שָׁמַיִם תְּחִלָּה וְאַחַר כָּךְ מְקַבֵּל עָלָיו עוֹל מִצְוֹת.

Rabbi Yehoshua ben Karcha said:

"Why did the Rabbis place the paragraph beginning with *Shema* before the paragraph beginning with *Vehayah im shamoa*?

"It is because one must first accept the rule of G-d, and only then one can commit to the *mitzvot*."

TEXT 13

NUMBERS 15:41, SHEMA, MORNING PRAYERS

אֲנִי ה' אֱלֹקֵיכֶם, אֲשֶׁר הוֹצֵאתִי אֶתְכֶם מֵאֶרֶץ מִצְרַיִם לִהְיוֹת לָכֶם לֵאלֹקִים. אֲנִי ה' אֱלֹקֵיכֶם.

I am the L-rd your G-d Who brought you out of the land of Egypt to be your G-d; I, the L-rd, am your G-d.

TEXT 14

RABBI SHNE'UR ZALMAN OF LIADI, *TANYA,* CHAPTER 47

וְהִנֵּה בְּכָל דּוֹר וָדוֹר וְכָל יוֹם וָיוֹם, חַיָּיב אָדָם לִרְאוֹת עַצְמוֹ כְּאִלּוּ הוּא יָצָא הַיּוֹם מִמִּצְרַיִם. וְהִיא יְצִיאַת נֶפֶשׁ הָאֱלֹקִית מִמַּאֲסַר הַגּוּף . . . לִיכָּלֵל בְּיִחוּד אוֹר אֵין סוֹף בָּרוּךְ הוּא עַל יְדֵי עֵסֶק הַתּוֹרָה וְהַמִּצְוֹת בִּכְלָל. וּבִפְרַט בְּקַבָּלַת מַלְכוּת שָׁמַיִם בִּקְרִיאַת שְׁמַע, שֶׁבָּהּ מְקַבֵּל וּמַמְשִׁיךְ עָלָיו יִחוּדוֹ יִתְבָּרֵךְ בְּפֵירוּשׁ, בְּאָמְרוֹ "ה' אֱלֹקֵינוּ ה' אֶחָד".

In every generation and on every day, a person must view oneself as if they left Egypt that day. This means freeing the G-dly soul from the domination of the body . . . in order to become one with the infinite G-d. Generally put, this is done through engaging in Torah and its *mitzvot*. More specifically, this is achieved through accepting G-d's rule when saying the Shema. When one says the words *Havayah Elokeinu*—the L-rd is our G-d—one acknowledges and experiences unity with G-d.

Exercise 4.1

Which theme of this lesson is most meaningful to you?

How can you utilize this theme to enhance your prayer experience?

Exercise for the Week

Love. This week, take a couple of minutes to reflect upon humanity's relative insignificance when contrasted with the sheer greatness and grandeur of the infinite G-d. Then, consider how fortunate you are that G-d not only notices you but also cares for you deeply and individually. Follow this up immediately with an out-loud reading of the Shema.

We'll discuss how it went during the next lesson.

KEY POINTS

1 The Shema prayer is flanked on either side by prayers that help frame its message.

2 Angels are spiritual beings with a heightened consciousness of G-d. They perceive the transcendent aspect of G-d and yearn for it. This is the meaning of their saying *kadosh*.

3 Despite G-d's transcendence, He contracted Himself to create our finite world because He desires to connect with us. This theme is reflected in the verse of *Shema Yisrael*.

4 Meditating on this arouses us to love G-d and inspires us to dedicate ourselves to fulfilling His will.

A book of Jewish customs, printed in 1723, and a machzor, *printed in 1735, teach us lots about prayer in the 18th century:*

MYJLI.COM/PRAYER

Additional Readings

THE HIDDEN BEAUTY OF THE SHEMA

BY LISA AIKEN, PHD

During World War II, countless Jewish parents gave their precious children to Christian neighbors and orphanages in the hope that the latter would provide safe havens for them. The parents expected that they, or their relatives, would take these children back if they survived the war.

The few parents who did not perish in the Holocaust, and were able to reclaim their children, often faced another horror. While the parents had summoned the strength to survive the slave labor and death camps, or had hidden out for years, those who took their children were busy teaching them to love Christianity, and to hate Jews and Judaism.

To add insult to injury, many Jewish children who were taken in by Christian orphanages, convents, and the like, had no parents or close relatives left after the Holocaust. When rabbis or distant relatives finally tracked down many of these children, the priests and nuns who had been their caretakers insisted that no children from Jewish homes were in their institutions. Thus, countless Jewish children were not only stripped of their entire families, they were also stripped of their souls.

In May, 1945, Rabbi Eliezer Silver from the United States and Dayan Grunfeld from England were sent as chaplains to liberate some of the death camps. While there, they were told that many Jewish children had been placed in a monastery in Alsace-Lorraine. The rabbis went there to reclaim them.

LISA AIKEN, PHD

Born in Baltimore, Maryland; noted author and speaker; served as chief psychologist at Lenox Hill Hospital in New York City from 1982–1989. Among her works are *Creating Healthy Marriages*, and *Faith, Meaning, and Self-Esteem*. She currently lives in Jerusalem.

When they approached the priest in charge, they asked that the Jewish children be released into the rabbis' care. "I'm sorry," the priest responded, "but there is no way of knowing which children here came from Jewish families. You must have documentation if you wish me to do what you ask."

Of course, the kind of documentation that the priest wanted was unobtainable at the end of the war. The rabbis asked to see the list of names of children who were in the monastery. As the rabbis read the list, they pointed to those that belonged to Jewish children.

"I'm sorry," the priest insisted, "but the names that you pointed to could be either Jewish or Gentile. Miller is a German name, and Markovich is a Russian name, and Swersky is a Polish name. You can't prove that these are Jewish children. If you can't prove which children are Jewish, and do it very quickly, you will have to leave."

One of the rabbis had a brilliant idea. "We'd like to come back again this evening when you are putting the children to sleep." The priest reluctantly agreed.

That evening the rabbis came to the dormitory, where row upon row of little beds were arranged. The children, many of whom had been in the monastery since the war started in 1939, were going to sleep. The rabbis walked through the aisles of beds, calling out, "Shema, Yisrael, Hashem Elokeinu, Hashem Echad!" ("Hear, Jewish people, the L-rd is our G-d, the L-rd is One!")

One by one, children burst into tears and shrieked, "Mommy!" "Maman!" "Momma!" "Mamushka!" in each of their native tongues.

The priest had succeeded in teaching these precious Jewish souls about the Trinity, the New Testament, and the Christian savior. Each child knew how to say Mass. But the priest did not succeed in erasing these children's memories of their Jewish mothers—now murdered—putting them to bed every night with the Shema on their lips.

(My thanks to Miriam Swerdlov for relating this story to me.)

G-d's Oneness

We say in the Shema that G-d is One, meaning that He is singular, unique, and incomparable. His uniqueness includes the idea that all else exists and functions only according to His will. He, of course, exists and functions without depending on anything else. The idea of G-d's singularity encompasses the first three of Maimonides' Thirteen Principles of Faith:

> *1. I believe with complete faith that the Creator, blessed is His Name, creates and guides all creations, and He alone made, makes and will make all things.*

This principle states that G-d has no "assistants" nor partners when He runs the world. This contrasts with pagan beliefs that many forces run the world and Christian beliefs that G-d is part of a trinity. This principle also includes the idea that the world only exists because of G-d's constant will for it to be sustained.

> *2. I believe with complete faith that the Creator, blessed is His Name, is unique, that there is no uniqueness like His in any way, and that He alone is our G-d who was, is, and always will be.*

G-d cannot be divided into component parts because He is a total unity that is indivisible.

> *3. I believe, with complete faith, that the Creator, blessed is His Name, has no body and is not affected by physical events, and He has absolutely no physical likeness.*

The idea of G-d's unity reminds us that our world's many creations do not function and exist independently. They all operate under G-d's providence. One of the Shema's main functions is to underscore this unity.

During Creation, the world expanded to the extent that G-d exclaimed, "If I create one more physical thing, the world will conceal Me so much that people won't be able to find Me. Enough concealment!" G-d wanted our world to operate via natural laws of cause and effect that would conceal His "directing the show" behind the scenes. At the same time, He wanted people to find Him. Some concealment was necessary to challenge us to use our free will to find and obey G-d. But He wanted us to grow from the challenges of the physical world, not assume that natural forces are in charge and that He is absent. Believing that the physical world is ultimate reality, and ignoring G-d's presence and will, negates the world's entire purpose.

The Almighty hides within the physical world and wants us to look for Him there. All life and blessing filters down here through Him, although we sometimes believe that other forces, such as nature, luck, fate, or people, ultimately make things happen. The more we believe that He is the only force that rules us, the less energy we waste compromising ourselves and trying to placate and control other forces. For example, if we believe that our efforts alone control our financial destiny and security, we might lie, act unethically, or compromise ourselves trying to get whatever financial benefits we can. If we believe that doctors restore our health, we look to them alone when we are sick and leave G-d out of the picture. If we think that we are fully responsible for our achievements, we try to accomplish goals on our own without asking for G-d's help.

The blessings that we receive actually depend upon how connected we are to our Source. The more we bond with and rely only upon Him, the more blessing we receive, and the less secondary forces distract us. Since "a servant can only serve one master," tying ourselves to extraneous forces makes us less available for a relationship with the Almighty. While He wants us to do our utmost to take care of our health, earn a living, and get what we need within the constraints of the physical world, we need always remember that G-d is the only *ultimate* Source. Finding a balance between having faith in Him while doing what we must to live in a material world is an ongoing, lifelong challenge.

When we get distracted by this world's superficiality, we think that it is ultimate reality. That prevents us from noticing the divine Presence behind the scenes. The more He seems absent, the more people tend to do negative things that fill the apparent void. That only makes Him even more hidden.

We can only see and appreciate G-d's unity and uniqueness by constantly searching for it. That is why the Hebrew word for "world" is *olam*. It derives from the word *he'elem* meaning "concealed." G-d designed a world that conceals His presence so that we can be rewarded for looking for Him. Searching for and finding Him lets us discover a hidden world of spiritual treasures that we aren't aware of otherwise.

Historical Background of the Shema

The Midrash (homiletical explanation of the Torah) gives two historical sources for the first two verses of the Shema prayer: "Hear, Israel, the L-rd is our G-d, the L-rd is One," and "Blessed is the Name of His glorious kingdom forever and ever."

One midrash describes our forefather Jacob being on his deathbed, surrounded by his children. He prophetically saw his descendants suffering so terribly that they questioned G-d's ways. He wanted to ensure that they would withstand the challenges and tribulations of exile while retaining their faith, by revealing to his sons the events that would lead to the coming of the Messiah. He was not going to tell them when the Messiah would arrive, nor could he, because the Jews' behavior will determine when the Messiah arrives. Rather, Jacob wanted to tell his children how the darkest times in their history would contribute to a good end. Unfortunately, he lost his prophetic vision and divine inspiration a moment before he could do this.

Jacob wondered if his children's blemished faith had caused G-d to prevent him from revealing how Jewish suffering would eventually lead to future goodness. If so, his sons must have unresolved theological questions that Jacob could help put to rest. Since his children were going to be the pillars of the Jewish nation, if they thought that G-d was unfair or unjust, how would their descendants fare millennia later? The latter would be so far removed from people like Jacob that their doubts would topple them spiritually.

This prompted Jacob to ask his sons, "Do you have any complaints about G-d?"

His children unanimously responded, "Hear, Israel (one of Jacob's names), the L-rd (who is compassionate) is our G-d (who metes out justice), the (compassionate) L-rd is One." Thus, they stated their belief that one loving G-d executes justice and runs the world.

Jacob was ecstatic when he heard their response. It reassured him that he would leave behind twelve sons who had perfect faith in G-d and who would be a strong foundation for the Jewish nation. He joyfully responded, "Blessed is the Name of His glorious kingdom forever and ever."

This midrash says that the Jewish people subsequently got the mitzvah of saying the Shema in the merit of Jacob's sons' response. The tribes' strong faith was also indelibly etched into the spiritual persona (collective unconscious) of the Jewish people forever. Our ancestors enabled every one of their descendants to believe that everything ultimately has a good purpose.

Throughout history, Jews suffered torture and martyrdom while declaring their faith in G-d as they said the Shema. For example, Rabbi Akiva died with the Shema on his lips as he bled from wounds inflicted by the Romans. During the Crusades and the Inquisition, Christians tortured and martyred hundreds of thousands of Jews who refused to renounce their religion and who expired while saying the Shema. The same happened when countless Jews were murdered by Nazis and Nazi sympathizers. This type of Jewish fortitude was possible because Jacob's children said the Shema around his deathbed.

A second midrashic explanation traces the Shema's roots to the giving of the Ten Commandments. G-d told the Israelites the First Commandment, "I am the L-rd, your G-d, who brought you out of the land of Egypt, out of the house of slaves." They responded, "Hear, Israel." Then He uttered the Second Commandment, "You shall have no other gods before Me." The Jews replied, "The L-rd is our G-d, the L-rd is One." When the Almighty uttered each successive commandment, the Jews responded with corresponding verses from the Shema. In this way, the Shema formed part of the Jews' acceptance of the Ten Commandments. According to this midrash, the Israelites' response merited G-d's commanding them and their descendants to recite the Shema.

These two midrashic explanations as to why we say the Shema apparently contradict each other. One says that we say the Shema because of Jacob's sons' faith, while the other attributes it to what the Israelites said when they received the Torah.

When two *midrashim* seem to contradict each other, it means that they are addressing different aspects of the same idea. One of the above *midrashim* refers to the aspect of the Shema which Jacob and his children emphasized: our faith that G-d directs everything and, notwithstanding the pain and suffering that surrounds us, that we will ultimately realize His total goodness. We proclaim this faith when what we know—that G-d is totally good—and what we see and experience—that the world is full of pain and evil—are not congruent.

But the Shema has a second aspect to it. It expresses our Torah knowledge, which the Jews had when they received the Torah at Mount Sinai. When we accepted the Torah, we were simultaneously given the ability to understand its wisdom and absorb its deepest levels of truth. We can relate to G-d's uniqueness and unity because of the knowledge that Torah study gives, not because we have blind, non-rational belief.

The Clarity of Torah

Torah is the best means for finding our inner selves. Its wisdom, truth, and energy can pierce the surface camouflages of G-d and let us discover what life is really about. Even if the rest of the world believes that their views of reality are true, Torah tells us that there is a spiritual system that is much more real than the purely physical world around us. Even when the physical world conceals G-d's singularity, our connection to Torah allows us to still see it.

When Jacob's sons surrounded his deathbed, they told him that they didn't understand G-d's ways, but believed in Him anyway. When the Jews received the Torah at Mount Sinai, they had clear knowledge and perceptions about G-d. They knew without a shadow of a doubt that He existed and was revealing absolute truth to them via the Torah. Their responding to each of the Ten Commandments with verses from the Shema meant that they saw G-d's unity through Torah. At that moment, they did not have to *believe* in G-d's unity—they *knew* it from their experience.

Throughout Jewish history, millions of Jews remained loyal to Judaism despite their lack of Jewish education because they inherited their faith from Jacob's children. Jews who are disconnected from Torah knowledge may still know the truth about G-d's existence and our obligation to be loyal to Him. When that happens, it is because they have blind faith, not because they understand the Almighty's ways.

Connecting to Torah gives us a certainty about how to live, despite what the rest of the world believes. A Jew who is strongly bound to Torah will survive the worst crises, while a Jew who is removed from Torah may or may not. Studying Torah always links us to what is happening behind the scenes and keeps us from despairing when we see only life's surface. This aspect of the Shema is rooted in the clarity and wisdom of Torah.

Because the Israelites in Egypt lacked this, they did not listen to Moses when he told them that they would soon go free. The Torah says that their "shortness of spirit and suffering from hard work" prevented them from believing him. "Shortness of spirit" means that they were not connected to Torah. When that happens, Jews do not appreciate the reality that underlies the superficial world and can easily be overwhelmed by its difficulties and burdens.

When we pray the morning or evening services, we precede the Shema with a blessing about G-d's tremendous love for the Jews. We ask Him to inspire us and give us the wisdom to understand the Torah, to do what it asks of us, to understand its secrets, and to be excited by it.

Shortly after rising every morning, we are supposed to thank the Almighty for the privilege of being able to study Torah before we begin learning it that day. If we forget to say that blessing, we can fulfill our obligation to say it by reciting the prayer before the Shema asking G-d to help us learn Torah.

We precede the Shema by yearning to learn Torah because we can only truthfully say, "Hear, Israel, the L-rd is our G-d, the L-rd is One" if we know Torah well. This verse expresses that we know G-d as clearly as the Israelites did at Mount Sinai. When the world around us seems full of injustice, and it is hard to believe that our lives are being guided by a divine Hand, only plumbing the depths of Torah and internalizing its message that G-d is running a purposeful world allows us to truly believe that He is One.

A midrash helps us understand how G-d can love and care for us when we feel that He has abandoned us. It describes a king who married his fiancée after exchanging many love letters and promising to give her many gifts once they got married. Shortly after the wedding, though, she became promiscuous. Her disloyalty angered her husband and he abandoned her. Many months passed and people told the queen that her husband would never come back. They advised her to marry someone else. They were so persuasive that she almost followed their advice. She cried, thinking that they might be right, and sequestered herself in her chambers. She read his love letters, reviewed his promises, and reminisced about their wonderful times together. She finally concluded that her husband would inevitably return.

When her husband finally did come back after a very long time, the first thing he asked was, "How did you have the strength to wait for me for so many years?"

She responded, "I honestly don't know. But every time that I was ready to break down and give up hope, I took out all of your letters. I read about all of the things that we had shared, and something convinced me that deep, deep down, we still shared an enduring love."

And so it is with G-d and us. He wed the Jews, then we strayed from the way that we had agreed to live. We devoted ourselves to many pursuits besides G-d, so He eventually "left." The nations of the world came to us and said, "Your G-d left. He hasn't been around for years. You might as well forget about Him ever coming back. Come and join us. You'll prosper, have a good time, and be accepted by the world."

Our connection to Torah is the only thing that guarantees that our love relationship with G-d never ends, no matter what the illusions of life suggest. Throughout history, Jews reached their breaking point and were about to renounce their belief in, and commitment to, G-d. But by entering our house of learning and prayer and reading the Torah, something always convinced us that G-d would come back.

G-d will openly return to us when the Messiah comes. The first thing He will ask is, "How did you have the strength to wait for Me for so many years?"

We will respond, "Had we not revived ourselves by studying Torah whenever we verged on giving up, we would not have made it. Its messages convinced us of Your undying love for us."

The Hidden Beauty of the Shema (Brooklyn: Judaica Press, 2004), pp. 17–19, 38–40, 44–50
Reprinted with permission of the author

SHEMA

BY RABBI NISSAN MINDEL, PHD

Part One

The Shema contains the essence of our faith, so much so, that countless Jewish martyrs calmly and bravely faced death with the words of Shema on their lips. They did so because they knew what these words meant.

The Shema consists of three chapters, taken from the Bible.

The first chapter[1] begins with the proclamation: "Hear, O Israel, G-d our G-d, G-d is One." It goes on to tell us that we must love G-d and dedicate our lives to the carrying out of His will. We can keep this faith alive only if we bring up our children in this belief. This section also contains the two Mitzvoth of Tefillin and Mezuzah which remind us that we are Jews.

The second chapter[2] contains a promise that if we carry out G-d's commands we shall be a happy people in our land. If not, we will suffer exile and hardships in strange lands, so that by suffering and trouble we will learn the ways of G-d and return to Him. We are again reminded to teach our children our true faith, and the Tefillin and Mezuzah are again mentioned, being the symbols of practical observance of G-d's commands.

The third chapter[3] contains the commandment of Tzitzith, the distinctive Jewish garment which is a constant reminder of all the precepts of the Torah. We are reminded also that G-d brought us out of Egypt and made us His people, and that we accepted Him as our G-d.

This, in short, is the theme of the Shema. Now we have to understand what all this means.

RABBI NISSAN MINDEL, PHD, 1912–1999

Secretary to the Lubavitcher Rebbe. Born in Latvia, Rabbi Mindel immigrated to the U.S., where he received a doctorate in Semitic languages from Columbia University. He translated many works into English, including the *Tanya,* the seminal text of Chabad philosophy, and was a prolific writer who authored numerous works including *Philosophy of Chabad* and *My Prayer.*

A little reflection on the contents of the Shema will reveal that the Shema is the highlight of our prayers and that all the prayers recited before the Shema are really but an introduction to it.

When we speak of the *essence* of Judaism we mean the foundations upon which our whole Jewish faith rests. These foundations are mentioned in the first chapter of the Shema:

The Unity of G-d—that G-d is the Creator and He is One, and that there are no other gods.

Submission to the reign of G-d—that is, to accept the Divine discipline (all the laws and precepts He gave us in the Torah) in our daily behavior, both in regard to our duties towards G-d and our duties towards our fellow-man.

Love of G-d—to understand that we owe everything to our good G-d, our Heavenly Father, Whom we must love with all our heart and soul.

Self-sacrifice—to be ready to give our very life rather than be forced to give up our faith.

The Study of the Torah and its Perpetuation—contained in the words: "And you shall teach them diligently unto your children and speak of them (of these foundations of Judaism) when you sit in your house, and when you walk by the way, and when you lie down, and when you rise up."

All this is contained in the first chapter of Shema, beginning with the word *Shema* ("Hear!") and ending with the word *ubishe'arecha* ("and in your gates"). It is a *Mitzvah* (a Divine command) to read the Shema every day, twice: in the morning and in the evening.

When we speak of the Shema, however, we do not mean only the first portion, but also the following two portions. For they also speak of the same foundations (although in different words) and contain the additional precepts of *Tzitzith* and the reminder of the liberation from Egypt.

Now, let us consider these basic principles of our faith:

The Unity of G-d: Many years ago people did not know that there is but One and Only G-d. They thought that there were many gods: a god of light and a god of darkness; a god of goodness, and a god of evil; a god of war, and a god of peace, and so on. They thought that the god of goodness wanted them to do good things, but the god of evil wanted them to do bad things. They did not know how to satisfy all the gods. They did terrible and cruel things thinking that by doing so they were making their gods happy.

Then came Abraham. Even when he was a little boy he knew there was but one G-d, Who created heaven and earth and everything. He knew that G-d was good and merciful and wanted the people to be good and merciful, so that they would be happy. He knew that G-d often puts people to the test to make them all the stronger, just as iron becomes strong when put through fire. He knew that everything G-d created and everything He does is good, but that people often bring trouble upon themselves by not knowing how to live. Abraham knew all this, and then G-d spoke to him and chose him to be the father of a great and holy nation, who would teach the whole world these truths.

Later, we received the Torah on Mount Sinai, in which G-d told us how we should live, and what we have to do in order to be happy. It is from this Divine Torah that the Shema is taken, and we repeat it every day of our lives, from the day when we are first able to speak.

Submission to the Reign of G-d: G-d is the Creator of the world. The whole world is His, and He is its King. A good king does everything for the benefit of his land and his people. He makes laws and gives orders so that the people could live in peace and harmony. Men who are near the king know *why* he has made these laws; others who are far away, perhaps in the country, or on a farm, do not understand them. But everybody knows that the laws are made for their benefit. It does not really matter whether one knows the reason or not; the main thing is to observe the laws, for the benefit comes from *observing* them.

In the same way, but much more so, we have to accept the laws which G-d, Our Father and Our King, has given us. They are all for our benefit, even if we are too young or of too little knowledge to know their importance. Even the wisest of men cannot understand the thoughts of G-d.

The Hebrew words for this submission to G-d are *Kabbalath ol malchuth shamaim*—"accepting the yoke of the heavenly kingdom." A "yoke," as we had occasion to note, is a harness put on an animal, so that its owner can lead it on the right way; it is not for the purpose of breaking its back under a heavy load. It is for the purpose of making the animal serve in the best way, for that is what the animal has been created for.

G-d never gives us a greater burden than we can carry. It is not a "burden" at all, if we have sense enough to understand the great benefits we get from accepting this "yoke." The unhappiest man is he who does not know what he has to do and whither he has to go. We Jews are very fortunate. G-d has given us wonderful laws and regulations. If we observe them faithfully, we are the happiest people on earth. They teach us all the good and wise things. By practicing them regularly in our daily life, they refine our character, for it becomes our habit—our very nature—to do what is good and right.

We are like soldiers in training. The soldier must not question the orders he receives. He must carry them out willingly and to the best of his ability. A good soldier is so well trained, that he does not have to think what to do in an emergency. He knows exactly what to do.

We are also like little children, whom a wise father wants to bring up well. A wise father does not spare the "rod" whenever the occasion requires it. When the child is too young to know why he has to wash his face and hands with soap and water, or clean his teeth, or behave like a little gentleman, he thinks all those things are unnecessary. When he grows up, he knows that but for the wise training of his father he would have become a hateful creature.

And so, when reading the Shema twice daily, morning and evening, we think of G-d's great Majesty. He is the Almighty Creator of the Universe, wise, kind, gracious, merciful. In his presence (and when are we not?) we must feel quite insignificant, even more insignificant than, by way of example, a worm in the presence of a great man. This gives us a feeling of humility. Knowing how good and kind G-d is to us, this leads us to the next thought of the Shema—love of G-d, contained in the words, "And you shall love G-d your G-d with all your heart, and with all your soul, and with all your might."

Part Two

> *And you shall love G-d, your G-d, with all your heart, and with all your soul, and with all your might.*

You may wonder how we may be *commanded* to love. If a stranger comes up to you and says to you, "You must love me," you may ask, "But why should I love you? I don't even know you." But suppose that the "stranger" turns out to be someone very close to you, someone who loves you, who has been watching over you, taking care of you, who has, perhaps, saved your life many times, who is kind, wise, generous, and so on. Would it be hard to love him then? For that matter, what about our own loving parents? We love them dearly, without even being *ordered* to do so.

Here, then, lies the explanation of the commandment to love G-d. What it really means is to remember that we owe everything to G-d: our life, our health, our parents, our home, our being able to think, understand, speak, walk, study, play; the sunshine, the very air we breathe—everything is a free gift from our benevolent G-d.

If we consider that *G-d does not owe us anything,* and that He has given us everything simply because He is good and kind—surely we could not help but love Him!

And so the commandment to love G-d simply amounts to an obligation on our part to reflect upon and appreciate G-d's kindness to us. *Shema* means not only *hear*, but *understand*. Of course, the more we think about it and the better we understand it, the greater will be our love for G-d. Our heart will be filled with love for G-d, with a great and intense love, a greater love than any other, a love that is truly "with all your heart, and with all your soul, and with all your might."

That is why our daily prayers do *not* begin immediately with the Shema. There is a great deal to say and to think before we come to Shema, so that by the time we come to the Shema G-d is no longer a "stranger" to us.

But what is meant by loving G-d?

When we love our parents truly, we will try to please them. We will be eager to obey them and do everything they want us to do. We will do our best never to make them angry or displeased with us in any way. We will never do anything that would show us to be ungrateful, or disrespectful.

It is the same in the case of our love of G-d. We must be eager to do all that G-d has commanded us to do. If we really love G-d, nothing will seem difficult. On the contrary. It will give us much pleasure to know that we are doing so many things for which G-d will love us all the more.

There is yet another meaning in the words "*And you shall love G-d your G-d.*" The Hebrew word for *And you shall love* (*ve'ahavta*) may be read in such a way (*ve'ihavta*) as to mean *And you shall make* (G-d) *beloved* (by others). This is to say, that through you—through your actions and conduct—G-d would be loved by all who know you. If you love G-d very much, you will want all your friends to feel that way too. Maybe they don't know why they should; maybe they never think about it. You may have many opportunities to tell them.

Being a living example of love of G-d, translated into action in the daily life and conduct, in itself goes a long way to make G-d beloved by others.

> *With all your heart, and with all your soul, and with all your might.*

With all your heart. In our heart all our desires are born, the good ones and the not so good. We have a "little good man" inside of our heart that tells us always to do good things. There is another "inner man" in our heart that tempts us to do bad things. (In Hebrew they are called *Yetzer-Tov* and *Yetzer-Hara*). They are always fighting each other, one trying to drive the other out and be the sole master. The heart cannot have two masters. When one is master, the other must be slave. Who shall be the master? Of course, the "Good Inner Man." We must help him.

This, our Sages tell us,[4] is the meaning of the words "with *all* your heart." Our whole heart must be filled with love of G-d; there should be no room in it for the "Bad Man"; if it cannot be driven out completely, it should be subdued and kept in check, so as to have no power over our actions. The voice of the inner "Bad Man" must be silenced; when there is something we *have* to do, there should be no inner voice saying "It's too hard," or "It can wait."

With all your soul. The Hebrew word *nefesh* (soul) also means *life.* This means that if we have to choose between G-d and a G-dless life, we should be prepared to give up our life.[5] To countless Jews throughout the ages these words were very real. During the time of Antiochus, during the reign of Hadrian, during the period of the Crusaders, the Inquisition, and, yes, down to the present time, Jews willingly chose torture and death rather than give up their love of G-d. They died *Al Kiddush Hashem*—for the sanctification of G-d's Name.

And with all your might. This, our Sages tell us[6] refers to our possessions, our wealth. We must love G-d more than all our most precious possessions. It may seem strange that after speaking of *self-sacrifice,* that is, being prepared to give up our very life, we should still speak of worldly possessions, wealth, money. But, sad to say, there are some people to whom money is more precious than their lives. Some people work themselves to death, or risk their life in a mad rush for gold. Even if the love for gold is so great, love for G-d should be greater.

> *And these words which I command you this day shall be upon your heart.*

We must study the Torah and learn to recognize G-d. This we do with our head, but the result will be that these words will fill our hearts and there our love for G-d will be born, and we shall love G-d with all our heart.

Note the words "this day" in the sentence quoted above. Here we are told[7] to think of the Torah as though it has been given *this day* for the first time. The Torah should *not* be thought of as a gift given us a long, long time ago, but as something new and fresh. When a person gets a new gift, it attracts his attention and holds his interest. So should we regard the Torah, with the exciting interest of a novelty. These are not mere words, for those who study the Torah know that it can never become stale, that there is always something new which they can discover in it. For the Torah is G-d's wisdom which knows no bounds.

> *And you shall teach them diligently unto your children and speak of them when you sit in your house and when you walk by the way and when you lie down and when you rise up.*

Here lies a very important commandment: the duty of Jewish parents to give their children a good Jewish education. The time to learn begins when Jewish boys and girls are young. The Torah and its precepts should become part of their life, at home and outside, in joy and in sorrow, in sickness and in good health. At all times the Torah is the Jew's guide in life and his constant companion.

Moreover, our Sages extended the duty of providing Jewish education also to *all* Jewish children, not merely to our own. Thus, they interpreted the word *l'vanecha* ("to your children") to mean "the pupils," for "pupils are also called children."[8]

The words, "when you lie down and when you rise up," contain the command that we should read the Shema twice daily, in the morning and evening service (that is why we do not say the Shema in the afternoon service). But "these words"—the words of the Torah—should be studied always, whenever we have a free moment, and we must live up to them in all our actions and movements.

> *And you shall bind them for a sign upon your hand and they shall be as frontlets between your eyes.*

Here the commandment of *Tefillin* is given. This commandment makes it the duty of every male Jew, from the age of 13 years and on, to observe the precept of Tefillin for the rest of his life. The details of the commandment were given to Moses orally, and they are to be found in the Mishnah and Talmud (the "Oral Law"). The details include instructions on how the

Tefillin are to be made, how they should be taken care of, and so on.
The Tefillin consist of two parts: the Hand-Tefillin and the Head-Tefillin. The former is placed on the left hand, facing the heart. The latter is placed on the head (*not forehead*) in the center (this is what is meant by the words "between your eyes"). Thus, the Tefillin symbolize that our thoughts, feelings and deeds should be dedicated to a life which is in accordance with the precepts of the Divine Torah.

The little boxes of the Head- and Hand-Tefillin contain scrolls of parchment upon which the words of the Shema are inscribed by hand by a Sofer (Scribe).

The Tefillin are a "sign"—the emblem of distinction, which we wear with pride, showing that we belong to the Jewish people. It is very much like the emblem or colors of a regiment by which it is distinguished and identified.[9]

Every day, except on the Sabbath and festivals, the Tefillin must be put on for the morning prayers. The exception is made because the Sabbath and the festivals are in themselves "signs" in the same sense.

> *And you shall write them upon the doorposts of your house and upon your gates.*

This is the concluding verse of the first chapter of the Shema. Here the Mitzvah of *Mezuzah* is given. The words of the Shema are inscribed on a parchment (in the same way as the Torah and Tefillin are inscribed on parchment). The parchment is rolled up and placed in a case and then affixed to the right hand side (on entering) of the doorpost. Every Jewish home must have a Mezuzah affixed on every doorpost.

The Mezuzah is a sign that the entire house and all our possessions therein belong to G-d, are dedicated to G-d, and are to be used in a way that would please G-d. It is our way of expressing gratitude to G-d for our possessions. Without first acknowledging that G-d is the real owner of everything, we would have no right to enjoy their use. This is also the thought behind the Berachah which we make before eating and drinking anything.[10]

Every time we enter or leave the house, the Mezuzah is there to remind us that we are Jews, and that both at home and outside (at work, in business) we must live up to the great ideals of our holy faith and to fulfill all the commandments of the Torah.

Finally, because the Mezuzah is a great and holy Mitzvah and contains the sacred words of the Shema, it is regarded as the ever watchful and faithful guardian of the Jewish home, blessing it with peace and harmony, health and happiness.

Part Three

The second chapter of Shema begins with the words:

> *And it will come to pass when you will hearken diligently unto My commandments . . . to love G-d your G-d and to serve Him with all your heart and with all your soul. Then I will give the rain of your land in its due season. . . .*

The first thing to note is that this chapter speaks in the second person plural, not in the singular as in the first chapter. This means that here G-d speaks to all of us together.

Secondly, this chapter contains everything that the first chapter does, but in addition it has something else: a promise of reward for following in the path of the Torah, and a warning of dire consequences if we should neglect the laws of the Torah.

This chapter, like the first, is taken from the Torah.[11] There are a few verses in the Torah immediately before this chapter which are of interest to us. They speak of the holiness of our Holy Land: It is different from all other lands; it is dependent upon the rains from the sky; G-d loves this land and watches it always. The welfare of this land is entirely bound up with the people of Israel and their loyalty to the Torah. If the Jewish people observe the commandments of the Torah, G-d will bless the land: He will send down the rain at the right time, everything will grow well and in abundance. But, G-d forbid, if the Jewish people neglect the Torah, then the Holy Land cannot suffer to hold them there. Famine, exile and suffering must follow, until Jews again realize their mistakes, and return to G-d.

Thus, while the Jew must be a Jew always and everywhere, and must observe all the Mitzvoth of the

Torah no matter in what land he lives, he must do so even more carefully in the Holy Land, where he especially is in the constant presence of G-d and under G-d's searching eyes.

After repeating the commandment of Tefillin, this chapter goes on to say:

> *And you shall teach them (these words of the Shema) to your children, to speak of them, when you sit in your house. . . .*

"And you shall teach them"—"you" in the plural. Here it is indicated that it is the duty of the community to see to it that all Jewish children should receive a full Torah-true Jewish education. It is a matter of Jewish law and custom that as soon as a child is able to speak, he should be taught to recite the Hebrew words *Torah tzivah lanu,* etc., meaning, "The Torah which Moses commanded us is the *inheritance of the congregation* of Jacob."[12] The whole congregation of Jacob is responsible to keep and guard this precious inheritance. To build and maintain Hebrew schools and Yeshivoth to provide Hebrew education for all Jewish children—is both a communal and individual responsibility.

The commandment of Mezuzah is repeated, then come the following words:

> *In order that your days and the days of your children be many upon the land which G-d swore unto your ancestors to give to them; like the days of the heaven upon the earth.*

G-d promises us many happy days upon our land if we will "hearken diligently" to His commands; not only for us but for our children and the coming generations as well. "Like the days of the heaven upon the earth" simply means "forever." But these words mean something else. Heaven and earth are a pair. Just as the earth cannot exist without the heavens, so would the heavens have no meaning without the earth. In the same way are the Jewish people and the Torah. By observing the Torah, the Jewish people bring the heaven down upon earth: they combine the holy and sublime with the earthly, and in this way lift up the earth to high heaven.

Part Four

> *And G-d spoke unto Moses, saying, "Speak unto the children of Israel, and bid them that they make them a fringe* (tzitzith) *upon the comers of their garments throughout their generations."*

The third chapter[13] of the Shema contains the commandment of Tzitzith and, as we will see later, mentions the Redemption from Egypt, when G-d redeemed Israel from Egyptian slavery and gave them the Torah; that is, when Israel began its life as a holy nation. When a king establishes a special regiment, a royal regiment bearing the king's name, he gives the members of the regiment a special uniform, or insignia to wear on their person always. The insignia gives the members of the regiment distinction, and at the same time reminds them that their conduct must always be of the highest, for by their conduct they bring either credit or shame upon the king.

The fringes are like such an "insignia." G-d wished to make our people a holy nation, bearing G-d's Name. That is why G-d gave us the holy Torah, which teaches us what our conduct should be, and how we are to lead our lives. The *whole* life of the Jew has to be consecrated, from the time he rises in the morning, until he retires to sleep at night, and from the day of birth, when he first opens his baby eyes, until his last day of life on this earth, when he goes to "sleep." Just as the member of that royal regiment is expected to be on his best conduct not only during a parade before the king, but at all times, so the Jew is never "off duty." He is in the presence of G-d always; he is always "on parade" before G-d, the King of kings. Therefore it is not only in the synagogue, during prayer, that the Jew must remember G-d, nor only during the study of the holy Torah, but during all of the day's activities. There is no activity in the Jew's life that is exempt from precepts (*Mitzvoth*). Before he sits down to eat, he washes his hands; he says grace before and after eating. When he is engaged in business, he has to observe the laws of honesty and truthfulness. If he is a farmer in Israel, he has many laws to observe in connection with his working on the soil. In the community he has his obligations in giving charity and supporting its institutions. Before going to bed he recites his prayers, and rising in the morning he recites prayers again. His *house* is Jewish by the Mezuzah, and by the observance of the Sabbath and festivals. His person is Jewish by the Mitzvah of circumcision, and by observing the precepts connected with his person, such as rest on the Sabbath. And even his *clothes* are Jewish, by the Mitzvah of Tzitzith and Shaatnes.[14]

> *And they shall put upon the fringe of each corner a cord of blue.*

The fringes are white woolen threads, four on each corner, folded in two, making eight threads in all. One of them (longer than the rest) is used as the "Shamash" to wind around the others. When the threads are threaded through the hole in the corner of the garment, they are folded and knotted twice. Then the Shamash is wound around the other threads seven times; the threads are separated and knotted again twice. The winding is continued, this time eight times, followed by a double knot, then eleven times, then thirteen times, with a double knot before and after. Thus we have five double knots in all.

In ancient days they also had a thread dyed with the color of sky-blue. This dye was obtained from the blood of a certain mollusk (called חילזון in Hebrew). Nowadays we do not know what kind of an animal it was, or where we can find it. Therefore we no longer have the thread of blue, but all the threads of the Tzitzith are white.

The purpose of the sky-blue thread or cord was to remind us of G-d. Said our Sages: "The blue cord of the Tzitzith resembles the sea, the sea reflects the heavens, and the heavens resemble the Throne of Glory."[15]

> *And it shalt be unto you for a fringe, that you may look upon it, and remember all the commandments of G-d, and do them.*

The Hebrew word וראיתם also means "that you may understand." For the Hebrew verb which means "to see" does not refer only to seeing with the physical eye, but also seeing with our intellectual eye.

As already mentioned, the Tzitzith are like a uniform to remind us of our special obligations as members of that holy "regiment" of G-d, called the people of Israel. How do the Tzitzith remind us of *all* the commandments of G-d? Rashi explained it in this way: The numerical value of the Hebrew word ציצית adds up to 600 (400—ת; 10—י; 90—צ); then there are eight threads and five knots in each of the fringes. The total is therefore 613, as many as there are commandments in the Torah.[16]

But remembering is not enough. *And you shall do them*, says the Torah. We cannot be good Jews in our hearts only; we must *practice* Judaism in our everyday life. All our precepts are based on action, for it is through action that the commands of G-d are fulfilled.

> *And you shall not go about after your own heart and after your own eyes, after which you go astray.*

Our Sages called the eyes and heart "the two agents of evil," for the eyes see and the heart desires.[17] That is why we are warned not to be led astray by the temptations of our eyes and heart.

There is an additional warning here not to rely upon our own judgment when it comes to the practice of our precepts. For as we said before, "seeing" in Hebrew means not only physical sight but also "mental" sight—thought and understanding. So the "eyes" and "heart" refer to external appearances and superficial judgments. Those who do not understand the deep significance of our holy Mitzvoth may think that the precepts have no meaning and no message for us in modern times. But they are led astray by their ignorance; they judge superficially, and have no idea of the deep inner meaning of each and every Mitzvah.

After warning us again to remember and *do* all the commands of G-d, and thus be holy unto our G-d, this section of Shema goes on to remind us of the Redemption of our people from Egypt.

This is not the first time in our prayers that we mention the liberation from Egypt. As a matter of fact, we mention this event many times in our prayers before reaching the Shema. And not only in our daily prayers, but also in Kiddush and in the prayers of the holy Sabbath day and of the holy festivals.

More than that. The first of our festivals—Passover—is dedicated to this event.

Why do we mention this event so many times and so frequently? Because the wonderful story of *Yetziath Mitzraim* (the liberation from Egypt) reminds us of at least five basic events and concepts relating to our early history which are always relevant to our existence and survival:

1. Our father Jacob came to Egypt with his family of 70 souls. Two centuries and ten years later a whole nation left Egypt. In a strange land and in suffering *our nation was born.*
2. G-d saw the terrible suffering of our people and kept His promise to our fathers Abraham, Isaac and Jacob, to free our people and set them up in the Promised Land. *G-d never forgets or forsakes us.*
3. In freeing our people from Egypt, G-d performed wonderful miracles. G-d showed that *He is the Master of the world and of all Nations, and that nothing is impossible or too difficult for Him to do.*
4. G-d punished the Egyptians for their wickedness, and rewarded the children of Israel for their suffering. *G-d loves justice, punishes the oppressor and protects the oppressed.*
5. G-d liberated the children of Israel from Egypt *in order to give us the Torah* that we should become a *Kingdom of Priests and a Holy Nation,*[18] so that we could teach the whole world the knowledge of G-d and His ways. And when all the peoples of the world will learn the ways of G-d, there will be no more oppressors and oppressed, no more bloodshed and war, but love and justice will reign everywhere, and mankind will enjoy the blessings of G-d.

My Prayer, vol. I (Brooklyn, N.Y.: Merkos L'inyonei Chinuch, 1972), pp. 152–168

Endnotes

1 Deut. 6:4–9.
2 Deut. 11:13–21.
3 Num. 15:37–41.
4 Sifre on Deut. 6:5. See also Zohar III, 268a.
5 Berachoth 61b, Rashi; Targum Jonathan on Deut. 6:5.
6 Berachoth 61b; Sanhedrin 74a.
7 Sifre on Deut. 6:6, quoted in Rashi.
8 Sifre on Deut. 6:7, quoted in Rashi.
9 See *Tefillin* by Alexander Cowen Brooklyn, N.Y.: Merkos L'inyonei Chinuch, 1945
10 Berachoth 31a, b.
11 Deut. 11:13–21.
12 Deut. 33:4.
13 Num. 15:37–41.
14 *Shaatnes* is the prohibition against wearing garments of wool and linen mingled together (Deut. 22:11).
15 Sotah 17a; Tanhuma, Shelach 15.
16 Rashi on Num. 15:39. See also Nedarim 25a.
17 Rashi on Num. 15:39. See also Sotah 8a.
18 Exod. 19:6.

Lesson 5

STANDING IN SILENCE

SYNTHESIZING DIVINITY AND MATERIALITY IN THE AMIDAH

Scene at a Synagogue, the Great Day of Atonement, 6th October 1897, Isaac Snowman, print from *The Illustrated London News.*

At the peak of our prayers, we expect to encounter prayers about the soul, G-d, and spirituality—temporarily abandoning all trivial and mundane matters. This lesson explores the Amidah prayer, the summit of our communion with G-d that, most surprisingly, is built around a series of requests for basic material needs. It offers deep and revolutionary insight into the relationship between G-d, spirituality, and our corporeal lives.

TEXT 1

RABBI SHALOM DOVBER SCHNEERSOHN, *SEFER HAMAAMARIM* 5680, P. 153

שְׁמוֹנָה עֶשְׂרֵה הוּא בִּיטּוּל אֲמִיתִּי וְהִתְכַּלְּלוּת בְּאוֹר אֵין סוֹף בָּרוּךְ הוּא מַמָּשׁ הַסּוֹבֵב כָּל עָלְמִין כו'. . . וְאֵינָהּ עוֹלָה בְּשֵׁם אַהֲבָה כְּלַל, רַק בְּחִינַת בִּיטּוּל בִּמְצִיאוּת לְגַמְרֵי, וְהַיְינוּ בְּחִינַת הִשְׁתַּפְּכוּת נַפְשׁוֹ אֶל חֵיק אָבִיהָ מַמָּשׁ לִהְיוֹת כְּאַיִן וְאֶפֶס מַמָּשׁ.

The Amidah is the experience of true surrender and immersion in the endless light of G-d that envelops all of existence. . . . This cannot be called love; rather, it is a sense of complete surrender. The soul melts into its Heavenly Father and feels literally as naught.

Silent · Speachless

Begin with the End in Mind

RABBI SHALOM DOVBER SCHNEERSOHN (RASHAB) 1860–1920

Chasidic rebbe. Rabbi Shalom Dovber became the fifth leader of the Chabad movement upon the passing of his father, Rabbi Shmuel of Lubavitch. He established the Lubavitch network of *yeshivot* called Tomchei Temimim. He authored many volumes of Chasidic discourses and is renowned for his lucid and thorough explanations of kabbalistic concepts.

"Amidah In-Depth," by ***Professor Lewis Glinert:***

MYJLI.COM/PRAYER

QUESTION FOR DISCUSSION

Can prayer be meaningful for people who do not experience this feeling of surrender during the Amidah? If yes, in what way?

The Sacrifice of Manoah, Ludwig Meidner, charcoal, London, c. 1950. (Museum Judengasse, Frankfurt)

QUESTION FOR DISCUSSION

Imagine yourself standing before a king. What emotions does this evoke within you?

TEXT 2a

PSALMS 51:17

ה' שְׂפָתַי תִּפְתָּח וּפִי יַגִּיד תְּהִלָּתֶךָ.

G-d, open my lips, and may my mouth speak your praises.

such a state of submission that we can't even open our mouth

TEXT 2b

RABBI YOSEF YITSCHAK SCHNEERSOHN, *SEFER HAMAAMARIM* 5682, P. 221

בִּתְפִלַּת שְׁמוֹנָה עֶשְׂרֵה, דְאָז הוּא כְּעוֹמֵד לִפְנֵי הַמֶּלֶךְ וּמִתְבַּטֵּל בְּמַהוּתוֹ, הִנֵּה הַתְחָלַת הַדִּיבּוּר הוּא ה' שְׂפָתַי תִּפְתָּח. וְהוּא לְפִי שֶׁאֵינוֹ יָכוֹל לְדַבֵּר כְּלַל בְּכֹחַ עַצְמוֹ, לִהְיוֹתוֹ בִּלְתִּי מַרְגִישׁ אֶת עַצְמוֹ כְּלַל בִּבְחִינַת יֵשׁ וּמְצִיאוּת דָבָר, שֶׁיּוּכַל לְדַבֵּר וּלְשַׁבֵּחַ. וְאֵין מִילִין בִּלְשׁוֹנִי כְּלַל.

The experience of the Amidah is akin to the complete surrender that one feels when standing before a king. We feel unable to utter a word because any form of speaking, including words of praise, requires a degree of self-awareness. Bereft of the ability to speak, we ask G-d to open our lips.

RABBI YOSEF YITSCHAK SCHNEERSOHN (RAYATS, FRIERDIKER REBBE, PREVIOUS REBBE) 1880–1950

Chasidic rebbe, prolific writer, and Jewish activist. Rabbi Yosef Yitschak, the sixth leader of the Chabad movement, actively promoted Jewish religious practice in Soviet Russia and was arrested for these activities. After his release from prison and exile, he settled in Warsaw, Poland, from where he fled Nazi occupation and arrived in New York in 1940. Settling in Brooklyn, Rabbi Schneersohn worked to revitalize American Jewish life. His son-in-law, Rabbi Menachem Mendel Schneerson, succeeded him as the leader of the Chabad movement.

Figure 5.1

Basic Laws and Customs of the Amidah

1	Stand upright.
2	Pray silently.
3	At certain points, bend at the knees and bow from the waist.

That's why! Three steps back, three step forward, explained by ***Rabbi Yossi Paltiel:***

MYJLI.COM/PRAYER

TEXT 3

TALMUD, BERACHOT 31A

כַּמָּה הִלְכְתָא גַּבְרְוָותָא אִיכָּא לְמִשְׁמַע מֵהַנֵּי קְרָאֵי דְחַנָּה: "וְחַנָּה הִיא מְדַבֶּרֶת עַל לִבָּהּ" (שְׁמוּאֵל א, א, יג) - מִכָּאן לַמִּתְפַּלֵּל צָרִיךְ שֶׁיְּכַוֵּין לִבּוֹ. "רַק שְׂפָתֶיהָ נָּעוֹת" (שָׁם) - מִכָּאן לַמִּתְפַּלֵּל שֶׁיַּחְתּוֹךְ בִּשְׂפָתָיו. "וְקוֹלָהּ לֹא יִשָּׁמֵעַ" (שָׁם) - מִכָּאן, שֶׁאָסוּר לְהַגְבִּיהַּ קוֹלוֹ בִּתְפִלָּתוֹ.

We infer many laws of prayer from the story of Chanah. "And Chanah spoke in her heart" (I SAMUEL 1:13); from this we learn that we must concentrate during prayer. "Only her lips were moving" (IBID.); this teaches us that the words of prayer must be articulated orally. "And her voice was not heard" (IBID.); from this we learn that it is forbidden to pray loudly.

BABYLONIAN TALMUD

A literary work of monumental proportions that draws upon the legal, spiritual, intellectual, ethical, and historical traditions of Judaism. The 37 tractates of the Babylonian Talmud contain the teachings of the Jewish sages from the period after the destruction of the 2nd Temple through the 5th century CE. It has served as the primary vehicle for the transmission of the Oral Law and the education of Jews over the centuries; it is the entry point for all subsequent legal, ethical, and theological Jewish scholarship.

"Is It Chutzpah to Pray?" A prophetess teaches us how to talk to G-d, by ***Mrs. Chana Weisberg***:

MYJLI.COM/PRAYER

A Woman of Valour, LN M, Canada, tempera on canvas.

Figure 5.2

Three Sections of the Amidah

CATEGORY	DESCRIPTION
First three blessings	Praising G-d
Thirteen blessings	Requests for our needs
Last three blessings	Thanking G-d

One prayer, 18 steps: An overview of the Amidah, by ***Rabbi David Aaron****:*

MYJLI.COM/PRAYER

Exercise 5.1

Together with a partner, review both columns of the chart below. When you are done, try to complete the three blank cells on your own. Why are they in this particular order?

	SUMMARY OF BLESSING	NOTES ON THE ORDER
1	We praise G-d as great, powerful, and awesome. We also describe His benevolence toward His children.	This blessing comes first because it describes G-d's benevolence, which is key to the granting of blessings.
2	We praise Almighty G-d for rainfall, supporting the fallen, healing the ill, and reviving the dead.	G-d protects us because He loves us. It follows that after praising G-d for His benevolence and love, we praise G-d for His might and protection.
3	We praise G-d's transcendence.	Here we transition from talking about things G-d does in the world to talking about His transcendence.
4	We ask G-d to grant us wisdom, knowledge, and understanding.	This is the first in a series of thirteen requests. We begin with a request for knowledge because the ability to distinguish between right and wrong, good and bad, is the most important value.
5	We ask G-d to accept our repentance.	
6	We ask G-d to forgive our sins.	

	SUMMARY OF BLESSING	NOTES ON THE ORDER
7	We ask G-d to save us from our daily adversaries, troubles, and distresses.	
8	We ask G-d to heal us and our loved ones from illness.	Having been forgiven, we are worthy of healing.
9	We ask G-d to provide for us and sustain us.	Having been forgiven, we are worthy of sustenance.
10	We ask G-d to gather all Jews who are scattered across the globe and bring them to Israel.	Here we transition from personal requests to requests on behalf of the collective Jewish people.
11	We ask G-d to restore the Jewish high court, which governed and taught the Torah from the Temple Mount.	After Mashiach leads the Jews back to Israel, the Jewish high court will be restored.
12	We ask G-d to eradicate sectarians who cause suffering to the Jewish people.	After Mashiach comes and Jewish governance is reestablished, we will no longer suffer at the hands of those who wish us harm.
13	We ask G-d to reward and never disappoint those who place their trust in Him.	When wickedness will cease, the star of the righteous will shine properly.
14	We ask G-d to rebuild Jerusalem and restore the seat of David's kingdom.	The righteous will shine most prominently in Jerusalem, which will be rebuilt in its full glory when Mashiach comes.

	SUMMARY OF BLESSING	NOTES ON THE ORDER
15	We ask G-d to bring the Mashiach, whose coming we await every day.	After we pray for the restoration of the seat of David's kingdom, we ask G-d that Mashiach, a descendant of King David, not tarry.
16	We ask G-d to listen to and accept all our prayers.	This is a general prayer that wraps up the request portion of the Amidah. It asks G-d to grant all our requests.
17	We ask G-d to accept us, the people of Israel, and our prayers.	This blessing serves to introduce the following one. It also serves as a summary of all our previous prayers.
18	We acknowledge and thank G-d for the many miracles that He performs for us daily.	This is the blessing of gratitude. In order to highlight its importance, it is preceded and followed by a blessing.
19	We ask G-d to bless us with peace.	We follow the prayer of gratitude with a plea for peace. It is a worthy ending because peace is the vehicle for all blessings.

TEXT 4

RABBI SHALOM DOVBER SCHNEERSOHN, *SEFER HAMAAMARIM* 5664, P. 79

אַתָּה קָדוֹשׁ וְשִׁמְךָ קָדוֹשׁ, וְלִכְאוֹרָה הֲוָה לֵיהּ לְמֵימַר אַתָּה וְשִׁמְךָ קָדוֹשׁ, וְלָמָּה מְחַלֵּק וְאוֹמֵר אַתָּה קָדוֹשׁ וְשִׁמְךָ כוּ'?

אַךְ הָעִנְיָן שֶׁאֵינָן דוֹמִים זֶה לָזֶה. דְשִׁמְךָ קָדוֹשׁ אִם הֱיוֹת שֶׁהוּא קָדוֹשׁ וּמוּבְדָּל . . . שֶׁאֵין עֲרוֹךְ לְהָעוֹלָמוֹת עִם שְׁמוֹ יִתְבָּרֵךְ עַד שֶׁהוּא קָדוֹשׁ וּמוּבְדָּל מֵהֶם, רַק הוֹדוֹ וְזִיווֹ שֶׁל שְׁמוֹ הוּא עַל אֶרֶץ וְשָׁמָיִם, דְהַיְינוּ רַק הֶאָרָה בְּעָלְמָא מִבְּחִינַת שְׁמוֹ כוּ', מִכָּל מָקוֹם, הֲרֵי הֶאָרָה מִמֶּנּוּ יְכוֹלִים לְקַבֵּל. וְאִם כֵּן בְּהֶכְרֵח לוֹמַר דְמַה שֶּׁשְּׁמוֹ נִשְׂגָּב מֵהָעוֹלָמוֹת וּמוּבְדָּל מֵהֶם אֵינוֹ בִּבְחִינַת הַבְדָּלַת הָעֵרֶךְ לְגַמְרֵי. וְלָכֵן יְכוֹלִים לְקַבֵּל עַל כָּל פָּנִים הֶאָרָה מִמֶּנּוּ כוּ'.

וְכָל זֶה הוּא בִּבְחִינַת שְׁמוֹ שֶׁהוּא בְּחִינַת מְמַלֵּא כָּל עָלְמִין בִּכְלָל . . . אַךְ פֵּירוּשׁ אַתָּה קָדוֹשׁ הוּא הַקָּדוֹשׁ בָּרוּךְ הוּא בִּכְבוֹדוֹ וּבְעַצְמוֹ, שֶׁלְּמַעֲלָה מִבְּחִינַת שְׁמוֹ. שֶׁאֲפִילוּ זִיו וְהוֹד לֹא הָיוּ הָעוֹלָמוֹת יְכוֹלִים לְקַבֵּל מִמֶּנּוּ כְּלַל, וְהַיְינוּ לְפִי שֶׁהוּא קָדוֹשׁ וּמוּבְדָּל לְגַמְרֵי, שֶׁאֵינוֹ בְּגֶדֶר הָעוֹלָמוֹת כְּלַל.

Why do we say, "You are transcendent, and Your name is transcendent"? Would it not make more sense for us to say, "You and Your name are transcendent"?

The answer is that "You are transcendent" and "Your name is transcendent" cannot be merged into one phrase.

"You" refers to the essence of G-d that completely transcends creation. "Your name" refers to the expression of G-d, a reflection of which is actually vested in creation, whereas "Your name" itself remains transcendent and distinct from the process of creation . . . to the point that there can be no comparison between them. Nevertheless, if the world can absorb a reflection of "Your name," then "Your name" is not completely removed from our world.

This is all with respect to "Your name," which connotes the expression of G-d that is vested in the creation of the finite world. . . .

However, the words "You are transcendent" refer to G-d's very essence that transcends even "Your name." The world cannot absorb even a reflection of G-d's essence because it is utterly and completely removed from the world.

This is why we mention the two phrases separately, "You are transcendent, and Your name is transcendent"—because they are not the same type of transcendence.

QUESTION FOR DISCUSSION

Why do you think we focus on our needs during the Amidah, a time that should be focused entirely and exclusively on G-d?

TEXT 5

I SAMUEL 1:13–14

וַיַּחְשְׁבֶהָ עֵלִי לְשִׁכֹּרָה. וַיֹּאמֶר אֵלֶיהָ עֵלִי עַד מָתַי תִּשְׁתַּכָּרִין הָסִירִי אֶת יֵינֵךְ מֵעָלָיִךְ.

Eli thought she was drunk. He said to her, "How long will you be drunk? Remove the effects of the wine!"

intoxicated with yourself - initial thought.

Exercise 5.2

Write down three important things that you need or would like to have that you consider G-d-oriented.

1	Love
2	Time
3	

Write down three important things that you need or would like to have that you would define as self-oriented. - can we be also self oriented

1	Comfortable home
2	Food
3	

TEXT 6a

THE REBBE, RABBI MENACHEM MENDEL SCHNEERSON, *LIKUTEI SICHOT* 19, P. 294

> אִין בַּקָשַׁת צְרָכָיו . . . אִיז נִיט אַרַיינְגֶעמִישְׁט אַ הֶרְגֵשׁ פוּן מְצִיאוּת הָאָדָם, וַוייל עֶר בֶּעט זַיי נָאר פַאר דֶעם אוֹיבֶּערְשְׁטְנְ'ס וֶועגְן. וְאַדְרַבָּה - דָאס קוּמְט דַוְקָא מִצַד דֶעם תַּכְלִית הַבִּיטוּל.

Our requests . . . are not marked by a sense of self, because we ask for them exclusively for G-d's sake. In fact, our requests stem specifically from an absence of self-awareness and an utter focus on G-d.

RABBI MENACHEM MENDEL SCHNEERSON 1902–1994

The towering Jewish leader of the 20th century, known as "the Lubavitcher Rebbe," or simply as "the Rebbe." Born in southern Ukraine, the Rebbe escaped Nazi-occupied Europe, arriving in the U.S. in June 1941. The Rebbe inspired and guided the revival of traditional Judaism after the European devastation, impacting virtually every Jewish community the world over. The Rebbe often emphasized that the performance of just one additional good deed could usher in the era of Mashiach. The Rebbe's scholarly talks and writings have been printed in more than 200 volumes.

Express your soul: A lesson from Hannah, by ***Mrs. Shimona Tzukernik:***

MYJLI.COM/PRAYER

Take It Away, Hank Mattson, United States, oil on canvas and cardboard.

TEXT 6b

RABBI YISRAEL BAAL SHEM TOV, *KETER SHEM TOV* 194

לָמָה בָּרָא הַקָּדוֹשׁ בָּרוּךְ הוּא דִבְרֵי מַאֲכָל וּמַשְׁקֶה שֶׁאָדָם תָּאֵב לָהֶם לֶאֱכוֹל וְלִשְׁתּוֹת? וְהַטַּעַם שֶׁהֵם מַמָּשׁ נִיצוֹצוֹת אָדָם הָרִאשׁוֹן שֶׁהֵם מִתְלַבְּשִׁים בְּדוֹמֵם, צוֹמֵחַ, חַי, מְדַבֵּר, וְיֵשׁ לָהֶם חֵשֶׁק לְהִדָּבֵק בִּקְדוּשָּׁה... וְכָל אֲכִילָה וּשְׁתִיָּה שֶׁאָדָם אוֹכֵל וְשׁוֹתֶה, הִיא מַמָּשׁ חֵלֶק נִיצוֹצוֹת שֶׁלוֹ שֶׁהוּא צָרִיךְ לְתַקֵּן.

וְזֶהוּ שֶׁכָּתוּב: "רְעֵבִים גַּם צְמֵאִים" (תְּהִלִּים קז, ה): כְּשֶׁאָדָם רָעֵב וְצָמֵא לָהֶם, לָמָּה זֶה? וְאָמַר: "נַפְשָׁם בָּהֶם תִּתְעַטָּף", בְּסוֹד גָלוּת בִּלְבוּשִׁים זָרִים. וְכָל הַדְּבָרִים שֶׁהֵם מְשַׁמְּשִׁין לָאָדָם הֵם מַמָּשׁ בְּסוֹד הַבָּנִים שֶׁלוֹ שֶׁהִלְבִּישׁוֹ.

Why did G-d create food and drink and make people crave them? Because sparks of our soul are embedded in everything: in the inanimate, in the vegetative, in the animal, and in the human, and these sparks have a desire to cleave to holiness. . . . When we eat or drink, we rectify the sparks in that specific food or beverage that our soul must rectify.

This is the deeper meaning of the verse, “Hungry and thirsty, their souls are enwrapped in them” (PSALMS 107:5). Why do our bodies hunger and thirst for specific things? Because sparks that are linked to our soul are enwrapped in those things. Indeed, every object that serves us contains sparks of our souls.

RABBI YISRAEL BAAL SHEM TOV (BESHT) 1698–1760

Founder of the Chasidic movement. Born in Slutsk, Belarus, the Baal Shem Tov was orphaned as a child. He served as a teacher's assistant and clay digger before founding the Chasidic movement and revolutionizing the Jewish world with his emphasis on prayer, joy, and love for every Jew, regardless of his or her level of Torah knowledge.

All sparks are diff.
We have a mission to correct those sparks to their Godly source + use them for a Godly purpose.

TEXT 6C

THE REBBE, RABBI MENACHEM MENDEL SCHNEERSON, *LIKUTEI SICHOT* 19, P. 296

דָאס וָואס אַ אִיד בֶּעט . . . אַז דֶער אוֹיבֶּערְשְׁטֶער זָאל אִים גֶעבְּן צְרָכָיו הַגַשְׁמִיִים וְהָרוּחָנִיִים, אִיז [אַף עַל פִּי אַז בְּחִיצוֹנִיוּת אִיז עֶס מִצַד דֶערוֹיף וָואס אִים זַיינֶען נוֹגֵעַ עִנְיָנִים פוּן בָּנֵי חַיֵי וּמְזוֹנֵי, אוּן זַיין מְצִיאוּת, אִיז אָבֶּער] דֶער אֶמֶת אוּן פְּנִימִיוּת פוּן דֶער שְׁפִיכַת הַנֶפֶשׁ - דֶער "הוּנְגֶער" פוּן נְשָׁמָה צוּ אוֹיסְפִירְן דִי כַּוָונָה הָעֶלְיוֹנָה צוּ מַאכְן פוּן דִי דְבָרִים גַשְׁמִיִים אַ דִירָה לוֹ יִתְבָּרֵךְ . . .

אוֹיף דֶעם הָאט חַנָה גֶעעֶנְטְפֶערְט "וָאֶשְׁפּוֹךְ אֶת נַפְשִׁי לִפְנֵי ה'" (שְׁמוּאֵל א, א, טו): נִיט נָאר אִיז אִיר תְּפִלָּה פַאר זֶרַע אֲנָשִׁים נִיט קֵיין עִנְיָן פוּן "שִׁכְּרוּת" חַס וְשָׁלוֹם אִין אֵייגֶעגֶע רְצוֹנוֹת, נָאר פַארְקֶערְט - דָאס אִיז אַן **אוֹיסְגוּס** פוּן **פְּנִימִיוּת** הַנֶפֶשׁ, וָואס דָאס דַוְקָא הָאט אַ שַׁיְיכוּת צוּם מַצָב פוּן שְׁטֵייעֶן "לִפְנֵי ה'".

On the surface, we plead with G-d . . . to provide for our physical and spiritual needs because we want those things for ourselves and because our health, children, and sustenance are important to us. Nevertheless, the inner truth is that these pleas are outpourings of the soul's yearning to fulfill G-d's wish that we make a home for Him through our physical possessions. . . .

This was Chanah's intent when she replied, "I poured out my soul before G-d" (I SAMUEL 1:15). Not only was her prayer for a child not a symptom of being "drunk" with selfish cravings, G-d forbid, but to the contrary, it was an outpouring of her inner soul, which is wholly appropriate when standing "before G-d."

Exercise 5.3

Reread the items you listed as G-d-oriented and the items you listed as self-oriented, and consider whether you want to change any of your entries in light of what we just learned.

TEXT 7

MODIM, EIGHTEENTH BLESSING OF THE AMIDAH

מוֹדִים אֲנַחְנוּ לָךְ, שָׁאַתָּה הוּא ה' אֱלֹקֵינוּ וֵאלֹקֵי אֲבוֹתֵינוּ לְעוֹלָם וָעֶד. צוּר חַיֵּינוּ, מָגֵן יִשְׁעֵנוּ, אַתָּה הוּא לְדוֹר וָדוֹר. נוֹדֶה לְּךָ וּנְסַפֵּר תְּהִלָּתֶךָ, עַל חַיֵּינוּ הַמְּסוּרִים בְּיָדֶךָ, וְעַל נִשְׁמוֹתֵינוּ הַפְּקוּדוֹת לָךְ, וְעַל נִסֶּיךָ שֶׁבְּכָל יוֹם עִמָּנוּ, וְעַל נִפְלְאוֹתֶיךָ וְטוֹבוֹתֶיךָ שֶׁבְּכָל עֵת, עֶרֶב וָבֹקֶר וְצָהֳרָיִם.

We thankfully acknowledge that you are our G-d and the G-d of our forefathers forever. You are the strength of our life and the shield of our salvation in every generation. We thank you and recount your praises—evening, morning, and noon—for our lives that are committed into your hand, for our souls that are entrusted to you, for your miracles that are with us daily, and for your continual wonders and kindnesses.

QUESTION FOR DISCUSSION

Is there one phrase that jumps out at you and resonates with you in a personal way?

TEXT 8

RABBI YOSEF YITSCHAK SCHNEERSOHN,
SEFER HAMAAMARIM KUNTREISIM 1, P. 167B

דְהִנֵה תְּפִלַּת שַׁחֲרִית הִיא בַּבֹּקֶר קוֹדֶם שֶׁהוּא הוֹלֵךְ לַעֲסָקָיו, וְאֵין זֶה חִידוּשׁ כְּלַל, וְוִי אִיז אַנְדֶערְשׁ? אַ אִיד שְׁטֵייט אוֹיף אִין דֶער פְּרִי אִיז דִי עֶרְשְׁטֶע זַאךְ הוֹלֵךְ לְבֵית הַכְּנֶסֶת לְהִתְפַּלֵּל בְּצִבּוּר . . . אֲבָל תְּפִלַּת הַמִּנְחָה שֶׁהִיא בְּאֶמְצַע הַיּוֹם כַּאֲשֶׁר הָאָדָם טָרוּד בַּעֲסָקָיו וְנִמְצָא בַּשְּׁוָקִים וּבָרְחוֹבוֹת, אוֹ הוּא בִּנְסִיעָה, וּפוֹנֶה אֶת עַצְמוֹ מִכָּל עֲסָקָיו וּמִתְפַּלֵּל – הִיא עֲבוֹדָה אֲמִיתִּית.

The morning service takes place before one goes to work. It is not at all surprising that a Jew goes to the synagogue to pray first thing in the morning upon waking. How can it be different? . . . However, *minchah* is different because it is in the middle of the day, when we are immersed in the affairs of our day and are in the market, on the streets, or on the road. Disengaging from our affairs in order to pray is a true service of G-d.

Exercise for the Week

Midafternoon Challenge. This week, arrange to take a brief break during your afternoon work hours. Use that precious time to recite the *minchah* Amidah. Before beginning your prayer, take a moment to meditate. Remind yourself that the *minchah* (afternoon) prayer is perched at the pinnacle of the prayer ladder, due to the tremendous achievement of successfully tearing yourself away from the busy demands of the daily grind in order to connect with G-d in focused prayer.

We'll discuss how it went during the next lesson.

KEY POINTS

1 The Amidah is the highest rung on the ladder of prayer. It is a time of complete focus on G-d and total emotional surrender.

2 Although it is primarily the soul that experiences this utter surrender, our objective is to tap into this feeling in our conscious minds as well. Reminding ourselves every day that we are standing before G-d allows us to expand our capacity for this kind of emotional surrender.

3 The Amidah contains praises of G-d and words of gratitude to G-d, but the heart of the Amidah is the section in which we make requests of G-d. In this section we pray for our personal needs as well as our collective needs.

4 Deep down, our desire for personal needs—such as health, success, and prosperity—is an expression of our soul's desire to fulfill the purpose of creation. Thus, we pray for our needs during the Amidah even though our focus is completely on G-d.

5 You don't need to be a holy Jew for G-d to listen to your prayer. Although Jews who immerse themselves in the Torah all day often have an easier time surrendering to G-d in prayer, the aspect of prayer that G-d cherishes most is when we take time off from our own pursuits to talk to Him.

6 This aspect of prayer is achieved primarily during *minchah*, the afternoon prayer. When we are engaged in our daily pursuits and yet tear away from our agenda to pray to G-d, we reach the highest state of prayer and the truest form of surrender to G-d.

Appendix

TEXT 9

TALMUD, BERACHOT 33B

הַהוּא דְנָחִית קַמֵיה דְרַ' חֲנִינָא, אָמַר: הָאֵ-ל, הַגָדוֹל, הַגִבּוֹר, וְהַנוֹרָא, וְהָאַדִיר, וְהָעִזוּז, וְהַיָרְאוּי, הֶחָזָק, וְהָאַמִיץ, וְהַוַדַאי, וְהַנִכְבָּד.

הִמְתִּין לוֹ עַד דְסַיֵים. כִּי סַיֵים אָמַר לֵיה, סַיֵימְתִּינְהוּ לְכוּלְהוּ שְׁבָחֵי דְמָרָךְ? לָמָה לִי כּוּלֵי הַאי? אֲנַן, הָנֵי תְּלַת דְאַמְרִינָן, אִי לַאו דְאָמְרִינְהוּ מֹשֶׁה רַבֵּינוּ בְּאוֹרַיְיתָא וְאָתוּ אַנְשֵׁי כְּנֶסֶת הַגְדוֹלָה וְתַקְנִינְהוּ בַּתְּפִלָה, לֹא הֲוֵינָן יְכוֹלִין לְמֵימַר לְהוּ. וְאַתְּ אָמְרַת כּוּלֵי הַאי וְאָזְלַתְּ?

מָשָׁל לְמֶלֶךְ בָּשָׂר וְדָם שֶׁהָיוּ לוֹ אֶלֶף אֲלָפִים דִינְרֵי זָהָב וְהָיוּ מְקַלְסִין אוֹתוֹ בְּשֶׁל כֶּסֶף. וַהֲלֹא גְנַאי הוּא לוֹ.

A certain fellow who led the service in the presence of Rabbi Chanina said, "O G-d, the great, mighty, awesome, powerful, firm, formidable, strong, fearless, sure, and honored one."

Rabbi Chanina waited until the man had finished and said, "Have you exhausted all the praises of your master? Why do you list so many praises? In fact, had Moses our master not mentioned these three praises [great, mighty, and awesome] in the Torah and had the Men of the Great Assembly not incorporated them into our prayers, we would not have been permitted to mention even these.

"This can be compared to an earthly king who possesses a million gold coins and someone praises him for possessing silver coins. Would this not be an insult to the king?"

TEXT 10

RABBI YOSEF ALBO, *SEFER HA'IKARIM* 4:35

וְאָמְרוּ: "אַתָּה גִבּוֹר לְעוֹלָם ה' מְחַיֶּה מֵתִים אַתָּה", כְּלוֹמַר אַתָּה גִבּוֹר וְיָכוֹל עַל כָּל דָבָר שֶׁיְצוּיַיר מְצִיאוּתוֹ אֵצֶל הַשֵּׂכֶל. וְאֵין גְבוּרָתְךָ כִּגְבוּרַת בָּשָׂר וָדָם. כִּי גְבוּרַת בָּשָׂר וָדָם הִיא לְהָמִית אֶת הַחַיִּים, וּגְבוּרַת הַשֵּׁם יִתְבָּרֵךְ הִיא בְּהֵפֶךְ שֶׁהִיא לְהַחְיוֹת אֶת הַמֵּתִים.

וְהִזְכִּירוּ בִּבְרָכָה זוֹ חֲסָדָיו שֶׁל הַקָדוֹשׁ בָּרוּךְ הוּא עִם בְּרִיּוֹתָיו בִּהְיוֹתָם בַּחַיִּים, וְאָמְרוּ, "מְכַלְכֵּל חַיִּים בְּחֶסֶד... סוֹמֵךְ נוֹפְלִים וְרוֹפֵא חוֹלִים וּמַתִּיר אֲסוּרִים וְכוּ'," לִרְמוֹז כִּי אֵין גְבוּרַת הַמָּקוֹם כִּגְבוּרַת בָּשָׂר וָדָם, כִּי גְבוּרַת בָּשָׂר וָדָם הִיא לְהַשְׁפִּיל הָאֲנָשִׁים וּלְהַכְנִיעָם, וּגְבוּרַת הַשֵּׁם יִתְבָּרֵךְ הִיא בְּהֵפֶךְ כִּי הוּא סוֹמֵךְ נוֹפְלִים. וְכֵן גְבוּרַת בָּשָׂר וָדָם הִיא לְהַכּוֹת, וְלִפְצוֹעַ, וּלְהַחְלִיא, וְהַשֵּׁם יִתְבָּרֵךְ בְּהֵפֶךְ כִּי הוּא רוֹפֵא חוֹלִים. וְכֵן גְבוּרַת בָּשָׂר וָדָם הִיא לַעֲנוֹשׁ נְכָסִים וְלַאֲסוּרִין, וְהַשֵּׁם יִתְבָּרֵךְ בְּהֵפֶךְ כִּי הוּא מַתִּיר אֲסוּרִים.

We say, "You are mighty forever, G-d, you resurrect the dead." By this we mean that You are mighty and capable of anything imaginable. But You use Your might differently from the way humans use their might. Humans use their might to kill the living, whereas G-d uses His might to resurrect the dead.

This blessing also mentions the kindnesses that G-d extends to the living. It reads, "He sustains the living with loving-kindness . . . supports the fallen, heals the sick, and releases the bound, etc." This implies once again that G-d's might is different from human might. Humans use their might to lower and oppress people, whereas G-d uses His might to support the fallen. Humans use their

RABBI YOSEF ALBO
C. 1380–1444

Spanish rabbi and philosopher. A student of Rabbi Chasdai Crescas, Albo is renowned for his philosophical work *Sefer Ha'ikarim* (*Book of Fundamentals*). The work stresses three fundamental aspects of Jewish belief: the existence of G-d, Torah from Sinai, and reward and punishment.

might to strike, maim, and inflict, whereas G-d heals the ill. Humans often hurt their victims and damage their property, whereas G-d releases the bound.

TEXT 11

MIDRASH TANCHUMA, VAYERA, CHAPTER 1

וּלְפִיכָךְ אֵין מִתְפַּלְלִין בְּשַׁבָּת שְׁמוֹנָה עֶשְׂרֵה, שֶׁאִם יִהְיֶה לוֹ חוֹלֶה בְּתוֹךְ בֵּיתוֹ, נִזְכַּר בְּרוֹפֵא חוֹלֵי עַמּוֹ יִשְׂרָאֵל, וְהוּא מֵיצֵר. וְהַשַּׁבָּת נִתְּנָה לְיִשְׂרָאֵל לִקְדוּשָּׁה, לְעֹנֶג וּלִמְנוּחָה, וְלֹא לְצַעַר. לְכָךְ מִתְפַּלֵּל ג' בְּרָכוֹת רִאשׁוֹנוֹת וְג' אַחֲרוֹנוֹת וְהַמְּנוּחָה בָּאֶמְצַע.

We don't recite the full eighteen blessings of the Amidah on Shabbat because one who has an ill family member would remember this person when praying for healing, which would lead to distress on Shabbat. The Shabbat was given to the Jewish people as a day of holiness, delight, and rest, not for distress. Therefore, we only recite the first three and last three blessings, with a blessing in the middle about rest.

MIDRASH TANCHUMA

A Midrashic work bearing the name of Rabbi Tanchuma, a 4th-century Talmudic sage quoted often in this work. Midrash is the designation of a particular genre of rabbinic literature usually forming a running commentary on specific books of the Bible. *Midrash Tanchuma* provides textual exegeses, expounds upon the biblical narrative, and develops and illustrates moral principles. *Tanchuma* is unique in that many of its sections commence with a halachic discussion, which subsequently leads into nonhalachic teachings.

Additional Readings

PERSONALIZING OUR PRAYER EXPERIENCE

BY RABBI ARYEH BEN DAVID

> *Blessed are You, L-rd,* our G-d and the G-d of our Fathers, *the G-d of Abraham, the G-d of Isaac, and the G-d of Jacob.*
> —Prayer book, opening words of the *Amida* prayer.

The peak moment of Jewish prayer, the standing, silent prayer (the *Amida*), teaches us the primacy of personalizing the prayer experience.

The *Amida* begins with the phrase "Our G-d and the G-d of our Fathers." These are two radically different experiences of the Divine.

"Our G-d" reflects the G-d of personal experience, the G-d of our lifetime. "Our G-d" refers to our personal and private relationship with G-d, which is unmediated by anyone else. No one else can create this for us. No one else can teach it to us. It is intimate and uniquely ours. This close, individual connection with G-d is sometimes referred to as a "vertical experience," a direct encounter with the beyond. The rabbis say that at Mount Sinai everyone heard a different voice—each person's relationship with G-d was unique.

"The G-d of our Fathers" is totally different. "The G-d of our Fathers" reflects the G-d of history. It is the G-d of Abraham, Isaac and Jacob. But it is not only the G-d of these three forefathers. It can also be understood to include all the people that preceded us. Everyone experiences G-d differently. This is the path that others have walked and that we can learn from. This experience of G-d is not accessed directly, nor is it the product of personal experience. Rather, it is learned through texts, stories, and a tradition conveyed by others. This indirect, mediated connection with G-d is sometimes referred to as a "horizontal experience," which is passed on through people, rather than through a direct experience with the transcendent.

We might have thought that the *Amida* would have begun with "the G-d of our Fathers" and then afterward mention "Our G-d." Their experience chronologically preceded our own. Nevertheless, we begin the *Amida* with "Our G-d." "Our G-d" precedes "the G-d of our Fathers."

Why?

First, we need to establish our own relationship with G-d. We need the "vertical" before the "horizontal." Only after this personal connection has been created can the teachings of "the G-d of our Fathers" resonate within us. The experience that others have had with G-d is meaningful only when we have already established our own experience of the holy.

Once, in the classroom, I asked if my students had ever been in love. One shook his head, saying "Never been." I said to him, "I love my wife very much. Do you have any idea how much I love my wife?" He answered, "No, not really, but it sounds nice." Since he had never been in love, he really had no idea what I was talking about. Then I asked a different student who *had* been in love before, "Do you have any idea how much I love my wife?" He nodded in confirmation and said, "Sure, I'm in love right now." Even though our experiences were probably completely different, he nevertheless could identify with my feelings, and we were able to carry on a discussion from a common platform.

RABBI ARYEH BEN DAVID

Rabbi Aryeh Ben David lives in Efrat, Israel. A lifelong educator, his passion is helping students engage with their spiritual heritage on a personal level. He blogs extensively, lectures internationally on the subject, and has authored two books. He is the founder of Ayeka, a center that develops and teaches pedagogical methods for bringing Jewish wisdom from the mind to the heart.

Only after someone has undergone a similar experience is it possible to fully identify and integrate the lessons from someone else's life. Otherwise, their experience will remain on a superficial level—that is, purely as intellectual information that does not affect a person deeply.

This is why "Our G-d" has to precede "the G-d of our Fathers." Only *after* we have had our own direct experience with G-d can we then benefit from someone else's experience of the Divine. Only *after* we have had our very own uniquely personal and distinct "spiritual" experience can we identify with, and take in, the experience of someone else.

This is one of the reasons why the words of the prayer book often do not resonate with people. They are the words of "our Fathers." They will only resonate with us after we have formed our own personal relationship with G-d.

The G-dfile

To develop your relationship with G-d, you have to click up your G-dfile. To click it up, you first have to write it.

What is a "G-dfile"? The G-dfile encompasses your relationship with G-d. It includes moments of overwhelming joy and of deep despair, of loving closeness and of painful distance. It consists of times when we are in dialogue with G-d and our belief is intact, and of times when we sorely feel an absence. Imagine now that all of the dimensions of this multifaceted relationship have been transcribed to a computer file entitled "The G-dfile."

Why might this metaphor be helpful? So often I have observed the frustration and disappointment of family members, friends and students—and certainly within myself as well—when the spiritual "lift" we expect at certain moments simply does not happen. Much of this frustration can be attributed to our mistaken expectations. We cannot expect to feel spiritually uplifted simply because of the uniqueness of the moment; we need to prepare ourselves in advance.

A personal example: When my wife and I were married in Jerusalem, my grandmother came to Israel for the first time for the wedding. She had been raised in a marginally connected Jewish home, and Judaism was not central to her life. We went to the Western Wall together, where she said: "Aryeh, I'm here at the Wall for the first time, and it is not doing anything for me. I don't feel anything special."

Why didn't the Wall do anything for my grandmother? I believe it is because she had not written her "Western Wall file" during her life. She had not come to Israel prepared for this potentially inspiring moment. Had she learned about this religiously significant and historical site and contemplated its meaning deeply, her visit might have been transformed into an overwhelmingly powerful experience:

Another example from routine, everyday life.

I am busy at work. In the middle of the day, I decide to call home to check in with my wife. Is it possible for us to have a brief, yet meaningful, interaction during a two or three-minute phone call? What of any consequence could possibly be expressed in these few minutes? The truth is that the amount of time is irrelevant. Even the briefest conversation offers the potential for a deep connection that is unrelated to the specific words that we will say. The conversation can be extremely meaningful and significant because over the past 25 years I have been developing and deepening my relationship with my wife, writing the "wife-file." The phone call itself will never *create* the beauty and depth of the relationship, but it can *maintain* it. This fleeting conversation is a chance to click on the wife file in the computer of my life, briefly calling up our shared history and reinforcing our commitment to a shared future.

Clearly, the conversation will only be as meaningful as the extent of the "file." I cannot create a relationship during a two-minute phone call, but I can build on the 20-year relationship that has already been developed and sustained. This history will imbue meaning to the conversation. "I love you, Sandra." Four short words carry with them all the connections, experiences and emotions built in our 20-year history.

If you take a break from your computer for a few minutes, the screen saver appears. Eventually you return to the computer, tap on the mouse, and the file that you were working on reappears on the screen. The file that appears is only as long or short, meaningful or shallow as what you had written before. When you click on the mouse, you never expect the tap to create the contents of the file. It only calls up whatever already exists.

Walking into a synagogue is like tapping on the mouse. It brings up a file. If you have written an extensive file, then all the emotions connected to that file will be evoked. If you have written only a small file, you can only expect to draw on the little that is already there.

Many of us walk into a synagogue with the expectation that a spiritual experience will descend upon us, regardless of how much or little we have written in our own personal G-dfile. We expect that the setting, prayer book, or maybe even the singing will elicit spiritual feelings. But in truth, neither the synagogue nor the prayer book can create a spiritual connection.

During the time of formal prayer, it is practically impossible to *create* a relationship with G-d. The synagogue can only serve to remind you of a relationship that already exists. Praying in a synagogue can certainly eclipse many of life's distractions, and help focus a relationship with G-d, but it is very unlikely that it will actually create the relationship. When no G-dfile has been written, and thus no file appears, frustration and disillusionment set in. The process is not magical. A file in which nothing has been written will produce just that—nothing. It is not the computer's fault. It is not the fault of the synagogue or the prayer book: they are simply tools designed to help us bring up the G-dfile. Just as in any relationship, it takes effort to build a relationship with G-d—effort that takes place in many settings besides the synagogue. Only you can write your own G-dfile.

Overcoming Obstacles to Writing Your G-dfile

We may find that in our path to writing a G-dfile, we encounter obstacles along the way, both internal and external.

Internal Obstacle #1: The Spiritual Stereotype

One common obstacle is the pervasive stereotype of the "spiritual type." Often I ask groups of students, "What do spiritual people do? What do they look like? What do spiritual people eat?" I inevitably receive the same answers: "They are mellow," says one. "They meditate a lot," says another. Others will say, "They do yoga, they sing, they dance; they are probably vegetarian or vegan; they wear flowing clothes, probably white." Then I ask the group, "How many of you fit into these categories?" Rarely does a hand go up.

"What is the goal of becoming more spiritual?" I persist. Again, the answers usually include such stereotypical notions as, "Being at peace with oneself, achieving nirvana, calmness and serenity. An inner glow."

Unfortunately, this characterization is terribly limiting. And since most people do not match this limited image, they believe that they themselves lack spirituality. These preconceived notions discourage most from ever trying to pursue a more spiritual path. I cannot begin to count the number of people who have told me, "I am simply not a spiritual person. I am not the spiritual type."

Overcoming the Obstacle: Breaking the Stereotype

I often ask people if they think they have a soul. They almost always respond affirmatively. "Well," I continue, "what does this soul do? What does it occupy itself with? Does it 'just sit there,' or is it active in any manner? Have you ever felt your soul communicating something to you? Have you ever had a spiritual moment?"

Invariably, one person begins to open up, and others begin to nod in agreement.

At the closing circle of one of our retreats, we invited everyone to talk for a few minutes about where they were spiritually. One elderly man had barely opened his mouth during our three days together. We hadn't expected him to say anything, so we were surprised when he began to talk and continued for over 20 minutes. Suddenly he stopped talking, and began to shake and cry. With tears welling up in his eyes, he whispered that all of his life he felt he had been on the outside of Judaism looking in. Now, for the first time, he felt as if someone had opened a door to let him in.

Who had locked this man out? Who created this "inside" and "outside" perception? Unfortunately, most of the time we do it to ourselves.

With an unrealistic stereotype of the "spiritual person" firmly embedded in our minds, we close the door to spirituality and lock ourselves out. The essential step in overcoming this obstacle, and placing ourselves back inside, is telling oneself, "I have a soul. I am a spiritual person."

Internal Obstacle #2: Fear of Change

Countering the desire within each of us for growth is an equally strong voice saying, "You're okay as you are, don't mess up your life. Who knows where change will lead? Why bother?"

According to the Talmud, we were all created with a drive that tricks us into complacency. We have a subconscious drive that urges us to remain static, to resist growth.

Sometimes when we see people after a long absence we observe that they haven't changed. Are they stable? Or are they stuck? One of the most difficult moments for students who return home after a year in Israel occurs when a relative or friend looks disapprovingly at them and remarks, "You've changed," subtly implying that change is a negative development reflecting a lack of stability.

At various stages in my life, an internal voice urged me to resist any kind of change. I convinced myself that more than anything, I needed to regain a sense of stability. I would often worry and feel uncertain about what a possible new stage might demand of me. Sometimes I simply lacked the energy and emotional strength to consider change and self-growth. For many years, I was aware that I had reached an impasse, and that I was spiritually stuck, yet I found myself incapable of overcoming this block. I was trapped in the daily routine of going through the motions.

Overcoming the Obstacle:
Finding the Will to Change

There is no single way to overcome this obstacle. Each person has his or her own personal demons. Personally, my desire to grow finally outweighed my drive to resist change. A spiritual block is like a black cloud that depletes joy and passion.

The crucial step in overcoming this obstacle requires asking ourselves three questions:

- Am I stuck?
- What exactly am I afraid of?
- What is holding me back?

External Obstacle #1:
The Synagogue—Where Is My Voice?

Did you ever feel like walking out of your synagogue?

Why is it that attending synagogue can be such a frustrating, and often empty, experience? Did you ever feel that it just was not working for you? You look around; everyone else is uttering the words, going through the motions. But the words of the prayer book are not your words; the pace of the service is not your pace. You're feeling lonely, alienated, out of it, and the feeling intensifies with each passing moment. Maybe you're wondering, "Am I the only one who feels like this? What's the matter with me?"

Perhaps you are asking yourself, "What am I supposed to be feeling at this moment? What is supposed to be happening now? Should I be asking for something? Should I be crying? Am I supposed to be feeling spiritual? Am I hoping for a mystical breakthrough? I know how to recite the words of the prayer book, but then what? What am I doing here? Where is my personal voice in all of this? There's no time or room for me to discover how I really feel about all of this. And, most painfully and poignantly of all, what is my voice supposed to be?"

At certain points in my life, the daily routine of praying in synagogue helped me build the stability of my faith. I enjoyed the connection with my friends in synagogue, the camaraderie before and after *davenning* (prayer) and the singing. But did the actual moment of prayer have any impact on my life? Was it meaningful?

I came to realize that for me—then—the answer was no.

Not only did my prayers lack meaning, but they often left me feeling deeply dissatisfied and frustrated, regardless of how many different synagogues I attended.

Overcoming the Obstacle: Finding Your Own Voice

Serious prayer should involve more than just the recitation of liturgical, or even informal, words. Prayer should be an authentically personal experience. It is not *someone's* prayer; it is *your* prayer. The Talmud refers to prayer as "the work of the heart." Prayer should reach the depths of your being and touch your heart.

The prayer book is supposed to be the springboard for this "work of the heart." Sometimes, however, the words of the prayer book take over, usurping your personal meditations. You follow the lines of the prayer book without personalizing them, without adding words or thoughts. You are not transformed. In fact, there is no "you" there.

You need to somehow find a place for yourself in the prayer book, to insert your own words, emotions and needs that you are feeling precisely at that moment. You need to bring yourself into the prayer experience.

Is this possible? Can you find room for yourself in the midst of an organized prayer service and fixed liturgy? Human beings are forever changing, but the prayer book does not: If the prayer book does not change, how can your own personal experience of prayer evolve to reflect your needs?

The rabbis themselves stressed the need to add personal prayers during the *Amida*, the silent standing prayer. During the "Listen to our voice" (*Shema Koleinu*) section of the *Amida*, one is encouraged to add personal thoughts. At the end of the *Amida*, and even during each blessing of the *Amida*, the rabbis encouraged the inclusion of personal insertions.

The essential step in overcoming this obstacle is saying to yourself, "I have a voice. I am allowed to add my personal prayers to the words of the prayer book. What personal words do I want to include?"

External Obstacle #2:
Public Nature of Prayer in Places of Worship

A second obstacle in creating one's own G-dfile is the focus of religious education on the "externals" of prayer, often at the expense of the "internals." Instead of concentrating on developing a rich internal life, and tapping into our spiritual beings, there has been a preoccupation with mastering the mechanics and technique of prayer.

I recognized this phenomenon while working with my students. They were talented young adults from all over the world. For many of them, this was their first serious encounter with Judaism. They began to learn about Jewish ideas and gradually incorporated more religious observances into their lives. They inevitably began to think about joining a Jewish community and wondered how they would fit in. How would they manage socially in this new milieu? Would it be awkward? Would they stand out? Would they feel self-conscious?

In their desire to integrate into Jewish communities, they pushed themselves to learn the essentials of Jewish public life: how to say the prayers, when to stand and when to bow. Some even learned how to lead the prayers. These were the easy things to teach and to learn.

Because of the public nature of places of worship, students became consumed with learning about the more visible and social dimensions of prayer. They often avoided the deeper question of how to use prayer to express their relationship with G-d.

Overcoming the Obstacle:
Finding Your Private Space in Places of Worship

Prayer comes in a number of forms. Certain forms center on the individual experience, a solitary figure sitting in solitude, in meditation, in supreme aloneness.

In community-centered prayer, the individual is swallowed up in the group experience. I remember being spellbound watching a Christian "revival" that culminated in a community singing of Halleluyah. In the frenetic energy of the congregation, the individuals seemed to merge into one communal being.

Which of these paradigms of prayer most reflects Judaism's approach—a solitary experience or a communal one? Actually, neither. Rather, the moment of encountering G-d in Jewish prayer reflects the fusion of these two models.

Although the *Shema* is probably the most well-known Jewish prayer, the central and most important moment in Jewish prayer is the silent standing prayer, the *Amida*. The *Shema* always precedes the *Amida*.

At the beginning of the *Amida*, one takes three steps backward, followed by three steps forward. Although one is now standing physically in the same spot, on a spiritual level, one moves into an entirely different place when entering the "*Amida* space." Despite being surrounded by others, the person praying is in a very private space—a space which draws upon the spiritual energy and mood of those around us, but that leaves us utterly alone at the ultimate moment of prayer. Students often refer to it as "the encounter" or "the zone" of standing in the presence of G-d.

Unfortunately, the social and communal nature of the synagogue and prayer often eclipse this precious moment. Extra effort is necessary to regain this sense and sanctity of private, solitary space. The rabbis of the Talmud instruct that one should not take any notice of any interruption—not even the entry of a king into the room or the sensing of a snake wrapped around one's legs. At this moment of silent prayer, one is entering a spiritual twilight zone, and nothing else exists but our relationship with G-d.

> *Three steps backward, three steps forward. You are alone with yourself: What are you thinking?*

Once you enter your "three steps forward" space, you enter sacred space, beyond time. You may find it helpful to pause, take several deep breaths, and repeat to yourself: "Three steps backward, three steps forward. I just entered into a different zone of being."

The rest of the congregation may be rushing forward with their own prayers, but you can and should take as long as you want during your private silent prayer. This is your time with G-d and everything else will simply have to wait.

After having taken three steps backward and three steps forward, what is supposed to happen now?

This moment cannot be captured through the words of the Jewish prayer book. It may be beyond all words. It is your opportunity to connect to the deepest part within yourself, to something greater than yourself. This is an experience that cannot be dictated for you by others, a moment of self-definition that only you can create for yourself. Only you will ever know what has transpired during this interval. Will this moment be meaningful? Or will it be empty?

Three steps backward, three steps forward. What kind of space have you entered? That depends on how you prepared yourself for this moment. The community cannot be held responsible for the depth, or lack of depth, of this spiritual moment. You have total control over the quality of the private space that you create during prayer. The important step in overcoming this obstacle is asking yourself, "Have I entered into a sacred space? What has changed within me? What does this open up within me?"

The G-dfile: 10 Approaches to Personalizing Prayer (Jerusalem: Devora Publishing, 2007), pp. 3–10, 25–33
Reprinted with permission of the author

THE *AMIDA*'S BIBLICAL AND HISTORICAL ROOTS: SOME NEW PERSPECTIVES

BY ALLEN FRIEDMAN

The opening of the *Amida* owes more to a few Biblical passages than we customarily think. The goal of this article is to understand the magnitude of that debt and thereby deepen our comprehension of the opening and of the *Amida* as a whole. We hope to achieve this through careful consideration of the source-texts and history of the *Amida*'s beginning phrases, viewing them in light of both the approach of *Hazal* and the fruits of modern scholarship.

The Opening Phrase

Every *Shemoneh Esre* opens with "Blessed are You L-rd, our G-d and G-d of our fathers, G-d of Abraham, G-d of Isaac, and G-d of Jacob."[1] This *matbe'a ha-berakha*—blessing template—differs from that used in almost all other blessings in Jewish liturgy or ritual. Almost all others begin by addressing G-d in the second person—"Blessed are You, L-rd our G-d"—and then immediately continue with a description of G-d as the *Melekh Ha-olam*.[2] By contrast, *Shemoneh Esre*'s opening continues with a reinforcement of that second person intimacy as it addresses G-d, not as the remote "King of the Universe," but as a familial "G-d of our fathers."[3]

The *Amida*'s opening phrase is noteworthy for a second reason: its separate invocation of each of the patriarchs and the separate association of each of the patriarchs with G-d—"G-d of Abraham, G-d of Isaac, and G-d of Jacob," a feature already discussed by *Hazal*.[4]

ALLEN FRIEDMAN

Allen Friedman is a managing director at J.P. Morgan Chase Tax Department. A graduate of Yeshiva University (BA) and Columbia University Law School, his writings have appeared in *Alei Etzion*, *Meorot*, and the *Torah U'Madda Journal*.

The Source of the *Amida*'s Opening Phrase

These two unique elements of the *Amida*'s opening are found in—and are simultaneously justified by—the source-text that the opening quotes almost verbatim: Exodus 3:15.[5] That verse reads:

> *And G-d said further to Moses, "Thus shall you say to the children of Israel,* 'The L-rd, G-d of your fathers, the G-d of Abraham, the G-d of Isaac, and the G-d of Jacob, *has sent me to you.' This is My name forever, and thus I am to be invoked in all ages."*[6]

Whenever you want to appeal to me, says G-d, from now until the end of time use this formulation: "*The L-rd, G-d of your fathers, the G-d of Abraham, the G-d of Isaac, and the G-d of Jacob*," or, to formulate this phrase from the perspective of the Israelites, who will refer to "G-d of *our* fathers" (rather than from G-d's perspective, who refers to Himself as "G-d of *your* fathers"), "*The L-rd, G-d of our fathers, the G-d of Abraham, the G-d of Isaac, and the G-d of Jacob.*"[7]

And, of course, Jews follow G-d's instructions to the letter every time they begin their appeal: they begin each *Shemoneh Esre* by appealing to "L-rd, [our G-d and] G-d of our fathers, G-d of Abraham, G-d of Isaac and G-d of Jacob." The only (other) change made to the quote is to add "our G-d" towards the beginning of the phrase, a point we discuss below.

Hazal were very conscious of this "borrowing," as indicated by the statement in the *Mekhilta de-Rabbi Yishmael* on Exodus 13:3 that cites Exodus 3:15 as the source-text for the opening of *Shemoneh Esre*—a statement we will look at later on to help complete our understanding of *Shemoneh Esre*'s message.

The Context of the Source for the Opening Phrase

The fact that G-d instructed Moses to use Exodus 3:15's formulation would be reason enough for the

Rabbis to word the opening of *Shemoneh Esre* as they did. But that instruction took place in a particular context—and we cannot fully understand the opening blessing of the *Amida*, or *Shemoneh Esre* as a whole, unless we examine and understand that context. As Reuven Kimelman put it:

> *The claim that [a particular verse] is the intertext [for a given prayer] implies that the liturgical text is to be understood in light of [the Biblical source]. The correct construal of meaning takes place in the mind of the reader who juxtaposes both texts. It is through the superimposition of the biblical text on the liturgical text that the liturgical meaning coalesces. In other words, the meaning of the liturgy exists not so much in the liturgical text* per se *as in the interaction between the liturgical text and the biblical intertext. Meaning in the mind of the reader takes place between texts rather than within them.*[8]

Put slightly differently, we cannot truly understand a prayer merely by translating its words. Rather, it can only be truly understood if we know its Biblical source, and understand the message that *Hazal* were conveying with the selection of that source. And, if this statement is true about prayer in general, it is certainly true about *Shemoneh Esre*, the prayer *par excellence*, and its opening phrase. The source-text for that opening, Exodus 3:15, is a continuation of a unit which opens with the last three verses of the second chapter of Exodus. Those verses read:

> *During those many days the king of Egypt died, and the people of Israel groaned because of their bondage and cried out, and their cry for help from the bondage rose up to G-d. And G-d heard their moaning, and G-d remembered His covenant with Abraham, with Isaac, and with Jacob. G-d saw the people of Israel—and G-d knew.*

Three points about these verses stand out. First, the verses record Israel's first collective prayer—"their cry for help . . . rose up to G-d."[9] Second, they are animated by four action verbs that describe G-d's response to His people's cry: "G-d heard;" "G-d remembered;" "G-d saw" Israel and its suffering; "G-d knew"—He understood His people's plight. Third, the verses link G-d's covenant with the children of Israel, of His promise to redeem His nation, with the separate mention of each of the patriarchs: "G-d remembered His covenant with Abraham, with Isaac, and with Jacob."

This third point—the linkage with the (separately-named) patriarchs found near the end of the second chapter—is repeatedly emphasized in the following chapters. In chapter three, G-d appears to Moses and tells him that He has seen His people's affliction and heard their cries and He has therefore decided to redeem them. Moses then asks G-d (verse 13), "When I come to the children of Israel and say to them, 'The G-d of your fathers has sent me to you,' and they ask me, 'What is his name?' what shall I say to them?" G-d responds with our source-text verse: "Thus shall you say to the children of Israel, '*The L-rd, G-d of your fathers, the G-d of Abraham, the G-d of Isaac, and the G-d of Jacob*, has sent me to you.' This is my name forever, and thus I am to be invoked in all ages."

Now, as if to make sure that Moses understands the importance of a formula that separately invokes each of the patriarchs and their relationship with G-d, this formula is repeated a third time in the very next verse, verse 16,[10] and yet a fourth time in Exodus 4:5.[11]

G-d's sudden engagement with the children of Israel and His invocation of the covenant with their patriarchs is especially remarkable in light of His seeming absence until now. Since G-d's revelation to Jacob on his way down to Egypt at the beginning of Genesis 46, G-d has not revealed Himself to, or (seemingly) involved Himself in the history of, Abraham's, Isaac's and Jacob's descendants. In fact, with one almost offhand exception,[12] G-d's name does not even appear in the book of Exodus until the end of chapter two (in the verses cited above). As the Bible itself emphasizes,[13] decades, then centuries pass as the Israelites sink deeper into exile and harsh servitude and G-d is seemingly nowhere to be found.[14]

To summarize, the source-text for the unique-in-Jewish-prayer opening of *Shemoneh Esre* draws our attention to the first several chapters of Exodus and the story they tell: Israel's descent into a long and harsh exile with no apparent evidence that G-d knows or cares—in fact, G-d seems conspicuously absent. As the burden of the exile becomes unbearable, the Israelites cry out to G-d in their first collective prayer and G-d responds, suddenly makes His presence known, and immediately begins their rescue because, G-d emphasizes, of the promises He made to each of the three patriarchs.[15]

Having established what the context is for the *Shemoneh Esre*'s opening source-text, we now must determine why *Hazal* wanted to evoke that context. We can answer this question once we (a) take into account key points about the history, narrative, and framework of the *Amida* that have been made by modern scholars and that are either made or alluded to by *Hazal;* and (b) determine when the *Amida*'s opening was composed.

The *Amida*'s History, Narrative, and Framework

The first two points to be noted concerning the *Amida*'s history are that (1) R. Gamliel and his colleagues in late first-century CE Yavneh created the institution of the *Amida*, its nineteen particular subjects,[16] and the order of those subjects, though not their fully fixed text,[17] and (2) this creation was a critical part of the Rabbinic response to the great theological challenge posed by the Second Temple's destruction and the ensuing exile: how to account for G-d's seeming abandonment of His people, and how to sustain hope for the future.[18]

The next point follows naturally from the first two. The overarching theme of Jewish prayer—and especially of The Prayer, the *Amida*—is the keystone of that Rabbinic response to the *hurban*: an unshakable belief in Israel's ultimate redemption. Joseph Heinemann put it this way: "The central motif in the world-view of the prayers is unquestionably the belief in the Redemption, and the longing for its realization."[19] Even a superficial examination of the *Shemoneh Esre*'s blessings reveals the truth of Heinemann's statement when applied to The Prayer: (i) most of the "heart" of the *Amida*—the middle, petitionary blessings—are explicitly devoted to the final redemption, and (ii) a majority of the "framework" blessings—the three introductory and three concluding blessings—have the Redemption as either their explicit subject (for example, the revivication of the dead, mentioned six times in the second introductory blessing, and restoration of the Temple service and the return of the Divine presence to Zion, the subjects of the first of the three concluding blessings) or as a very important subtext (for example, the invocation of G-d, in the opening blessing, as the One who will bring the redeemer: "*u-mevi go'el le-venei veneihem*").[20]

Dating the Composition of the *Amida*'s Opening

In the absence of an explicit statement of authorship—something that, with the possible exception of *ve-laMalshinim*, the *Amida*'s blessings lack—or a datable text—something that does not exist in the case of the *Amida* before the time of the Cairo Genizah texts and the siddurim of Amram Gaon and Saadiah Gaon (9th century CE and later)—the attribution of authorship of the *Amida*'s opening to a particular time period must rely on circumstantial evidence. There are, however, several pieces of strong circumstantial evidence, all of which point to or are consistent with conclusions that:

- The incorporation of Exodus 3:15 into the liturgy postdates the Second Temple's destruction.
- This liturgical incorporation took place in the *Amida*'s earliest days, in the decades immediately after the Second Temple's destruction.
- The incorporation was, in the standard liturgy, exclusive to the *Amida*.

The principal evidence that Exodus 3:15 was first incorporated into the liturgy post-*hurban Bayit Sheni* is perhaps most accurately characterized as evidence of absence: we know of no instances of the liturgical use of Exodus 3:15 before the Second Temple's destruction. That is, although we have many examples of pre-*hurban Bayit Sheni* prayers, blessings, and other precursors to significant portions of the *Shemoneh Esre* and to the standard liturgy, none of those examples invoke Exodus 3:15.[21]

Conversely, there are a number of examples of the liturgical use of Exodus 3:15 (outside of the standard liturgy), all of which are post-Second Temple.[22]

If, as we contend, the liturgical use of Exodus 3:15 postdates *hurban Bayit Sheni*, we must determine when in the post-*hurban Bayit Sheni* period that use arose. The answer to that question is suggested by the near identity of the opening words of the *Amida* in all *nusha'ot*—an identity that exists with almost no other portion of the *Amida* (other than with many of the *hatimot*). This near-identity points to an early standardized use of Exodus 3:15 and pushes the time of the composition of that opening back toward the earliest days of the *Shemoneh Esre*—the decades immediately following the Second Temple's destruction. This is consistent with an assumption that even if the text of (many of the) individual blessings remained fluid for some time—as it appears was likely the case[23]—R. Gamliel would have standardized the opening of the *Amida*.

The dates of the earliest attestations to the use of Exodus 3:15 to open the *Amida* are also consistent with the early post-*hurban Bayit Sheni* hypothesis. Explicit attestations date from the early decades of the third century CE,[24] while strong allusions to the use of Exodus 3:15 date from the early to mid-second century CE.[25] These sources would provide us with a *terminus ad quem* for the composition of the *Amida*'s opening that (while after the time of R. Gamliel de-Yavneh) would be considerably before the earliest date-certain for the composition of almost all other specific wordings of the Prayer.

How the Scholarship and Historical Evidence Informs Our Understanding of the *Amida*'s Opening

We have seen that:

a. The *matbe'a ha-berakha* that opens the *Amida* is unique to the *Amida* and, in sharp contrast to that used in virtually every other blessing in the Jewish liturgy, emphasizes the relationship between G-d, Israel, and its founding ancestors.[26]
b. This *matbe'a ha-berakha* is a near quote of Exodus 3:15.
c. The biblical context of Exodus 3:15 is the response of a heretofore seemingly absent G-d to Israel's despairing cry to rescue it from a long and harsh exile.
d. The Midrash and the text of the *Amida* acknowledge and play off this context.[27]
e. The institution of the *Amida* and its content were critical elements of the Rabbis' response to the theological challenge posed by the destruction.
f. The overall and pervasive theme of the *Amida* is the keystone of that response: an unshakable belief in Israel's ultimate redemption.
g. The *Amida*'s basic framework was put into place in the decades following the Second Temple's destruction.
h. As best we can tell, the opening of the *Amida* was written in that same post-Second Temple destruction era, even as much of the rest of the *Amida*'s text remained fluid.

These eight points, taken together, make it clear that Exodus 3:15 was chosen to open the *Amida* not "merely" because that is what G-d instructed, and not just because so doing invokes Israel's first redemption. Rather, it was chosen because the context of Exodus 3:15—the unfolding of the first exile and redemption in the last chapters of Genesis and the first chapters of Exodus—paralleled the nation's current condition and foretold its future one: the children of Israel—then (in Egyptian bondage), as now (after the *hurban*)—find themselves in harsh exile; then, as now, G-d has seemingly abandoned His people and yet they remember the promise that G-d made to their ancestors; then, as now, Israel cries out to Him, invoking that promise and emphasizing the relationship with each of the patriarchs. And His people express their confidence that G-d will hear their prayers, remember them and His promise now, as He did then, and end their suffering and redeem His people; that G-d is, as the Midrash states, the *shomea tefilla*[28]—the one who hears His people's prayers—even as His seeming absence and the suffering of His people might cause them to think otherwise.

That the liturgical use of Exodus 3:15 was reserved for the *Amida* alone reinforces and dovetails with the points just made: the most logical explanation for the reservation is that Exodus 3:15 was set aside for the prayer most related to the context in which the quoted words originally appeared—a prayer whose wording and order took shape in the aftermath of (and largely in reaction to) the Temple's destruction, and a context that had special resonance in that post-*hurban* period: G-d's appearance as Israel's Redeemer from an oppressive exile after His seeming abandonment of His people.

Two further points need to be made to round out this portion of our discussion. First, we need to explain why "our G-d" is inserted into the quote/paraphrase of Exodus 3:15 in the opening of *Shemoneh Esre*: "Blessed are You our L-rd, *our G-d* and G-d of our fathers, G-d of Abraham, G-d of Isaac and G-d of Jacob."

On the most obvious level, the insertion preserves the standard *matbe'a ha-berakha* to a greater extent than would be the case without that insertion.

On a more fundamental level, the insertion reinforces Israel's faith that it has a continuing relationship with He Who spoke the words of Exodus 3:15 3,300 years ago: G-d is not 'merely' the G-d of generations past, but is the G-d of every following generation as well—a reinforcement that was particularly necessary in the post-Second Temple destruction period in which *Shemoneh Esre* took its current form. Additionally, and related to this *point, the insertion picks up on the phrase "Ehyeh Asher Ehyeh"* "I Will Be What I Will Be" that appears in Exodus 3:14—the verse that precedes our key source-text of Exodus 3:15—and, specifically, *Hazal*'s understanding of Exodus 3:14, quoted by Rashi in his comment on that verse: "I am with them in this affliction as I am with them in all future exiles"—precisely the point that is emphasized by the insertion of "our G-d."[29]

We complete this discussion by noting the context in which the *Mekhilta* observes that Exodus 3:15 is the source-text for the opening of *Shemoneh Esre*. It is not a coincidence that the immediately preceding part of the *Mekhilta* contains an extended discussion—much of which is familiar to many thanks to its inclusion (in a variant form) in the Haggadah—of the relationship between the redemption from Egypt and the future redemption:

> *13:3* And Moses said to the people, etc. *Until now, I am only aware of an obligation to remember the Exodus from Egypt during the day. Whence the obligation to remember it at night? As it is written, "so that you should remember the day you went out," etc. "the days of your life"—telling me of an obligation to remember it during the day.* "All *the days of your life"—to include the nights, as Ben Zoma stated. And the Sages say: "the days of your life" refers to this world; "all the days of your life" comes to add the days of the Messiah. . . . And how do we know that we recite "Blessed are You L-rd, our G-d and G-d of our fathers, G-d of Abraham, G-d of Isaac and G-d of Jacob"? As it is written, "And G-d said further to Moses, 'Thus shall you say to the children of Israel,* "The L-rd, G-d of your fathers, the G-d of Abraham, the G-d of Isaac, and the G-d of Jacob."'"
>
> *This juxtaposition of the future redemption, the Exodus, and the source-text for the opening of the* Amida *reinforces our thesis that the selection of Exodus 3:15 to open* Shemoneh Esre *is intended to connect the people's first, past redemption with their final, future one.*[30]

Conclusion

We examined the source-text for the opening words of *Shemoneh Esre*, and the context of that source-text, and saw how that examination allowed us to see this most-familiar of prayer openings with fresh eyes. We then looked at the message of the *Amida* as a whole and its history as they are understood by many contemporary scholars, and discussed the evidence pointing to the post-Second Temple destruction composition of the opening of the *Amida*. We saw how these elements reinforced and deepened our understanding of the relationship between the opening of the *Shemoneh Esre* and the body of the prayer. It is hoped that, in the process, we have at least partly lifted the veil of familiarity that can obscure the meaning of this most familiar of Jewish liturgical routines.

Tradition: A Journal of Orthodox Jewish Thought, Vol. 45, No. 3 (Fall 2012), pp. 21–34.

Endnotes

[1] All translations of excerpts from the siddur are from Jonathan Sacks, *The Koren Siddur*, (Jerusalem: Koren Publishers, 2009). The *Amida*'s opening phrase quoted in the text is the one used in all *nusha'ot* as well as in virtually all the texts from the Cairo Genizah that include the first blessing of *Shemoneh Esre*. See Yehezkel Luger, *The Weekday Amidah in the Cairo Genizah* (Jerusalem: Orhot Press, 2001), 41–43.

[2] There has been much discussion of how this second person/third person formula came to be. For an analysis and summary of traditional and modern scholarship on the issue, see Joseph Heinemann, *Prayer in the Talmud—Forms and Patterns* (Berlin-New York: Walter de Gruyter, 1977), 104–122.

[3] The power of this point is magnified if one adopts Rashi's understanding of the principle of *berakha ha-semukha le-havertah*, under which the remaining eighteen blessings "borrow" this opening as their own; see Rashi in *Berakhot* 46b, s.v. *ve-yesh me-hen hotem ve-lo poteah*. The prayer is thus, in this view, addressing each blessing of the *Shemoneh Esre* not to a distant King of the Universe but to a familial Deity.

Interestingly, the *Amida*'s first blessing does eventually refer to G-d by the term "King," but, instead of referring to Him as "King of the Universe," it refers to Him as the "King Helper, Savior, and Protector," again emphasizing the personal, direct relationship. This formulation—with occasional slight variations—is found in all modern *nusha'ot* as well as in most of the texts from the Cairo Genizah that include the first blessing of *Shemoneh Esre*, Luger, 48–49.

How the lack of a reference to G-d as "King of the Universe" can be harmonized with the halakhic requirement that every blessing contain "*shem*"—G-d's name—and "*malkhut*"—a reference to G-d as King—is a much discussed issue that is beyond the scope of this article. See, generally, *Encyclopedia Talmudit*, "Blessings," 294.

[4] See *Pesahim* 117b. This statement is best known through its citation by Rashi commenting on Genesis 12:2.

[5] Much of *Shemoneh Esre*—and of our daily prayer—is of course a paraphrase of, or is clearly inspired by, verses from the Bible, and those Biblical source-texts often provide clues as to the meaning of the prayer. See n. 8 and accompanying text.

[6] Translations of Biblical verses are adapted from *The New JPS Translation* and Robert Alter, *The Five Books of Moses—A Translation with Commentary* (New York: W.W. Norton & Company, 2004).

[7] For a similar change in perspective—from G-d's (first person) to the prayer's (second person)—when a verse is adapted for use in the *Amida*, compare Jeremiah 9:23's "*haskeil ve-yadoa oti*" to its paraphrase in the fourth blessing of *Shemoneh Esre*: "*me-ittekha de'ah . . . ve-haskeil*." For a similar change in perspective—from G-d's (first person) to the prayer's (second person)—when the last seven words of 'our' source-text are paraphrased later in the Bible, see Psalms 135:13: "*Ado-nai shimcha le-olam, Ado-nai zikhrekha le-dor va-dor*."

[8] Reuven Kimelman, "The Shema Liturgy—From Covenant Ceremony to Coronation" in *Kenishta: Studies of the Synagogue World*, Joseph Tabory, ed., (Ramat-Gan: Bar Ilan University Press, 2001), 28.

[9] See n. 15 for a discussion of how we know—and how we know that the Rabbis assumed—that the phrase "their cry for help rose up to G-d" refers to prayer and not (just) to a cry of desperation.

[10] "Go and gather the elders of Israel together and say to them, 'The L-rd G-d of your fathers has appeared to me, the G-d of Abraham, of Isaac, and of Jacob, saying, 'I have taken note of you and of what is being done to you in Egypt.'"

[11] "That they may believe that the L-rd, the G-d of their fathers, the G-d of Abraham, the G-d of Isaac, and the G-d of Jacob, did appear to you."

[12] The exception is Exodus 1:15, where G-d blesses two individuals (the midwives) whom the text does not even identify as Israelite; see exegetes cited in *The Jewish Study Bible* (New York: Oxford University Press, 2004), 108 on the verse.

[13] The unit opens in Exodus 2:23 with "During those many days."

[14] I am grateful to Rachel Friedman, who first brought these points to my attention.

[15] A Midrash commenting on Exodus 2:23 reinforces the point that *Hazal*'s near-quote of Exodus 3:15 was intended to evoke that verse's context—the nation's first collective prayer and G-d's response to it in the closing verses of Exodus 2. That Midrash explicitly connects those closing verses and The Prayer *par excellence* that Jews recite three times a day:

> When the children of Israel groaned and cried out to G-d and He heard their cry, as it says "and the people of Israel groaned because of their bondage and cried out, and their cry for help from the bondage rose up to G-d," [Exodus 2:23] immediately the ministering angels opened up and said, "Blessed are You G-d, who listens to prayers [*shomea tefilla*]."

Midrash quoted in *Torah Shelema, Exodus* v. 1, 105, and J. D. Eisenstein, *Otsar Midrashim* (Israel 1915), 584. The Israelites cry out in their first collective prayer—"their cry for help rose up to G-d"—and the angels respond with "Blessed are You G-d, who listens to prayers," the coda of *Shemoneh Esre*'s petitionary blessings: that first collective prayer becomes the model for their future *tefillot*.

There are also two textual reinforcements of the relationship between the first collective prayer and that same *shomea tefilla* blessing. First, the opening words of that blessing in most *nusha'ot* are "hear our voice L-rd our G-d" "*shema koleinu Ado-nai Elo-heinu*." This opening evocatively paraphrases the recounting in Deuteronomy 26:7 (in the *hava'at bikkurim* ceremony) of G-d's response to that collective prayer: "We cried out to the L-rd, G-d of our fathers, *and the L-rd heard our voice*" "*va-yishma Ado-nai et koleinu*."

Second, a widespread early version of the *shomea tefilla* blessing, a version that survives in the *nusah* of Aram Tsova (Aleppo) and Persia, adds the phrase "*u-shema na'akateinu ka-asher shamata na'akat avoteinu*." This phrase is unquestionably an allusion to Exodus 2:24: "And G-d heard their moaning [*va-yishma Elo-him et na'akatam*], and G-d remembered his covenant with Abraham, with Isaac, and with Jacob." Thus, the last of the petitionary blessings explicitly loops back to the opening of the first blessing of *Shemoneh Esre*.

Full discussion of these points is beyond the scope of this article.

[16] Discussion of the variations that had seventeen or (even post-*ve-laMalshinim*) eighteen blessings is beyond the scope of this article.

[17] With the possible exception of the *hatimot* and—as discussed in the text—the opening of the *Amida*, the overwhelming scholarly consensus reflected in the sources just cited is that the text of the *Shemoneh Esre* remained fluid for an extended period after the time of R. Gamliel. See, *e.g.*, Joseph Tabory, "Prayers and Berakhot" in *The Literature of the Sages*, Second Part, Shmuel Safrai, Zeev Safrai, Joshua Schwartz, and Peter Tomson, eds., (Amsterdam: Royal Van Gorcum Fortress Press), 308–311; Richard S. Sarason, "Communal Prayer at Qumran and Among the Rabbis: Certainties and

Uncertainties," in *Liturgical Perspectives: Prayer and Poetry in Light of the Dead Sea Scrolls*, Esther Chazon, ed. (Boston, Leiden: Brill, 2003), 168; Lee Levine, *The Ancient Synagogue: The First Thousand Years*, (New Haven & London: Yale University Press, 2005), 548-549. But see the contrasting (and singular) views of Ezra Fleischer, "On the Origins of Mandatory Prayer in Israel" in *Likkutei Tarbiz VI Studies in Jewish Liturgy*, Hananel Mack, ed. (Jerusalem: Magnes Press, 2003). Put slightly differently (and *pace* Fleischer) R. Gamliel likely mandated the order of the blessings, and the text of the *hatimot* and (we maintain) the opening, but not the text of the individual blessings. That there was not a mandated text seems almost self-evident from the multiplicity of *nusha'ot* found in the Cairo Genizah and in use in many communities to this day. See discussion of related points in the following footnote and n. 20.

18 Key questions concerning *Shemoneh Esre*'s composition—including when it was (or specific elements of it were) composed, who composed it (or a given element thereof), whether there was a full "ur-text" of *Shemoneh Esre* (as opposed to merely a mandated schematic outline), what (if any) is the relationship between "our" *Shemoneh Esre* and (what some see as) pre-*hurban* partial proto-*Shemoneh Esres* found in Qumran, Ben Sira and elsewhere, and what the role of R. Gamliel and his colleagues was in this process—are probably the most discussed ones in the study of Jewish prayer. Except to the limited extent discussed in the following sections of the article (concerning the opening phrase of the *Amida*), resolution of these questions is not necessary for establishing the validity of the statements made in the text; for a summary of and references to many of the sources that discuss this subject, see Levine, chapters five and sixteen.

19 Heinemann, 33. For a citation to, and discussion of, early Rabbinic sources emphasizing the idea of the *Amida* as a prayer for redemption, *see* Kimelman, "Daily Amidah," 178–179, 194–196.

20 Many modern scholars in fact extend this understanding of *Shemoneh Esre* as an articulation of the yearning for the future redemption and of Israel's confidence in its inevitability to each of the (a) framework blessings—the first and last three that begin and end every *Shemoneh Esre*—and (b) middle (petitionary) blessings of *Shemoneh Esre*. One succinct summary (by Ezra Fleischer) summarizes all the middle blessings as "a chronologically organized plan, in logical sequence, for the rebuilding of the nation from its post–[Second Temple] destruction historical reality to its spiritual and political restoration in the ideal future." Ezra Fleischer, "The Shemoneh Esre: Its Character, Internal Order, Content and Goals," in *Likkutei Tarbiz VI Studies in Jewish Liturgy*, Hananel Mack, ed. (Jerusalem: Magnes Press, 2003), 198; translation from the Hebrew is from Kimelman, "The Penitential Part of the Amidah and Personal Redemption" in *Seeking the Favor of G-d Vol. 3: The Impact of Penitential Prayer Beyond Second Temple Judaism* (Atlanta: Society of Biblical Literature, 2008), 81. Kimelman (and others), while still strongly endorsing the overall 'redemption-centric' view, disagree with the way Fleischer relates blessings 4 (*honen hada'at*) through 9 (*mevarekh ha-shanim*) to the redemption. See Kimelman, "The Penitential Part of the Amidah," 83.

For discussions of the "redemption-centric" view, see Kimelman, "Daily Amidah and the Rhetoric of Redemption"; Fleischer, "The Shemoneh Esre"; Lawrence Hoffman, *My People's Prayer Book, Vol. 2—The Amidah* (Vermont: Jewish Lights Publishing, 1998), 32–34; Maurice Liber, "Structure and History of the Tefilah," *The Jewish Quarterly Review* 40 (1949), 331; and Leon Liebreich, "The Intermediate Blessings of the 'Amidah,'" *The Jewish Quarterly Review* 42 (1952), 423.

It is important to emphasize that a "redemption-centric" understanding of the *Amida* is held by scholars who have very different views as to the time of the composition of the prayer. It is held, for example, by Ezra Fleischer, perhaps the most prominent member of the "redemption-centric" school, who asserted that "there existed at [the end of the Second Temple period] no sort of verbal worship that resembled the liturgy that was established at Yavneh. . . . At the time it was promulgated at Yavneh, the *Shemoneh Esre* was an utter innovation on all levels, whether institutional, functional, or theological." Ezra Fleischer, "On the Origins of the Amidah: Response to Ruth Langer," *Prooftexts* 20:3 (2000), 381. See also Fleischer's seminal article, "On the Origins of Mandatory Prayer in Israel." The "redemption-centric" understanding is held by Maurice Liber—the inspiration for Kimelman's "redemption-centric" understanding (see Kimelman, "Daily Amidah," 181 n. 57)—who sees at least significant parts of "our" *Shemoneh Esre* as predating the Second Temple's destruction. Maurice Liber, "Structure and History of the Tefilah," 353 ff. Even Heinemann, who is at the opposite end of the authorship debate from Fleischer—believing that "[t]he custom of reciting precisely eighteen benedictions must have crystallized sometime during the century before the destruction of the Temple (at the very latest) . . . [though] the exact content and order of these benedictions . . . was not yet uniform" (Heinemann, 224)—noted (in the words quoted in the text) the centrality of the redemption in Jewish prayer and would not, I believe, see any inconsistency between his views on authorship and a redemption-centric understanding of *Shemoneh Esre*.

That is, even Heinemann's "minimalist" understanding of R. Gamliel's and his court's contribution is consistent with the view that they reorganized and reworded either pre-existing groups of, or individual, benedictions so as to lay out the redemption narrative in the way that the *Shemoneh Esre* now does. Cf. Lee Levine's conclusion (Levine, 548): "There can be little doubt that the obligatory daily *Amidah* prayer . . . was first implemented in the post-70 period under the auspices of Rabban Gamliel. However . . . these prayers were not created ex nihilo. There were many precedents, and the Yavnean *tannaim* incorporated earlier materials, reworking, reformulating, and structuring them so as to fashion a prayer that would be obligatory for Jews everywhere."

Finally, it should be noted that viewing R. Gamliel's and his court's role as the reworking and re-ordering of pre-existing prayers and benedictions is consistent with the Talmud's discussion of *Shemoneh Esre*'s composition. See, e.g., *Megilla* 17b & 18a.

21 For a summary of (what assorted scholars see as) the precursors to the *Amida*, see Heinemann, 219–220 and Daniel Falk, *Daily, Sabbath & Festival Prayers in the Dead Sea Scrolls* (Leiden: Brill 1998), 76–78. For a list of secondary sources that discuss those precursors, see (in addition to the Heinemann and Falk references just cited) those cited in Stefan C. Reif, *Judaism and Hebrew Prayer* (Cambridge: Cambridge University Press, 1993) 346 n. 19.

For a discussion of the one (or perhaps two) pieces of evidence that imply a pre-*hurban Bayit Sheni* existence of an *Amida*—though with no indication as to what the text (or at least the opening text) of that *Amida* might have looked like—see Fleischer, "On the Origins of Mandatory Prayer in Israel," 425; Falk, *Prayer in the Dead Sea*

Scrolls, 249 n. 102; David Levine, "A Temple Prayer for Fast Days" in *Liturgical Perspectives: Prayer and Poetry in Light of the Dead Sea Scrolls*, Esther Chazon, ed. (Leiden, Boston: Brill, 2003), 102; Heinemann, 96 n. 26; Lee Levine, 549 n. 80.

22 Kimelman, "Daily Amidah" n. 57. This is not to say that pre-*hurban Bayit Sheni* prayers separately invoking each of the three patriarchs by name are unknown—on the contrary, it would appear that such invocations were fairly widely used, see Martin Rist, "The G-d of Abraham, Isaac and Jacob: A Liturgical and Magical Formula," *Journal of Biblical Literature* 57 (1938), 289. Given the frequent use of the "three patriarch" formula in the Bible, these usages are not at all surprising. What is somewhat surprising—and what the text focuses on—is that the opening of the *Amida* is the only source in the standard liturgy (and one of the few liturgical sources anywhere) that couches the invocation in language that consciously evokes Exodus 3:15.

23 See discussion in n. 17 and sources cited there.

24 See *Sanhedrin* 107a, which quotes a statement from R. Yehuda in the name of Rav that contains the opening words of the *Amida*. Rav died in 247 CE. Three other attestations date from perhaps several decades later. One is the quote of the *Amida's* opening words found in *Pesahim* 117b (noted in the text accompanying n. 4). The statement is attributed to Resh Lakish, who died in 299 CE. The next two are the *Midrash Tanna'im le-Devarim*, 33:2 (sometimes referred to as the *Mekhilta le-Devarim*) and the *Mekhilta de-Rabbi Yishmael* on Exodus 13:3 cited towards the beginning of this article (and discussed in more detail towards the article's conclusion). Each of the two *Mekhiltot* explicitly quotes the opening words of the *Amida*, and the compilation of each is dated to around the middle of the third century CE, with much of the material considerably older than that. It must be noted, however, that some scholars date *the Mekhilta de-Rabbi Yishmael* passage that includes the attestation to the *Amida*'s opening somewhat later than the rest of the *Mekhilta*, although they do not see this later dating as bearing on the antiquity of the composition of the *Amida*'s opening. See Binyamin Katzoff, "'G-d of our Fathers': Rabbinic Liturgy and Jewish-Christian Engagement," *Jewish Quarterly Review* 99:3 (Summer 2009), 306.

25 See Mishna Bikkurim 1:4 and Mishna Rosh Hashanah 4:5, which refer to the opening blessing of the *Amida* as "Avot."

26 The implicit assumption in the text is that the liturgically-ubiquitous phrase *melekh ha-olam* was already in use in the first century CE Yavnean era, and that the use of Exodus 3:15—with its emphasis on G-d as a familial Deity—was thus intended as a sharp contrast to the standard *matbe'a ha-berakha*'s emphasis on G-d as King of the Universe. In fact, we now have strong evidence, based on a recent archeological find in the Judaean desert, that this was the case—that is, that *melekh ha-olam* was in fact in use at that time; see Kister, "Liturgical Formulae in the Light of Fragments from the Judaean Desert," *Tarbiz* 77 (2009), 331–356. This conclusion is at odds with the tendency among some scholars to date the standard *matbe'a ha-berakha*—especially the phrase *melekh ha-olam*—to sometime in the second century CE—see Heinemann, 94—or perhaps as late as the opening decades of the third century—see Reuven Kimelman, "Blessing Formulae and Divine Sovereignty in Rabbinic Liturgy" in *Liturgy in the Life of the Synagogue—Studies in the History of Jewish Prayer*, Ruth Langer & Steven Fine, eds., (Winona Lake, Indiana: Eisenbrauns, 2005)—both dates, of course, being after the late-first century CE period of R. Gamliel. It should be noted, however, that Heinemann's and Kimelman's statements were made before the aforementioned archeological discovery came to light.

27 See discussion in n. 15; see also the penultimate paragraph of this article (highlighting the eschatological context of the *Mekhilta*'s connecting the opening of the *Amida* to Exodus 3:15).

28 See the Midrash on Exodus 2:23 quoted in n. 15.

29 The reasons given in the text for the insertion of "our G-d" in the paraphrase of Exodus 3:15 that opens the *Amida* also apply to—and explain—the insertion of "our G-d" in the paraphrase of Deuteronomy 26:7—"hear our voice L-rd *our G-d*"—that opens the last of the *Amida*'s petitionary blessings. See n. 15.

30 See Eliezer Halevi, *Torat Hatefilah* (Tel Aviv: Abraham Zioni, 1967), 104–105, for a full discussion of this point.

Lesson 6

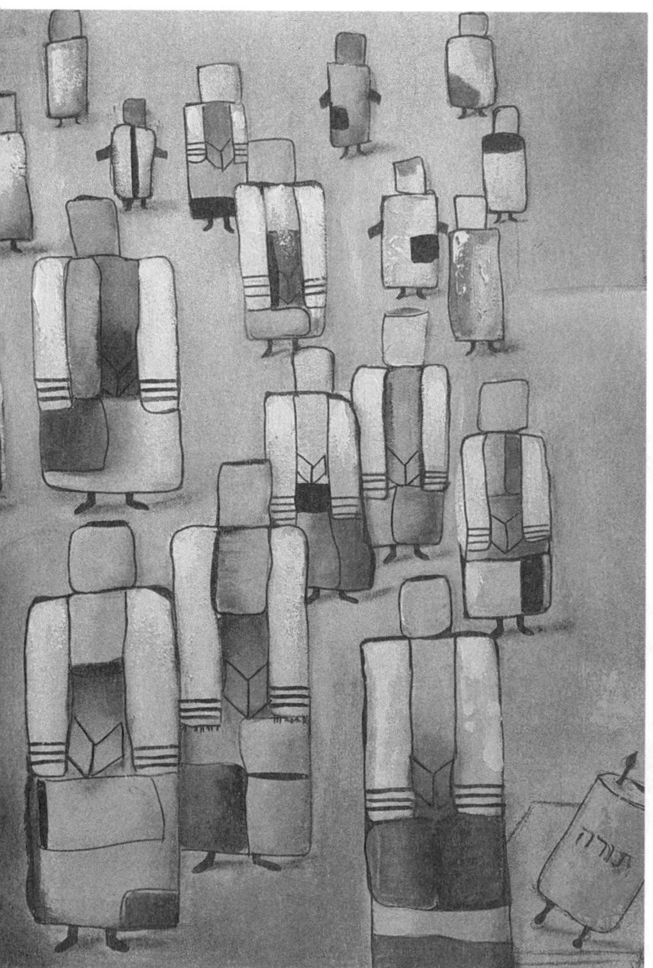

Morning Services, Sharon Feldstein, United States; paint, ink, charcoal on canvas.

COMMUNITIES THAT PRAY TOGETHER

FINDING MEANING IN COMMUNAL PRAYER

Solitude seems most appropriate for soulful reflection and meditation and for experiencing a highly personal moment with G-d. This lesson examines the role of communal prayer, to which Judaism lends enormous weight, and leads us to the realization that solo prayer is severely limited in terms of our greater goals. It offers practical methods of balancing the personal and communal elements of genuine prayer to arrive at the ultimate prayer experience.

shifts to communal prayer.

TEXT 1

RABBI YOSEF CARO, SHULCHAN ARUCH, *ORACH CHAYIM* 90:9

יִשְׁתַּדֵל אָדָם לְהִתְפַּלֵל בְּבֵית הַכְּנֶסֶת עִם הַצִבּוּר.

One should endeavor to pray in a synagogue together with a congregation.

RABBI YOSEF CARO (MARAN, *BEIT YOSEF*) 1488–1575

Halachic authority and author. Rabbi Caro was born in Spain but was forced to flee during the expulsion in 1492 and eventually settled in Safed, Israel. He authored many works, including the *Beit Yosef, Kesef Mishneh*, and a mystical work, *Magid Meisharim*. Rabbi Caro's magnum opus, the Shulchan Aruch (Code of Jewish Law), has been universally accepted as the basis for modern Jewish law.

Morning Prayers, Ernest Kathelin, Belgium, active 1863–1879, oil on canvas. (The Jewish Museum, New York)

Exercise 6.1

List some of the advantages and disadvantages of praying alone and praying with a group.

	ADVANTAGES	**DISADVANTAGES**
PRAYING ALONE		
PRAYING WITH A GROUP		

TEXT 2

TALMUD, SUKKAH 51B

רַבִּי יְהוּדָה אוֹמֵר, מִי שֶׁלֹּא רָאָה דְיוּפְלוּסְטוֹן שֶׁל אֲלֶכְּסַנְדְּרִיָא שֶׁל מִצְרַיִם לֹא רָאָה בִּכְבוֹדָן שֶׁל יִשְׂרָאֵל. אָמְרוּ, כְּמִין בַּסִילֵקִי גְדוֹלָה הָיְתָה, סְטָיו לִפְנִים מִסְטָיו . . . וְהָיוּ בָּהּ ע"א קַתֶּדְרָאוֹת שֶׁל זָהָב כְּנֶגֶד ע"א שֶׁל סַנְהֶדְרִי גְדוֹלָה . . .

וְלֹא הָיוּ יוֹשְׁבִין מְעוֹרָבִין, אֶלָּא זֶהָבִין בִּפְנֵי עַצְמָן וְכַסָּפִין בִּפְנֵי עַצְמָן וְנַפָּחִין בִּפְנֵי עַצְמָן וְטַרְסִיִּים בִּפְנֵי עַצְמָן וְגַרְדִּיִּים בִּפְנֵי עַצְמָן. וּכְשֶׁעָנִי נִכְנָס שָׁם הָיָה מַכִּיר בַּעֲלֵי אוּמָנְתוֹ וְנִפְנֶה לְשָׁם, וּמִשָּׁם פַּרְנָסָתוֹ וּפַרְנָסַת אַנְשֵׁי בֵיתוֹ.

Rabbi Yehudah says: One who did not see the great synagogue of Alexandria of Egypt never saw the glory of Israel. They said that it was like a large basilica, with a colonnade within a colonnade. . . . In it there were seventy-one golden chairs, corresponding to the seventy-one members of the Great Sanhedrin. . . .

The members of the various crafts would not sit mingled. Rather, the goldsmiths would sit among themselves, the silversmiths among themselves, the blacksmiths among themselves, the coppersmiths among themselves, and the weavers among themselves. When a poor stranger entered there, he would recognize people who shared his craft and would join them. His colleagues would find him work in that craft, helping him secure a livelihood for himself and his family.

Power of group prayer!!

BABYLONIAN TALMUD

A literary work of monumental proportions that draws upon the legal, spiritual, intellectual, ethical, and historical traditions of Judaism. The 37 tractates of the Babylonian Talmud contain the teachings of the Jewish sages from the period after the destruction of the 2nd Temple through the 5th century CE. It has served as the primary vehicle for the transmission of the Oral Law and the education of Jews over the centuries; it is the entry point for all subsequent legal, ethical, and theological Jewish scholarship.

A renowned Dutch engraver depicted an Amsterdam synagogue in the year 1700. Learn about this engraving:

MYJLI.COM/PRAYER

TEXT 3a

TALMUD, YEVAMOT 49B

אָמַר רָבָא, מֵידַן דַיְינֵיהּ וְקַטְלֵיהּ.
אָמַר לֵיהּ . . . מֹשֶׁה רַבָּךְ אָמַר "מִי . . . כַּה' אֱלֹקֵינוּ בְּכָל קָרְאֵנוּ אֵלָיו" (דְבָרִים ד, ז), וְאַתְּ אָמַרְתְּ, "דִרְשׁוּ ה' בְּהִמָצְאוֹ" (יְשַׁעְיָהוּ נה, ו).

Rava said: Manasseh judged Isaiah and then killed him.

Manasseh said to Isaiah, . . . "Moses, your master, said, 'Who is like our G-d, Who is near to us whenever we call upon Him?' (DEUTERONOMY 4:7). But you said, 'Seek G-d while He may be found; [call upon Him while He is near]' (ISAIAH 55:6)."

TEXT 3b

TALMUD, IBID.

מִכָּל מָקוֹם קָשׁוּ קְרָאֵי אַהֲדָדֵי . . .
דִּרְשׁוּ ה' בְּהִמָּצְאוֹ, הָא בְּיָחִיד הָא בְּצִבּוּר.
וְיָחִיד אֵימַת? אָמַר רַב נַחְמָן אָמַר רַבָּה בַּר אֲבוּהַּ, אֵלּוּ עֲשָׂרָה יָמִים שֶׁבֵּין רֹאשׁ הַשָּׁנָה לְיוֹם הַכִּפּוּרִים.

In any case, these verses appear to contradict each other. . . .

[The Talmud responds:] Isaiah's prophecy, "Seek G-d *while* He may be found," was said with regard to the individual. Whereas the verse, "whenever we call upon Him," is stated with regard to a community.

And when is G-d found near the individual? Rabbi Nachman said in the name of Rabbah bar Avuha, "These are the ten days between Rosh Hashanah and Yom Kippur."

TEXT 4

TALMUD, SOTAH 34A

וּגְמִירֵי דִטְעוּנָא דְמַדְלֵי אִינִישׁ לְכַתְפֵיה תִּילְתָּא דִטְעוּנֵיהּ הָוֵי.

It has been taught: The weight of a load that we can lift onto our shoulders is one-third of the weight of the load that we can carry when others load it onto our shoulders.

Untitled (A Heavy Load), Diego Rivera, offset lithograph on paper, 1945.

TEXT 5

RABBI MOSHE DI TRANI, *BEIT ELOKIM, SHAAR HATEFILAH*, CHAPTER 11

מִפְּנֵי שֶׁאֵינוֹ דוֹמֶה מוּעָטִים הָעוֹשִׂים אֶת הַמִּצְוָוה לִמְרוּבִּים הָעוֹשִׂים אֶת הַמִּצְוָוה, כִּי הִיא מִתְעַלֵּית יוֹתֵר הַרְבֵּה מִכְּפִי הָעֵרֶךְ לְכָל אֶחָד בִּהְיוֹתָהּ נַעֲשֵׂית בַּחֲבוּרַת בְּנֵי אָדָם.

כִּי אֲפִילוּ בִּדְבָרִים הַגַּשְׁמִיִּים עוֹשֶׂה אָדָם יוֹתֵר מִכְּפִי הָעֵרֶךְ בְּהִשְׁתַּתְּפוֹ עִם אֲחֵרִים בִּמְלָאכָה, וּכְמוֹ שֶׁאָמְרוּ... דְּכָל טוּנָא דְּמַדְלֵי אִינִישׁ לְכַתְפֵיה וְאֵין אַחֵר מְסַיְּיעוֹ תִּלְתָּא דִטְעוּנֵיהּ הוּא כְּשֶׁמַּטְעִינוֹ אַחֵר (סוֹטָה לד, א)...

וְאִם כֵּן, כָּל שֶׁכֵּן בִּדְבָרִים הָאֱלוֹקִיִּים.

A few people performing a mitzvah does not compare to the masses performing a mitzvah. When we perform a mitzvah as a group, it is of greater value than a mitzvah performed by individuals.

This is true even regarding physical activities. We can accomplish more by partnering with others, as our sages said, . . . "The weight of a load that we can lift onto our shoulders is one-third of the weight of the load that we can carry when others load it onto our shoulders" (TALMUD, SOTAH 34A). . . .

If this is true regarding physical activities, it is certainly true regarding spiritual activities.

RABBI MOSHE OF TRANI (MABIT) 1505–1580

Rabbi and scholar. Rabbi Moshe was born in Ottoman-ruled Salonika, Greece. At the age of 16, he left for Safed, Israel, to study under the tutelage of Rabbi Yaakov Beirav. Later, he served as the rabbi of Safed for 55 years, during which time he penned many books on philosophy, halachic responsa, Talmud, and the Bible. These include *Bet Elokim* and *Kiryat Sefer*. He is buried in the ancient cemetery in Safed, near the Arizal.

TEXT 6

RABBI YEHUDAH HALEVI, *KUZARI* 3:17–19

וּמָשָׁל מִי שֶׁהִתְפַּלֵּל לְצוֹרֶךְ עַצְמוֹ, כְּמָשָׁל מִי שֶׁהִשְׁתַּדֵּל לְחַזֵּק אֶת בֵּיתוֹ לְבַדּוֹ וְלֹא רָצָה לְהִכָּנֵס עִם אַנְשֵׁי הַמְּדִינָה בְּהֶעְזְרָם עַל חִזּוּק חוֹמוֹתָם, הוּא מוֹצִיא הַרְבֵּה וְעוֹמֵד עַל הַסַּכָּנָה, וַאֲשֶׁר יִכָּנֵס בְּמַה שֶּׁנִּכְנָסִים בּוֹ הַצִּבּוּר, מוֹצִיא מְעַט וְעוֹמֵד בְּבִטְחָה, כִּי מַה שֶּׁמְּקַצֵּר מִמֶּנּוּ אֶחָד מַשְׁלִימוֹ אַחֵר, וְתָקוּם הַמְּדִינָה בְּתַכְלִית מַה שֶּׁיֵּשׁ בִּיכוֹלֶת, וְיִהְיוּ אֲנָשֶׁיהָ מַגִּיעִים כֻּלָּם אֶל בִּרְכָתָהּ בְּהוֹצָאָה מוּעֶטֶת . . .

שֶׁמְּעַט הוּא שֶׁתִּשְׁלַם תְּפִלָּה לְיָחִיד מִבְּלִי שְׁגָגָה וּפְשִׁיעָה. וּמִפְּנֵי כֵּן קָבְעוּ לָנוּ שֶׁיִּתְפַּלֵּל הַיָּחִיד תְּפִלַּת הַצִּבּוּר . . . כְּדֵי שֶׁיַּשְׁלִים קְצָתָם מַה שֶּׁיֶּחְסַר בִּקְצָתָם בִּשְׁגָגָה אוֹ בִּפְשִׁיעָה, וְיִסְתַּדֵּר מֵהַכֹּל תְּפִלָּה שְׁלֵמָה בְּכַוָּנָה זַכָּה וְתָחוּל הַבְּרָכָה עַל הַכֹּל . . .

כִּי הַיָּחִיד בִּכְלַל הַצִּבּוּר כְּאֵבֶר הָאֶחָד בִּכְלַל הַגּוּף. אִילוּ הָיָה מַקְפִּיד הַזְּרוֹעַ עַל דָּמוֹ כְּשֶׁהוּצְרַךְ אֶל הַהַקָּזָה, הָיָה נִפְסָד הַגּוּף כּוּלוֹ וְנִפְסָד הַזְּרוֹעַ בְּהֶפְסֵדוֹ.

Praying on our own can be compared to attempting to fortify our home by ourselves rather than joining the people of the city in reinforcing the city walls. It is more expensive and less effective, whereas joining the people of the city is less expensive and more effective. When we act as a group, what one lacks, the other completes, resulting in much better security at a much lower cost. . . .

It is uncommon for an individual's prayer to be complete without any inadvertent or negligent deficiency. This is why they established that the individual should join in congregational prayer. . . . In this way, people will

RABBI YEHUDAH HALEVI
C. 1075–1141

Noted author, physician, and poet. Rabbi Yehudah Halevi is best known as the author of the *Kuzari*, a philosophical work written in the form of a discussion between a Jew, a Christian, and a Muslim before the King of the Khazars. In addition to the *Kuzari*, he wrote thousands of poems, of which only a few hundred survive today.

complement each other's prayer, thus producing a complete prayer with pure intent, resulting in blessing for all. . . .

An individual in a community is like a limb in a body. If an arm would resist giving its blood when necessary, the entire body would deteriorate, and the arm would also suffer.

***Professor Jonathan Sarna** analyzes the history of the prayer for the government:*

MYJLI.COM/PRAYER

Large group of men and small girl pray in a sanctuary, Jean Mohr, photograph, 1958, Wroclaw, Poland. (American Jewish Joint Distribution Committee Archives, New York)

TEXT 7

THE REBBE, RABBI MENACHEM MENDEL SCHNEERSON, *SEFER HAMAAMARIM MELUKAT* (*TORAT MENACHEM* EDITION), 2, P. 77

צִבּוּר רָאשֵׁי תֵּיבוֹת צַדִּיקִים בֵּינוֹנִים וּרְשָׁעִים. שֶׁכָּל ג' סוּגִים אֵלּוּ הֵם מְצִיאוּת אַחַת.

The Hebrew word *tsibur*, congregation, can be seen as an acronym for *tsadikim*, *beinonim*, and *reshaim*—the righteous, intermediate, and wicked people. These three types combine to form a single unit.

RABBI MENACHEM MENDEL SCHNEERSON 1902–1994

The towering Jewish leader of the 20th century, known as "the Lubavitcher Rebbe," or simply as "the Rebbe." Born in southern Ukraine, the Rebbe escaped Nazi-occupied Europe, arriving in the U.S. in June 1941. The Rebbe inspired and guided the revival of traditional Judaism after the European devastation, impacting virtually every Jewish community the world over. The Rebbe often emphasized that the performance of just one additional good deed could usher in the era of Mashiach. The Rebbe's scholarly talks and writings have been printed in more than 200 volumes.

QUESTION FOR DISCUSSION

Is our prayer liturgy more consistent with the "teamwork approach" or the "collectivist approach"?

TEXT 8

TALMUD, BERACHOT 7B–8A

אָמַר לֵיהּ רַבִּי יִצְחָק לְרַב נַחְמָן, מַאי טַעֲמָא לֹא אָתֵי מָר לְבֵי כְּנִישְׁתָּא לְצַלּוּיֵי? אָמַר לֵיהּ, לֹא יָכִילְנָא . . .

וְלֵימָא לֵיהּ מָר לִשְׁלוּחָא דְצִבּוּרָא בְּעִידְנָא דִמְצַלֵּי צִבּוּרָא לֵיתֵי וְלוֹדְעֵיהּ לְמָר.

אָמַר לֵיהּ, מַאי כּוּלֵּי הַאי? אָמַר לֵיהּ דְאָמַר רַבִּי יוֹחָנָן מִשּׁוּם רַבִּי שִׁמְעוֹן בֶּן יוֹחָאי, מַאי דִכְתִיב "וַאֲנִי תְפִלָּתִי לְךָ ה' עֵת רָצוֹן" (תְּהִילִים סט, יד), אֵימָתַי עֵת רָצוֹן, בְּשָׁעָה שֶׁהַצִּבּוּר מִתְפַּלְּלִין . . .

רַבִּי נָתָן אוֹמֵר, מִנַּיִן שֶׁאֵין הַקָּדוֹשׁ בָּרוּךְ הוּא מוֹאֵס בִּתְפִלָּתָן שֶׁל רַבִּים, שֶׁנֶּאֱמַר "הֵן אֵ-ל כַּבִּיר וְלֹא יִמְאָס" (אִיּוֹב לו, ה).

Rabbi Yitschak said to Rabbi Nachman, "Why did your honor not come to the synagogue to pray?" Rabbi Nachman replied, "I was weak and unable to attend." . . .

Rabbi Yitschak suggested another option, "Your honor should ask the congregation to notify you when they are praying so that you can pray at home simultaneously."

Rabbi Nachman asked, "Why go to such lengths?" Rabbi Yitschak answered him that Rabbi Yochanan said in the name of Rabbi Shimon ben Yochai, "The verse states, 'May my prayer to You, G-d, be in a time of favor' (PSALMS 69:14). When is it a time of favor? When the congregation prays. . . ."

Rabbi Natan says, "How do we know that G-d does not spurn the prayer of the masses? Because the verse says, 'The mighty [i.e., the masses], G-d will not spurn' (JOB 36:5)."

TEXT 9

RABBI YOSEF YITSCHAK SCHNEERSOHN, *SEFER HAMAAMARIM* 5688, PP. 148–152

אָמְרוּ רַזַ"ל, תְּפִלַּת רַבִּים אֵינָהּ נִמְאֶסֶת, שֶׁנֶּאֱמַר הֵן אֵ-ל כַּבִּיר וְלֹא יִמְאָס. שֶׁהָרַבִּים בִּתְפִילָּתָם מַמְשִׁיכִים י"ג מִדּוֹת הָרַחֲמִים.

Our sages taught, "The prayer of the masses will never be spurned, as is implied by the verse, 'The mighty [i.e., the masses], G-d will not spurn.' This is because communal prayer channels the Thirteen Attributes of Mercy."

RABBI YOSEF YITSCHAK SCHNEERSOHN (RAYATS, FRIERDIKER REBBE, PREVIOUS REBBE) 1880–1950

Chasidic rebbe, prolific writer, and Jewish activist. Rabbi Yosef Yitschak, the sixth leader of the Chabad movement, actively promoted Jewish religious practice in Soviet Russia and was arrested for these activities. After his release from prison and exile, he settled in Warsaw, Poland, from where he fled Nazi occupation and arrived in New York in 1940. Settling in Brooklyn, Rabbi Schneersohn worked to revitalize American Jewish life. His son-in-law, Rabbi Menachem Mendel Schneerson, succeeded him as the leader of the Chabad movement.

Yom Kippur prayers, France, from *The Illustrated London News*, c. late 1800s.

TEXT 10

EXODUS 34:6–7

ה' ה' אֵ-ל רַחוּם וְחַנּוּן אֶרֶךְ אַפַּיִם וְרַב חֶסֶד וֶאֱמֶת. נֹצֵר חֶסֶד לָאֲלָפִים נֹשֵׂא עָוֹן וָפֶשַׁע וְחַטָּאָה וְנַקֵּה . . .

G-d, G-d, benevolent G-d, compassionate and gracious, slow to anger and abounding in kindness and truth. He preserves kindness for two thousand generations, forgiving iniquity, transgression, and sin, and He cleanses. . . .

Woman Praying 20th Century, Arno Nadel, (1878–1943). (Leo Baeck Institute at the Center for Jewish History, New York)

TEXT 11

RABBI YOSEF YITSCHAK SCHNEERSOHN, *SEFER HAMAAMARIM* 5688, PP. 148–152

דְהִנֵה, תְּפִלָּה עִנְיָנָה הוּא בְּחִינַת הַעֲלָאָה מִלְמַטָּה לְמַעְלָה, הַיְינוּ דְבְּאִתְעַרוּתָא דִלְתַתָּא אִתְעֲרוּתָא דִלְעֵילָא, דִלְפִי אוֹפֶן הָאִתְעַרוּתָא דִלְתַתָּא כַּךְ הִיא הָאִתְעַרוּתָא דִלְעֵילָא. וּתְפִלַּת הָרַבִּים הוּא מַה שֶׁהָרַבִּים עַל יְדֵי תְּפִלָּתָם מַמְשִׁיכִים . . . אִתְעֲרוּתָא דִלְעֵילָא שֶׁלֹא לְפִי עֶרֶךְ הַהַעֲלָאָה שֶׁלָּהֶם . . .

וְזֶהוּ שֶׁאוֹמֵר "הֵן אֵ-ל כַּבִּיר וְלֹא יִמְאָס", דְאִם הָיָה הָאִתְעַרוּתָא דִלְעֵילָא לְפִי עֶרֶךְ הַהַעֲלָאָה אֵינוֹ שַׁיָּיךְ לוֹמַר עַל זֶה לֹא יִמְאָס, שֶׁהֲרֵי זֶהוּ שֶׁמַּגִיעַ עַל יְדֵי הַעֲלָאַת מַיִין נוּקְבִין, אֶלָּא דִבִּתְפִלַּת הָרַבִּים הִנֵה הַהַמְשָׁכָה הִיא שֶׁלֹא לְפִי עֶרֶךְ הַהַעֲלָאָה מִשּׁוּם מַעֲלַת הָרַבִּים.

וּכְמוֹ תְּפִלַּת יָחִיד בַּעֲשֶׂרֶת יְמֵי תְּשׁוּבָה שֶׁאָמְרוּ רַזַ"ל "וְיָחִיד אֵימַת, בַּעֲשָׂרָה יָמִים שֶׁבֵּין רֹאשׁ הַשָּׁנָה לְיוֹם הַכִּיפּוּרִים", שֶׁמַּמְשִׁיךְ בְּחִינַת י"ג מִדּוֹת הָרַחֲמִים כְּמוֹ הָרַבִּים, הֲרֵי שֶׁזֶהוּ שֶׁלֹא לְפִי עֶרֶךְ הַהַעֲלָאָה, וְלָכֵן הוּא בַּעֲשֶׂרֶת יְמֵי תְּשׁוּבָה דַוְקָא מִפְּנֵי שֶׁאָז הוּא עֵת רָצוֹן. וּכְמוֹ כֵן, הִנֵה הָרַבִּים בִּתְפִלָּתָם בְּכָל הַשָּׁנָה מַמְשִׁיכִים י"ג מִדּוֹת הָרַחֲמִים שֶׁהוּא אִתְעֲרוּתָא דִלְעֵילָא שֶׁלֹא לְפִי עֶרֶךְ הַהַעֲלָאָה.

Prayer is a process of ascendance initiated from below. The stimulation from below evokes a parallel stimulation from above—the nature of which is commensurate with the stimulation from below. Communal prayer, however, defies this principle; it channels . . . a stimulation from above that is incommensurate with the stimulation from below. . . .

On this basis, we can understand our sages' interpretation of the verse, "The mighty [i.e., the masses], G-d will not spurn." Were the stimulation from above commensurate with the stimulation from below, this wouldn't be possible because the response from above would be dependent on our initiative from below. However, with regard to communal prayer, the stimulation from above is not commensurate with the stimulation from below. Thus, it is possible to be certain that G-d will not spurn communal prayer.

Similarly, individual prayer during the Ten Days of Repentance—regarding which our sages said, "When is G-d found near the individual? During the ten days between Rosh Hashanah and Yom Kippur,"—channels the Thirteen Attributes of Mercy. This stimulation from above is also incommensurate with the stimulation from below. As communal prayer throughout the year channels the Thirteen Attributes of Mercy—a stimulation from above incommensurate with the stimulation from below—so does individual prayer during this time of Divine favor.

Kaddish: Its meaning, structure, and messages, *by* ***Rabbis Eli Silberstein*** *and* ***Leibel Fajnland****:*

MYJLI.COM/PRAYER

TEXT 12

RABBI CHAIM VITAL, *PERI ETS CHAYIM, SHAAR HAKAVANOT, DRUSHEI BIRCHOT HASHACHAR*

> קוֹדֶם שֶׁהָאָדָם יְסַדֵּר תְּפִילָּתוֹ בְּבֵית הַכְּנֶסֶת . . . צָרִיךְ שֶׁיְּקַבֵּל עָלָיו מִצְוַת וְאָהַבְתָּ לְרֵעֲךָ כָּמוֹךָ. וִיכַוֵּין לֶאֱהוֹב כָּל א' מִבְּנֵי יִשְׂרָאֵל כְּנַפְשׁוֹ, כִּי עַל יְדֵי זֶה תַּעֲלֶה תְּפִילָּתוֹ כְּלוּלָה מִכָּל תְּפִילּוֹת יִשְׂרָאֵל, וְתוּכַל לַעֲלוֹת לְמַעְלָה וְלַעֲשׂוֹת פְּרִי.

Before beginning to pray in the synagogue . . . we must undertake to fulfill the commandment of "love your fellow as yourself." . . . Thereby, our prayers will ascend and merge with the prayers of all Jewish people and bear fruit."

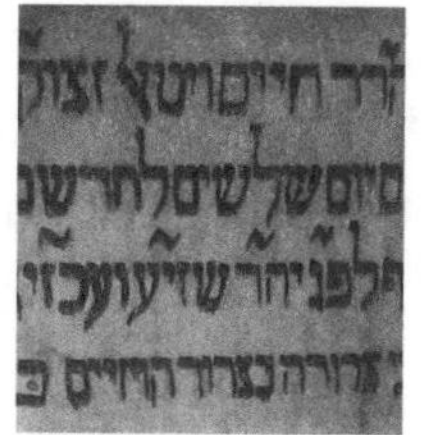

RABBI CHAIM VITAL
C. 1542–1620

Lurianic kabbalist. Rabbi Vital was born in Israel and lived in Safed and Jerusalem, and later in Damascus. He was authorized by his teacher, Rabbi Yitschak Luria, the Arizal, to record his teachings. Acting on this mandate, Rabbi Vital began arranging his master's teachings in written form, and his many works constitute the foundation of the Lurianic school of Jewish mysticism. His most famous work is *Ets Chayim*.

TEXT 13

HAREINI MEKABEL, RECITED BEFORE THE MORNING PRAYERS (IN PRAYER BOOKS FOLLOWING THE TRADITION OF ARIZAL)

> נָכוֹן לוֹמַר קוֹדֶם הַתְּפִילָּה: הֲרֵינִי מְקַבֵּל עָלַי מִצְוַת עֲשֵׂה שֶׁל וְאָהַבְתָּ לְרֵעֲךָ כָּמוֹךָ:

It is proper to make the following statement before prayer: "I hereby undertake to fulfill the positive commandment to love your fellow as yourself."

TEXT 14

RABBI YOSEF YITSCHAK SCHNEERSOHN, *SEFER HASICHOT* 5700, PP. 156–157

מָאנְטָאג, י"ב תַּמוּז, אִין טָאג פוּן מַיין בַּר מִצְוָה . . . אַ זֵייגֶער זֶעקְס הָאט מֶען זִיךְ גֶעוַואשְׁן צוּ דֶער סְעוּדַת מִצְוָה. הוֹד כ"ק אאמו"ר הרה"ק אִיז גֶעוֶוען זֵייעֶר אוֹיפְגֶעלֵייגְט . . . אוּן מִיט דֶעם סִגְנוֹן הָאט הוֹד כ"ק אאמו"ר הרה"ק בַּא דֶער סְעוּדָה פוּן מַיין בַּר מִצְוָה מִיךְ אָנְגֶערוּפְן בַּיים נָאמֶען אוּן גֶעזָאגְט: יוֹסֵף יִצְחָק, פְּרֶעג עֶפֶּעס.

הָאבּ אִיךְ גֶעפְרֶעגְט בַּא הוֹד כְּבוֹד קְדוּשַּׁת אאמו"ר הרה"ק: אִין סִידוּר שְׁטֵייט נָכוֹן לוֹמַר קוֹדֶם הַתְּפִילָּה הֲרֵינִי מְקַבֵּל עָלַי מִצְוַת עֲשֵׂה שֶׁל וְאָהַבְתָּ לְרֵעֲךָ כָּמוֹךָ, אִיז פַארְוָואס שְׁטֵייט דָאס דַוְקָא קוֹדֶם הַתְּפִילָּה. אוּן אוֹיבּ אַהֲבַת יִשְׂרָאֵל דַארְף זַיין תֵּיכֶף בַּבֹּקֶר, הָאט מֶען דָאס בַּאדַארְפְט קוֹבֵעַ זַיין צוּזַאמֶען מִיט בִּרְכוֹת הַשַּׁחַר.

הָאט הוֹד כְּבוֹד קְדוּשַּׁת אאמו"ר הרה"ק מִיר גֶעעֶנְטְפֶערְט: וֶוען אַ טַאטֶע הָאט אַ סַךְ קִינְדֶער אִיז דֶער עִיקָּר הַתַּעֲנוּג זַיינֶער וֶוען עֶר זֶעט אַז אַלֶע זַיינֶען זֵיי בְּאַחְדוּת אוּן הָאבְּן זִיךְ אֵיינֶער דֶעם אַנְדֶערְן לִיבּ. תְּפִילָּה אִיז דָאךְ בַּקָּשַׁת צְרָכִים רוּחָנִיִּים, אִיז קוֹדֶם הַבַּקָּשָׁה דַארְף מֶען מַאכְן אַ נַחַת רוּחַ לְאָבִינוּ שֶׁבַּשָּׁמַיִם, אוּן דֶערִיבֶּער הָאט מֶען קוֹבֵעַ גֶעוֶוען דֶעם לְקַבֵּל מִצְוַת עֲשֵׂה פוּן אַהֲבַת יִשְׂרָאֵל קוֹדֶם הַתְּפִילָּה דַוְקָא.

On Monday, the twelfth of the month of Tamuz, the day of my bar mitzvah . . . at about six o'clock, my father washed his hands for the festive mitzvah. His cheerful spirits were apparent. . . . He called me by name, "Yosef Yitschak, ask something."

I asked, "It is written in the siddur that it is proper to say before the Morning Prayer, 'I hereby undertake to fulfill the positive commandment to love your fellow as yourself.' Why does this instruction appear as a preface to the prayer? After all, since the obligation to love our fellow is incumbent upon us from the beginning of the day, shouldn't the instruction have been inserted in the Morning Blessings that are recited first thing in the morning?"

My father answered, "When a father has many children, he derives the greatest pleasure from seeing their unity and love for each other. Prayer is a request for one's needs, both material and spiritual. Before making a request, we must grant our Father in Heaven pleasurable *nachas* [satisfaction]. This is why the instruction to undertake the mitzvah to love our fellow appears as a preface to the prayer."

Jewish Symbols, Janet and Emmanuel Snitkovsky, United States, 20th century, oil on canvas.

TEXT 15

RABBI YOSEF YITSCHAK SCHNEERSOHN, *SEFER HAMAAMARIM* 5709, P. 99

הוד כְּבוֹד קְדוּשַּׁת אֲבוֹתֵינוּ רַבּוֹתֵינוּ הַקְּדוֹשִׁים זצוקללה"ה נבג"מ זי"ע פָּסְקוּ לַהֲלָכָה, לְאֵלּוּ שֶׁשָּׁאֲלוּ בְּעִנְיַן תְּפִילָּה בְּצִיבּוּר: אֵיךְ יְקַיְּימוּ שְׁנֵיהֶם, לַעֲסוֹק בַּעֲבוֹדָה שֶׁבַּלֵּב בַּאֲרִיכוּת הַתְּפִלָּה וּלְהִתְפַּלֵּל בְּצִיבּוּר? . . .

וְסִידְרוּ לָהֶם כִּי יִשְׁמְעוּ כָּל הַתְּפִילָּה, קַדִּישִׁים, בָּרְכוּ, קְדוּשָּׁה, קְרִיאַת הַתּוֹרָה, וְהַקַּדִּישִׁים דִּתְפִילַּת הַצִּיבּוּר, וְאַחַר כָּךְ לְהִתְפַּלֵּל בִּמְתִינוּת אִישׁ אִישׁ כְּפִי הַשָּׂגַת יַד שִׂכְלוֹ בְּהָעֲבוֹדָה שֶׁבַּלֵּב . . .

כִּי אֲמִיתַּת עִנְיַן דִּתְפִילָּה בְּצִיבּוּר שֶׁהוּא תְּפִילַּת הָרַבִּים הוּא לִכְלוֹל עַצְמוֹ בִּכְלַל תְּפִלַּת יִשְׂרָאֵל, וְהוּא עַל יְדֵי אֲמִירַת "הֲרֵינִי מְקַבֵּל עָלַי מִצְוַת עֲשֵׂה שֶׁל וְאָהַבְתָּ לְרֵעֲךָ כָּמוֹךָ" קוֹדֶם הַתְּפִלָּה.

The question has been asked: How does one balance the need for meditative prayer with the obligation to pray together with the congregation? . . .

The rebbes of Chabad instructed their followers to listen to the entire congregational service, including the *Kaddish, Barchu, Kedushah*, and the Torah reading, and then proceed with meditational prayer, each according to their ability.

The true point of communal prayer is that our prayer merges with the prayer of all Jews. This is achieved through declaring, "I hereby undertake to fulfill the positive commandment to love your fellow as yourself," before beginning to pray.

TEXT 16

RABBI YOSEF YITSCHAK SCHNEERSOHN, *SEFER HASICHOT* 5709, P. 319

אַמָאלִיגֶע חַסִידִים פְלֶעגֶען מַאכֶען יֶעדֶען טָאג אַ קְנֵייטְשׁ אִין סִידוּר, הַיינְט הָאבּ אִיך גֶעדַאוֶועוְנְט בִּיז דָא.

עֶר פְלֶעגְט כְּמוּבָן גוֹמֵר זַיין דֶעם גַאנְצֶען דַאוְונֶען, נָאר "גֶעדַאוֶועוְנְט" הָאט עֶר נָאר בִּיז דַאנֶען. מָארְגֶען פְלֶעגְט עֶר דַאוְונֶען נָאךְ אַ שְׁטִיקֶעלֶע אוּן דָארְט מַאכְן דֶעם קְנֵייטְשׁ אִין סִידוּר.

There were Chasidim in the past who would fold an ear of a page in the siddur every day, indicating, "Today I prayed until this point."

Of course, they would complete the prayers in their entirety. But their deep, contemplative prayer was only until that point. The next day they would continue their contemplative prayer where they left off and meditate on another part of the prayers. They would then make another fold where they concluded.

Exercise 6.2

At the beginning of Lesson One, we each wrote down what we hoped to gain from this course. At this point, let's return to page 2 and take a minute to reflect on whether our goals were met.

If you are willing to share those thoughts, please do so.

TEXT 17

RABBI YITSCHAK BEN SHESHET, *RESPONSA* 157

רַבִּי שִׁמְשׁוֹן מִקִּינוּן זִכְרוֹנוֹ לִבְרָכָה, שֶׁהָיָה רַב גָדוֹל מִכָּל בְּנֵי דוֹרוֹ . . . הָיָה אוֹמֵר אֲנִי מִתְפַּלֵל לְדַעַת זֶה הַתִּינוֹק.

Rabbi Shimshon of Chinon, of blessed memory, who was the greatest rabbi in his generation . . . would often say, "I pray with the thoughts of a child."

RABBI YITSCHAK BEN SHESHET (RIVASH) 1326–1408

Halachist. Rivash studied under Rabbi Nisim of Gerona (Ran) in Barcelona and served as rabbi there and in other important Jewish communities in Spain. Because of the eruption of anti-Jewish riots in 1391, he fled to North Africa and settled in Algiers. He was the first to address the halachic status of Marranos. Rivash's halachic responsa are his most important work; they contain sources no longer extant and serve, in part, as a basis for the Code of Jewish Law.

RABBI SHIMSHON OF CHINON 14TH CENTURY

Talmudist and halachic authority. Rabbi Shimshon authored several Talmudic and halachic works, primary among them was *Sefer Hakritut*, an important commentary on Talmudic methodology that gained wide acceptance among Talmudic scholars. He was a leading scholar and an important halachic authority in his day.

Solomon's Wall, Jean-Léon Gérôme, Oil on canvas, 1867. (The Israel Museum, Jerusalem)

Exercise for the Week

Collective Experience. This week, join your fellow Jews for a group prayer. It could be a Shabbat prayer at the synagogue, or any of the many weekday services. As you pray, be mindful not only of the personal energies you invest in your prayers, but also the powerful collective energy emerging from the group. Sense your own inner voice, amplified by the energies of the people around you, and then hear your own contribution echo within the collective prayer, greatly strengthening its combined potential.

KEY POINTS

1 Joining others and praying together as a congregation is a major theme in Jewish life, and for good reason: it dramatically enhances our prayers.

2 Synagogues play a key role in Jewish social life: in ancient communities, the synagogue was even set up to assist people in finding employment.

3 Communal prayer works like teamwork, and *everyone*—from the wicked to the righteous and all in between—has something to contribute to the group effort.

4 Praying together makes our prayers most acceptable on High, and our unity brings G-d *nachas*.

5 A critical part of the prayers is verbally and *truly* accepting the mitzvah to love every Jew as you start to pray.

6 You can pray at your own pace and still be a part of the community's prayer.

Appendix

TEXT 18

RABBI YAAKOV REISCHER, *RESPONSA SHEVUT YAAKOV* 2:25

דְּכוּלֵּי עַלְמָא מוֹדוּ, דְּקוֹדֶם שֶׁנִּקְבַּר הַמֵּת, דְּכֵיוָן שֶׁפָּטוּר מִן הַתְּפִילָּה,
דְּאֵינוֹ מִצְטָרֵף כְּלַל לְמִנְיַן עֲשָׂרָה.

The halachic consensus is that a mourner whose next of kin has yet to be buried is not counted in a *minyan* because he is exempt from prayer.

RABBI YAAKOV BEN YOSEF REISCHER
C. 1670–1733

Renowned rabbi, halachic authority, and author. He served on rabbinical courts in Prague, Ansbach, Worms, and Metz. He was accepted by contemporary rabbis as the ultimate authority on halachic issues, and problems were addressed to him from all over the Diaspora and Israel. His most famous works are *Chok Yaakov*, an exposition on the section of the Shulchan Aruch pertaining to the laws of Passover, and his responsa *Shevut Yaakov*.

TEXT 19

TALMUD, BERACHOT 28B

וּכְשֶׁאַתֶּם מִתְפַּלְּלִים - דְּעוּ לִפְנֵי מִי אַתֶּם עוֹמְדִים.

When you pray, know before Whom you stand.

Additional Readings

SHELIACH TZIBBUR: HISTORICAL AND PHENOMENOLOGICAL OBSERVATIONS

BY GERALD BLIDSTEIN, PHD

IN MEMORY OF RABBI NISSAN TELUSHKIN

Although the "representative of the community" (*sheliach tzibbur*) plays a significant role in Jewish prayer, there is surprisingly little discussion of the history and function of that role. Rabbinic literature contains one famous exchange on the question, in which the Sages say to R. Gamliel that the function of the *sheliach tzibbur* is to pray on behalf of those who lack the knowledge to pray themselves.[1] But the assertion that the *sheliach tzibbur* prays for those who do not themselves know the prayer seems too fragile fully to account for the genesis of the institution; certainly, it offers little phenomenological basis for its continuity in Jewish history. Moreover, the dialogue in question is late, for our purposes; it dates from the first decades after the Destruction of the Temple, and mirrors the difficulties encountered when new halakhic responsibilities and structures are grafted onto older forms. Thus, rather than aiding us to solve our problem, this discussion becomes part of the problem.

Some scholars suggest that the model for the *sheliach tzibbur* was the priest, who represented the community at the Temple altar.[2] The daily *tamid* sacrifice especially was brought on behalf of all Israel, and the officiating priest thus performed his ministry for all Israel. And the Prayer, R. Joshua L. Levi tells us, was instituted "as against" the *tamid* sacrifice.[3] Indeed, a late *midrash* explicitly states that the praying "representative of the community" brings the offering of the community.[4] But this reconstruction of the office of *sheliach tzibbur* does not at all do justice to the rich and complex history of liturgic development.

A second suggestion has greater merit, I believe. Louis Finkelstein has argued that the origins of the synagogue lay in the "prophetic prayer-meetings" of the First Commonwealth. He also remarked that "the position of the leader of the congregation is sufficiently . . . akin to that of the early prophet when he 'besought the L-rd' for those who came to him, to make it likely that the one is an outgrowth of the other."[5] Finkelstein presented little incontrovertible evidence for the existence of "prophetic prayer-gatherings," nor was his second contention well-documented. Yechezkel Kaufmann has since shown, however, that the prophetic role did include petition for the unfortunate individual and, more notably, for the entire community.[6] It was to this role, I believe, that the *sheliach tzibbur* succeeded. Early rabbinic data supports this contention, as it portrays the "representative of the community" as performing a rite for the community that has little to do with his vicarious prayer for those who cannot themselves pray.

Prime occasions for communal prayer in Biblical times were the times when the community was threatened—times of war, pestilence, and drought. Evidence for prayer-gatherings at such crises is abundant in the Biblical, Hasmonean, and Rabbinic eras.[7] A prominent feature of these gatherings is the prayer of the exemplary virtuoso on behalf of the community. One thinks of Samuel at Mizpah ("And Samuel said, 'Gather all Israel to Mizpah, and I will pray for you unto the L-rd.'" I Sam. 7:5), of Choni Ha-Me'aggel, R.

GERALD BLIDSTEIN, PHD, 1938–

Professor Emeritus at Israel's Ben-Gurion University of the Negev. He is an Israel Prize laureate in law (2006) and has been a member of the Israel Academy of Sciences since 2007. A graduate of Columbia (MA) and Yeshiva University (PhD), he has authored and edited many books on Jewish law, history, and philosophy.

Akiba, R. Eliezer, and so on. The Mishnah describes the normal procedure thus:[8]

> *How did they order the matter on the last seven days of fasting? They used to bring out the Ark into the open space in the town. . . . They stood up in prayer, sending down[9] before the Ark an old man, well versed in prayer, one that had children and whose house was empty, so that he might be whole-hearted in the prayer. He recited before them the twenty-four Benedictions: the Eighteen of daily use, adding to them yet six more.*

The antiquity of this procedure, which can be dated back to pre-Destruction times, is generally recognized.[10] Here, then, we have the first clear account of the function of the *sheliach tzibbur.* He is carefully selected for his piety, fluency in prayer, and sincerity—for he speaks for the community, even if they do pray themselves. As Choni himself reportedly said, some 150 years before the destruction of the Second Temple, "O L-rd of the world, your children have turned their faces to me, for I am like a member of your household (*ben bayyit*). . . . I will not stir . . . until you have pity on your children."[11] The prayers of Moses on behalf of the people were similarly described as "prayers of the individual for the community (*rabbim*),"[12] and he was described, we shall see, as a *sheliach tzibbur.*

Another Mishnah also implies that the representative of the community prayed on its behalf over and above the prayers that might be offered by individuals: [13]

> *If one makes a mistake in his prayer it is a bad sign for him, and if he is the representative of the community it is a bad sign for those who have commissioned him, because a man's agent is equivalent to himself. It was related of R. Chanina ben Dosa that he used to pray for the sick and say, "This one will die, this one will live." They said to him, "How do you know?" He replied, "If my prayer comes out fluently, I know that he is accepted, but if not, then I know that he is rejected."*

The point of the Mishnah is that the mistake of the *sheliach tzibbur* reflects upon, and indeed condemns, the *tzibbur* that delegated him; the logic of the Mishnah is that the entire community—both the learned and the ignorant, those who can pray and those who cannot—is bodied forth before G-d in their single representative. Furthermore, while the placing of the sayings of R. Chanina ben Dosa in our Mishnah is primarily determined by the idea that an error in prayer betokens its rejection, a secondary point of congruence is suggested as well: the representative of the community stands in the same relationship to the community as R. Hanina stands to the sick; in both cases one offers prayer on another's behalf.

In distinction to the Mishnah *Ta'anit* cited earlier, we do encounter here the explicit designation of he who prays before the people as *sheliach tzibbur*, "the representative of the community." This designation is not without significance, I believe: it betokens a shift in the way he who prayed before the community as its time of distress was authenticated.[14] In Tannaitic literature, the term *shaliach* has the connotation of delegated responsibility and answerability.[15] The authority of a *shaliach* is granted by those who send him. The prayer of the *sheliach tzibbur* was now not the more powerful because of his own personal piety or power. Rather, it was significant and potent because he had been delegated by the community, and served as its spokesman. G-d would listen to him because G-d was committed to the community of Israel. Nonetheless, it did not hurt if the community chose a man of exemplary piety and charisma to represent it. Thus, though Simeon ben Shetach disapproved of Choni's display of personal charisma, Jewish communities of Tannaitic and Amoraic times continued to have their prayers at times of drought and distress presented to G-d by figures of exemplary piety. The rabbis responded to the communal needs, but apparently sought to temper the popular interpretation of events:

> *(R. Eliezer prayed before the ark and it did not rain; R. Akiba prayed, and it did rain.) A heavenly voice came forth and proclaimed: "R. Akiba is not greater than R. Eliezer, but the one is of a conciliatory disposition and the other is not."* (Ta'anit 25*b)*

The "power" of R. Akiba was indeed greater than that of R. Eliezer, but the specific virtues that are decisive are the ethical ones of humility and the pursuit of peace.[16]

Two rabbinic sources further clarify the role of the *sheliach tzibbur*, particularly in reference to the fast-day liturgy.

In the Mekhilta we are told that "no less than three men should go before the ark on a public fast,"[17] based on the fact that Aaron and Hur supported Moses' hands at the battle with Amalek. This teaching is anonymous, and we cannot date it with certainty. We do know, however, that R. Joshua (who was at least 30 years old when the Temple was destroyed) claimed that Moses fasted the entire day of the battle, and R. Eleazar of Modi'in (1st third of 2nd cen.) claimed it was a public fast day. Both the practice of having "no less than three men go before the ark on a public fast" and its exegetical base may date to one of these two figures.[18] What was its purpose? It is quite conceivable that this procedure demonstrated that the charisma and merit of no single individual was crucial; rather, three men prayed before the ark and stressed thereby that they petitioned G-d as representatives of the community. For when it came to synagogue governance a Palestinian *baraita* reported that "three men of the synagogue are as the entire synagogue," and this same rubric held for prayer on the fast-day, too.[19] Thus, R. Judah the Patriarch sends R. Hiyya and his sons—R. Hiyya had two sons—down before the Ark on a fast-day.[20]

One final source documents something of the content of the prayer of the *sheliach tzibbur*; it is a relatively late source, but nonetheless may point to more ancient practice.

R. Yochanan (who died in 279) comments on Exodus 34:6–7 (". . . the L-rd passed before him and proclaimed, 'The L-rd! The L-rd! A G-d compassionate and gracious,' etc."):[21]

> *Were it not written in Scripture, it could not be said! We learn hence that the L-rd wrapped himself [in a* tallit*] like a* sheliach tzibbur *and showed Moses the order of prayer. G-d said to him, "Whenever Israel sins, let them perform this order of prayer before me, and I shall forgive them."*

In the third century, then, the *sheliach tzibbur* says a special prayer on behalf of his people "when they sin." But since no group prays when "it sins," but only when it suffers and interprets its experience as punishment for its newly-acknowledged sins, we may safely say that the recitation of the "thirteen attributes" by the *sheliach tzibbur* took place on fast days called to avert drought or other catastrophes.[22]

Who recited the "thirteen attributes"? Our printed texts state, "let *them* perform this order of prayers before me, and I shall forgive them." This may mean that the entire assembled group sent one of its members to act as its representative, but it may also mean that the entire group recited the passage in question. But in any case, our text is not the only one: *She'iltot*, the commentary of R. Hanan'el, and *Midrash Ha-Gadol*[23] all have a text reading, "(G-d said to Moses) whenever Israel sins, you perform (singular verb) this order of prayers before me. . . ."; so too in a parallel cited in *Tanchuma*.[24] Furthermore, the passage is more coherent if we assume that the *sheliach tzibbur* recited the "thirteen attributes": according to the *aggadah* it is G-d who first recited these attributes, and He functions as the *sheliach tzibbur*. It is clear, then, that the recitation of the "thirteen attributes" on the fast-day was not only a community ritual, but was also delegated to the *sheliach tzibbur*.

We cannot claim that the practice of the recitation of the "thirteen attributes" pre-dates R. Jochanan or the mid-third century. At the same time, it would not be surprising to discover that we have before us a ritual much older than that. Moses is reported by the Bible (Numbers 14:18) to have pleaded for his people after the incident of the twelve spies by passionately reminding the L-rd of His merciful attributes.[25] The prophet Joel pins his hopes, on a day of fast and prayer, to these same qualities of G-d, and Jonah incorporates them into his prayer as well, suggesting that G-d would not destroy the Ninevites because of His merciful nature.[26] The Divine attributes function in a similar way in the Apocryphal literature.[27] It is not impossible, then, that R. Yochanan refers to a liturgic practice that predated his own period of activity.

We have seen that the model, and possibly the actual source, for the "representative of the community" in prayer is the prophet who prayed for his people. The exemplary individual prays for his community because of his superior gifts, but his prayer is also uniquely potent because the claims of the community as a whole, as a *tzibbur*, crystallize in him as its representative. With the destruction of the Temple and the concomitant requirement that each individual say the *Tefillah*, a new role was added: the *sheliach tzibbur* prays on behalf of those who cannot pray themselves.[28] But even then, the *sheliach tzibbur* functions in this way because he is the representative of the entire community; indeed, many claim that he can so function only when he actually represents a *tzibbur*, that is, with a *minyan*, but not in a one-to-one relationship with the unlettered.[29]

It would seem that the ability to pray on behalf of the ignorant derives its impetus from the broader (and more basic) possibility of prayer for, and of, the community; one might argue that it is only the prayer of the community which can do service for the ignorant individual, and that it is only as the unlettered individual fuses with the community in the person of the *sheliach tzibbur* that their prayer is his. The new role of the *sheliach tzibbur* is, then, an organic expression and extension of the old. The original concept provided not only the conceptual and halakhic scaffolding for this new role, but also the phenomenological and experiential vitality of the entire institution.[30]

Tradition: A Journal of Orthodox Thought, vol 12, No. 1 (Summer 1971), pp. 69–77
Republished with permission of the Rabbinical Council of America

Endnotes

*Some of the ideas contained in this paper resemble motifs I have heard circulated in the name of Rabbi J. B. Soloveitchik. If these reports are accurate, I acknowledge my indebtedness.

1 *Tosefta Rosh Ha-Shanah* IV (II). 12 (ed. Zukermandel, p. 214, 1.7); b. *Rosh Ha-Shanah* 34b.

2 I. Sonne, "Synagogue," *Interpreter's Dictionary of the Bible*, IV, 490. See also M. Landsberg, "Sheliach Tzibbur," *Jewish Encyclopedia*, XI, 261; E. Halevi, *Yesodei Ha-Tefillah*, 86–87 (Halevi's citation of b. *Nedarim* 35b is inaccurate.); R. Patai, *Man and Temple*, 208.

3 *Berakhot* 26b. The idea (though not necessarily the phrase, *keneged*) is undoubtedly much older. Interestingly, the Talmud (26a) also uses the term *bimkom*.

4 See p. *Berakhot* 4:4, 8b; and L. Ginzberg, *Perushim* (Heb.), III, 350–354.

5 "The Origin of the Synagogue," *Proceedings of the American Academy for Jewish Research* (1928–30), 49–59, esp. p. 59.

6 *Toledot Ha-'Emunah Ha-Yisre'alit*, II, 499–500.

7 See A. Buechler, *Types of Jewish-Palestinian Piety*, 213ff.

8 *M. Ta'anit* II, 1–2.

9 Prof. Danby's rendering. "They stood up in prayer and sent down before the Ark an old man. . . ." is not quite accurate, and distorts the situation. I prefer, "they stood up in prayer, sending down . . . an old man." Thus it is clear that the communal prayer is in fact the prayer of the "old man." Buechler, *op. cit.*, p. 214, gives as well: "When about to begin the prayer, they send down an old man . . ." See also L. Blau, "Liturgy," *JE*, VIII, 137.

10 See Buechler, *op. cit.*, Kohler's reservations ("The Development of the Amidah," *HUCA I* (1924), 387ff.) mainly concern the antiquity of specific liturgical formulae.

11 *M. Ta'anit* III, 8.

12 See *Sifre*, Deut. 27 (ed. Finkelstein, p. 42). *Rabbim* and *tzibbur* are identical for our purposes, though a difference in nuance probably distinguishes them. See also *Mekhilta*, *Nezikin*, 18 (ed. Horowitz-Rabin, 314–315), and E. Uhrbach, *Chazal*, p. 398, n. 14.

13 *M. Berakhot* V, 5.

14 The term itself may be derived from the use of the verb *s-l-h* in Jeremiah 42:5, 9, where the prophet is "sent" by the people to pray for them. Actually the form *sheliach tzibbur* is not at all remarkable, and needed no special literary stimulus for its origin. See also S. Krauss, *Synagogale Altertumer*, 131–133. It is noteworthy that the term *sheliach tzibbur* does not denote any other community functionary; but see Krauss, above. *P. Ta'anit* 1:4: 64b, though suggestive, does not support the identification of the *sheliach tzibbur* with the *parnas*, as Halevi (*op. cit.*) claims.

15 See, e.g., *Mekhilta*, *Pischa*, 1 (ed. Horowitz-Rabin, p. 4). P. Borgen, "G-d's Agent in the Fourth Gospel," *Religions in Antiquity*, ed. J. Neusner, 137–148, claims that some rabbis developed the identity of the agent and his sender into a "judicial mysticism," but his evidence is sparse and unconvincing. A more interesting discussion would have emerged had Borgen noted the *shelichut* structure in prayer; indeed Mishnah *Berakhot*, cited above, is the only Mishnaic citation of the teaching that "a man's agent is equivalent to himself" (see also L. Ginzberg, "*Al Ha-yachas . . .*" *Studies in Memory of M. Schorr* [Heb.], 70). Moreover, A. Gulack, *Yesodei Ha-Mishpat Ha-Ivri*, I, 42–43, argues for the "sacramental character" of *shelichut* on the basis of its limitation in Jewish law to Jews. But this is still wide of "judicial mysticism."

16 In the Palestinian version (p. *Ta'anit* 3:5: 66b–c) R. Akiba says that G-d fulfilled his request and not that of R. Eliezer because the L-rd enjoys the company of the latter, and so forces him to stay and pray longer, while he, R. Akiba, is not so precious to G-d and so is quickly dismissed with his request fulfilled. The Talmud then comments that this explanation was offered so as to relieve the embarrassment of R. Eliezer.

17 Mekhilta, I (*op. cit.*, pp. 180–1).

18 See Buechler, *op. cit.*, p. 217. The rabbis also opposed the reading and translating of the Torah by one and the same person: see *P. Megillah* 4:1, 74d, for 3rd cen. Palestine.

19 *P. Megillah* 3:2; 74a. In the Book of Judith, the town of Betuliah is governed by a council of three (6:15; ed. J. Grinitz, p. 120).

20 *Baba Meziah* 85b: *Tosafot* 86a, *s.v. ahtinhu*.

21 *Rosh Ha-Shanah* 17b.

22 See *Siddur Rav Amram Ga'on*, I, 35; Rashi, R. H., *ad loc.*

23 *Midrash Ha-Gadol*, Exodus, ed. M. Margaliot, p. 707; *She'iltot*, 66.

[24] *Midrash Tanchuma*, ed. S. Buber, I, 46a. Especially noteworthy is *Seder Eliyahu Zuta,* ch. 23 (ed. M. Friedmann, pt. II, p. 42), which argues from the statement of R. Yochanan that the exemplary individual must be ready to offer himself as pleader, *sanegor*, for the people Israel.

[25] This Biblical incident is probably a stimulus for R. Yochanan's teaching, cited above. Moses pleads the "13 attributes" in Numbers 14 because the L-rd had taught him to do so in Exodus 34.

[26] Joel 2:12–14; Jonah 4:2.

[27] See the Prayer of Manasseh, 7; IV Ezra, 5:132–139.

[28] See n. 1, above; see also I. Elbogen, *Der juedische Gottesdienst*, 254ff.

[29] See *Tur, Orah Hayyim*, 594; the exploration of these different views could proceed along lines laid down above. The communal role of the *sheliach tzibbur* is presupposed by many paragraphs of *Shulkhan Arukh*, O.H., 124.

[30] A full discussion of the *sheliach tzibbur* as an institution would draw on other materials, too, such as the practice of *pores al shema*, etc., many of which presuppose the presence of a *minyan*.

MY BELOVED *MECHITZAH*

BY JOELLE KEENE

I didn't know these lovebirds, but they were obviously just that, standing at Sabbath morning services amid a sea of men and women with his arm around her waist, she leaning into his shoulder and the two of them swaying gently back and forth to the sound of the prayers. How nice, I thought, that they're learning Torah together. Where it will take them no one can say, but they're together on a great and splendid journey.

Since then, my own journey, begun in part in that same room, has led me to a place where I could not possibly stand in prayer with my husband's arm around my waist. Praying might just be the most important thing we humans do, setting the stage for all of the rest of our behavior, but it is not the easiest. For most of us it takes tremendous concentration, a great erasing of everything outside and at the same time a bringing of everything we are into one small moment framed by a particular piece of ancient text. The problem is that love is so powerful—especially love for a spouse, but even premonitions of love like crush and curiosity—that in any given moment, prayer cannot compete.

Perhaps that's why Judaism promotes something called the *mechitzah*, surely the most widely maligned—I would say misunderstood—of any institution in Judaism today. A *mechitzah*, literally "separation," is a screen or other barrier in a traditional synagogue that separates women from men during worship; in this separation, some say, the women are demeaned. The religious idea is that men should not be able to see women while they're praying, for if they do, their prayer will not be heard. To me, that's not demeaning; it's a statement of obvious fact. It's hard enough to pray when you're alone.

Try this exercise: Imagine that you need to speak with G-d. Imagine that you need something very, very badly, and that G-d really is all-powerful and the only One Who can grant it to you. Or imagine that you've done something terribly wrong and need some great forgiveness, or that your first child has just been born and you want to offer thanks. Close your eyes. Find the words. Now try, really try, to send them up to heaven.

Could you do this while cuddling with your spouse? Could you do it while ogling the latest beauty to join the synagogue, or that guy you see each Saturday who's so cute it makes you laugh? Maybe you could—everyone's different—but I strive mightily just to sense G-d's listening when I pray.

Sometimes I picture great tree limbs, an overarching Father seeing every word and deed, or see myself as human clay addressing Him who formed it. Or I conjure up an awesome, holy Throne bathed in rays of light, considering with mercy my so tiny, distant plea. Yet with all these tools and more, still it's hard. We need all the help we can get.

And so we have a curtain—to center us perhaps, to make a place that forms a space where we can pray. There are as many kinds of *mechitzahs* as there are synagogues—I've seen sleek wood carved in modern shapes, and balconies where height is the *mechitzah*, and gathered lace on curtain rods that roll.

But all *mechitzahs* hold us back from one another and group our prayers by gender rising heavenward. Perhaps this helps G-d hear us, too; perhaps we sound clearer, are more ourselves, unmediated by our opposites. Judaism loves categories and celebrates them every way—night and day, milk and meat, Sabbath versus holidays and ordinary days—and gender's no exception.

The men's section is front and center because men have more ritual commandments in the synagogue, while women are responsible for bringing Torah into

JOELLE KEENE

Mother of three, currently teaches music and journalism at Shalhevet High School in Los Angeles. Joelle previously worked as an award-winning newspaper reporter for the *Los Angeles Herald Examiner* and *The Seattle Times*. Additionally, she was a music critic, and served as associate editor of *OLAM Magazine*.

the home. Synagogue becomes one place where we can be with our own gender, something not without a pleasure all on its own.

So you can say the *mechitzah* exists to keep women out, that the genders are identical and all else is cultural conceit. For many of us, though, the *mechitzah* opens a door in, perhaps into a more concentrated experience of who we are and certainly into the presence of G-d where holiness and much direction lie. In prayer, we reach outside our earthly yearnings and search for something different, something that ennobles us, sets our sights high and improves us from the inside out. In love, we find an outlet for those improvements, for our goodness, kindness, generosity. Love is arguably our most G-d-like activity, and also our greatest earthly reward; in its physical expression, it is said to bring G-d's presence to rest on us directly. Each paves the way for the other; I'm a better wife for praying, and drawn closer to G-d through the love my marriage brings. Each creates a chasm we can cross.

And so I wonder again about those Sabbath lovebirds, trying to make their yearnings heard above the din of daily life, studying Torah and singing psalms, arms linked, perhaps journeying down paths deep into wisdom.

There's no one way to pray, and none of us can say for sure whose prayers are heard. But perhaps their love has grown so much that they can't sit together in services anymore, or their love for G-d has grown in such a way that they don't want to. Maybe it would take more than a curtain to keep them apart—and perhaps just a curtain to link them.

Hear O Israel, Leopold Pilichowski (1866–1934), oil on board. (Ben Uri Gallery, London)

THE HOW OF JEWISH PRAYER

Jewish prayer is a powerful and highly calibrated tool to connect, communicate, petition, and discover G-d. But for many today, it is a lost art, due partly to unfamiliarity with its language, structure, setting, and texts. "The How of Jewish Prayer" is a game-changing step-by-step guide to daily prayer, congregational prayer, and the prayer book.

I. Introduction to Prayer

A. *NUSACH*—PRAYER RITE

The prayer book that we know today evolved over millennia, drawing from the experiences and contributions of multiple Jewish communities. The process was launched in the third century BCE, when the Jewish leader known as Ezra the Scribe, in partnership with a venerable body of sages referred to as the Men of the Great Assembly, established the basic structure of standardized prayers. Future sages and communities continued to build on this initial framework for centuries thereafter. Many of our prayers are selected readings from ancient biblical sources; other contributions, such as *lecha dodi*, the poetic-mystical prayer chanted on Friday night to welcome the Shabbat, were penned as recently as the sixteenth century.

As the Jewish nation spread further in exile, diverse liturgical customs and textual nuances took hold in various communities, countries, and continents. Several, but not all, of these colorful variations are extant today. The two most widely-adopted varieties today are *Ashkenaz*, rooted in the ancient tradition of Germanic Jewry, and *Sefard*, based on the ancient tradition of Spanish Jewry. Despite the various liturgical styles and disparities between Jewish prayer texts, the core elements and order of the prayers, as articulated in the Talmud, are identical across all traditions.[1]

When faced with a choice of liturgical style (*nusach*), it is generally appropriate to pray in the *nusach* that has remained in one's family tradition for centuries. If this information has been lost or

1 See *Responsa Maharshdam, Orach Chayim* 35.

cannot be identified, one should consult a rabbi about choosing an appropriate *nusach*.

Before presenting a brief overview of the standard prayers and their appropriate order, it is important to note that most of what is said below pertains across all traditions, but some of the information is not true for every *nusach*. In these cases, the information presented here is based specifically on the Chabad custom, which is rooted in the mystical teachings of one of Jewish history's foremost and revered mystics, Rabbi Yitschak Luria (sixteenth century), referred to as the Arizal (hence the identification of the style as *Nusach Ari*).

All references to the prayer book are taken from *Siddur Tehilat Hashem* (New York: Merkos L'Inyonei Chinuch, 2004).

B. THREE DAILY PRAYERS

According to Jewish law and custom, Jews open their hearts in prayer three times a day: *shacharit* in the morning, *minchah* in the afternoon, and *arvit* in the evening.

Ancient tradition traces the origin of these three daily prayers, although not their precise content, to the earliest dawn of Jewish history: Abraham established *shacharit*, Isaac established *minchah*, and Jacob established *arvit*.[2] After the destruction of the Second Temple, these three daily prayers assumed an entire new significance and degree of obligation, whereby the Jewish people adopted them as substitutes for the daily offerings that were brought in the Temple.[3]

2 Talmud, Berachot 26b.

3 Ibid.

The three prayers can be located in the prayer book as follows:

- *Shacharit*, the weekday morning service, begins on page 27 and ends on page 81. *Shacharit* for Shabbat can be found on pages 181–221.
- *Minchah*, the weekday afternoon service, begins on page 101 and ends on page 117. *Minchah* for Shabbat can be found on pages 253–269.
- *Arvit*, the weekday evening service, begins on page 118 and ends on page 135. *Arvit* for Friday night can be found on pages 154–176.

One who is unable to recite the entire *shacharit* should recite the following three segments as a minimum: the Blessings of Gratitude (pp. 6–7), the Shema and its blessings (pp. 39–45), and the Amidah (for weekdays, pp. 45–54; for Shabbat, pp. 211–217). If praying three times a day is unachievable, one should recite as many of the daily prayers as personal circumstances permit.

C. WHERE

Praying together with a congregation is the optimum choice by far, and should be attained whenever possible. Our sages revealed that congregational prayer is more glorifying to G-d than individual prayer[4] and that G-d accepts the congregation's prayers irrespective of whether its members are deserving.[5]

It is best for the congregation to include a *minyan*—a quorum of at least ten Jewish men age thirteen or older—because our

4 *Shulchan Aruch HaRav, Orach Chayim* 90:10.

5 Ibid., and 52:1.

sages taught that G-d is particularly present in the presence of a *minyan*.[6]

If attending a *minyan* is not a viable option, one should schedule one's prayers to coincide with the *minyan*'s prayer at the synagogue. If that is not feasible, it is preferable to pray alone in the synagogue despite the lack of a congregational service because (a) it is appropriate to pray in a sacred location, and (b) prayers recited in a synagogue are received more favorably by G-d.[7] If that is not an option, one may pray at home or any location that is conducive to focused concentration.

Unstable surfaces or wide-open spaces are not recommended for prayer because the need to maintain balance or vigilance is likely to disturb one's concentration.[8] The best place for undistracted prayer is in front of a plain wall.[9]

One should designate a permanent, personal place at home or at the synagogue for daily prayer.[10] Praying in an established location each day turns the spiritual exercise of prayer, and the sincere bond with G-d that it enables, into a permanent feature of our minds, hearts, and lives.[11] It also makes it obvious to spectators that one is praying, and they will recognize the need to avoid disturbances or interruptions.[12]

6 *Ethics of the Fathers* 3:6.

7 *Shulchan Aruch HaRav, Orach Chayim* 90:10; *Kitsur Shulchan Aruch* 12:7.

8 *Shulchan Aruch HaRav, Orach Chayim* 90:1, 5.

9 Shulchan Aruch, *Orach Chayim* 90:21.

10 Shulchan Aruch, *Orach Chayim* 90:19.

11 Maharal, *Nesiv Avodah*, chapter 4.

12 *Shulchan Aruch HaRav, Orach Chayim* 90:18.

D. LANGUAGE OF PRAYER

It is best to pray in Hebrew. Hebrew is the unique language of the Jewish people, the native expression of the Jewish soul, and the sacred tongue in which the Torah was written. Furthermore, the majority of our prayers were composed in this language, and they are far more accurate, potent, and rich in their original. In addition, the sages who composed these prayers encoded in their subtle choices of Hebrew words, letters, and vowels various esoteric intentions that are key to the soul of prayer and are entirely lost in translation.

That said, it is crucial to the function of the prayers to understand their plain meaning. This concern outweighs the benefits of praying in Hebrew, so one who does not understand Hebrew should rightfully pray in a familiar language. Nevertheless, it is preferable to aim for the best of both options: to recite the prayers in a language that is understood while taking additional time to study the meaning of the Hebrew prayers, enabling a gradual transition to Hebrew.[13]

There is another option for one who wishes to pray in Hebrew specifically, despite not understanding the meaning of the prayers: to maintain an overall meditation while praying by reflecting on the greatness of G-d and the comparative insignificant stature of the human being, and also to picture the degree of undistracted focus appropriate at an intimate audience with a mortal monarch, and then consider the far greater focus required when standing in prayer before the King of all kings, the Creator of the universe.[14] At the same time, it is appropriate to petition G-d to accept one's prayers as if they were offered with all the appropriate understandings, intentions, and meditations.[15]

13 *Shulchan Aruch HaRav, Orach Chayim* 101:5.

14 *Shulchan Aruch HaRav, Orach Chayim* 98:1.

15 Rabbi Yosef Yitschak Schneersohn, *Igros Kodesh* 3:144.

E. PREPARATION FOR PRAYER

Jewish tradition offers several activities as appropriate preparations for prayer:

1. *Proper attire:* The standards of attire for prayer are largely determined by what is commonly considered acceptable at highly formal interviews in one's culture and region.[16] Nevertheless, the requisite for modest attire overrides cultural norms, and this includes a head covering for men.[17]

2. *Ritual washing of the hands:* Fill a washing cup with water. Pour it over the right hand from wrist to fingers, and then proceed to do the same over the left hand. Repeat this procedure three times. Those who are left-handed simply reverse the order, and begin with the left hand.[18] If one washed the hands ritually earlier in the morning, it is sufficient to simply rinse the hands under running water before prayer.

3. *Donate to charity:*[19] This can be a nominal amount, but it should be given before praying (except on Shabbat and Jewish festivals, when handling money and making transactions is prohibited).

4. *Mental focus:* To enhance concentration during prayer, it is necessary to spend several minutes beforehand in quiet reflection, in order to remove distracting thoughts that might result from previous activities, and to focus the mind and settle the emotions in readiness to focus on G-d and converse with Him in prayer.[20]

16 Shulchan Aruch, *Orach Chayim*, 91:5.

17 Ibid., 91:3.

18 *Kitsur Shulchan Aruch* 2:3.

19 Talmud, Bava Batra 10a.

20 Shulchan Aruch, *Orach Chayim* 93:1–3 and 98:1.

5. Men don a *talit* (prayer shawl) before *shacharit* and wear it for the duration of the service. On weekdays, men also don *tefilin* (phylacteries) for *shacharit*. A man who is unable to recite *shacharit*, or who cannot do so with *tefilin*, should make an effort to wear *tefilin* briefly at any point later in the day and recite the Shema while wearing them.

F. VERBALIZING PRAYER

A prayer in the heart is a healthy start, but one's personal obligation to pray has not been satisfied until the words are verbalized. Prayer must be *from* the heart but should not *remain* in the heart. In order for the experience to embrace not just the soul but also the physical body and human condition, it must find tangible expression.[21] Preferably, the words should be audibly vocalized; however, there is no need to raise one's voice. The exception is the Amidah prayer, which should be verbalized in an undertone so that the words are audible only to the one uttering them.

G. STANDING AND SITTING

It is customary to stand for certain prayers and sit for others. We stand for prayers in which we address G-d directly, such as the Amidah, or to highlight the significance of specific prayers. Most prayer books indicate the prayers for which it is considered appropriate to stand. In a congregational setting, we also stand to honor the Torah as it is carried to and from the ark.

21 *Tanya*, chapter 37.

II. *Daily Prayer, Step-by-Step*

A. MORNING

1. Modeh Ani—"I Offer Thanks"

We collapse into bed at night, weary and weak from a long day, but as the sun climbs back into the skies, we arise rejuvenated and refreshed. It is most appropriate to offer our sincerest thanks to our Creator at the start of each day for the precious gift of life, and our sages therefore minted a powerful, single-sentence prayer to be recited immediately upon awakening.[22] (In the siddur, it appears on p. 5.) Some have the custom to recite this prayer while sitting up in bed with the head bowed toward the chest, and with the fingertips held against each other.[23]

2. Morning Blessings and Preliminary Readings

Our morning prayers begin with a series of brief blessings to thank G-d for many elements of daily life that might otherwise be taken for granted (pp. 6–9), such as the ability to see, sit up, stand upright, and walk. We also thank G-d for providing us with clothes, shoes, and so forth, as well as the privilege of being Jewish and having been given the Torah and its sacred laws.

3. *Karbanot*—The Sacrificial Offerings

The subsequent section in the prayer book describes the sacrificial and incense offerings in the Holy Temple (pp. 17–24). Before entering this topic, however, we declare our love for our

22 *Kitsur Shulchan Aruch* 1:2.
23 *Sefer Haminhagim, Minhagei Chabad*, p. 1.

fellow Jews (p. 12);[24] we then read a biblical passage that describes Abraham's binding of Isaac (pp. 13–14), followed by the Shema declaration that is Judaism's ultimate proclamation of faith in G-d (p. 16).

After reading a description of the daily offerings (pp. 17–21), we read the thirteen principles that govern the derivation of Jewish law from Torah passages, as formulated by the ancient sage Rabbi Ishmael.

In a congregational prayer with a *minyan*, the leader recites *Rabbanan Kaddish* (p. 26) after the teaching of Rabbi Ishmael. For more information about Kaddish, see below.

B. SHACHARIT— THE MORNING PRAYER

1. *Hodu*—"Offer Praise"

The formal start of the *shacharit* prayer is the passage that begins *hodu*, "Offer praise to the L-rd" (pp. 27–29). This section is a collage of verses culled from diverse biblical sources, all of which offer praise to G-d and describe the Creator's providence over our people.

On Shabbat, several additional prayers are inserted into this section (pp. 184–191).

2. *Pesukei Dezimrah*—Passages of Praise

This section (pp. 30–38) is built of entire paragraphs and chapters from biblical texts that descriptively sing G-d's praises. It is

24 *Igros Kodesh Rayats* 3, p. 143.

designed to awaken feelings of admiration, gratitude, awe, and love for G-d. This section is introduced with a poetic blessing and signs out with another, as described below.

Baruch She'amar ("Blessed is He Who spoke") (p. 30). This blessing sets the tone for *pesukei dezimrah.* It is customary for men to recite it while grasping the front two *tsitsit* (fringes of the *talit*) in the left hand.[25] Some run the *tsitsit* lightly over the eyes and then kiss them at the conclusion of *Baruch She'amar.*[26]

There are two parts to *pesukei dezimrah.* Its first half is primarily comprised of Psalms 145–150. Our sages taught that one who recites Psalm 145 three times daily is assured of a share in the World to Come. This psalm includes the verse, "You open your hand and satisfy the needs of every living thing," which testifies to G-d's providence over creation, a central message of *pesukei dezimrah.*[27] Psalm 145 is followed by Psalms 146–150, because each chapter in this series begins and ends with the words "praise the L-rd," which is the ultimate goal of this stage of our morning prayers.[28]

The second half of *pesukei dezimrah* is comprised of selections from Chronicles, Nehemiah, and Exodus that praise G-d for creation and for the miracles He performed for us during the Exodus and at the Sea of Reeds.

The grand finale of this section is *yishtabach* ("may Your Name be praised forever"), a blessing filled with expressions of praise derived from the preceding passages.[29] On Shabbat, an additional prayer, *nishmat* ("the soul of every living being"), is inserted before *yishtabach* (pp. 199–201).

25 *Shulchan Aruch HaRav, Orach Chayim* 51:2.

26 *Sefer Haminhagim, Minhagei Chabad*, p. 9.

27 *Shulchan Aruch HaRav, Orach Chayim* 51:8.

28 Ibid. 51:1.

29 Ibid.

In a congregational prayer with a *minyan*, *yishtabach* is followed by "half Kaddish" (p. 38), which is in turn followed by *barchu* (p. 39). These will be explained further below.

3. *Birchot Keri'at Shema*—Blessings Surrounding the Shema

The next step in our ladder of prayer is the Shema that is preceded by two blessings and trailed by a third blessing (pp. 39–45):

The initial blessing preceding the Shema mentions the enormity and brilliance of G-d's creation[30] and contains the *kedushah*—a prayer that describes the loving and reverential prayers offered by the angels in Heaven. On Shabbat, the first blessing is modified and expanded (pp. 203–205).

The second blessing describes G-d's eternal love for us and our profound devotion to Him. During this blessing, men gather the four *tsitsit* of the *talit* and grasp them in the left hand (those who are left-handed gather them into their right hand).

4. Shema

The Shema consists of three distinct portions from the Torah. The first (Deuteronomy 6:4–9) is a declaration of our faith in G-d's unity and our love for G-d. The second (Deuteronomy 11:13–21) describes the rewards earned by the observance of the divine commandments and the consequences that result from disobeying them. The third (Numbers 15:37–41) defines the mitzvah of *tsitsit* and the imperative to recall our Exodus from Egypt.

The opening verse of the Shema is traditionally recited aloud to enhance concentration. It is customary to cover the eyes with the

30 During the first blessing (p. 39), it is customary for men who are wearing *tefilin* to touch the hand-*tefilin* at the words *yotser or* ("Who forms light"), and to touch the head-*tefilin* while reciting *uvorei choshech* ("and creates darkness") (*Kaf Hachayim, Orach Chayim* 59:2).

right hand while reciting this verse, to avoid distractions. Those who are left-handed cover their eyes with the left hand. Our sages taught that the final word, *echad* ("one"), should be extended long enough to reflect on the idea that G-d is King over everything that exists in every direction—east, west, north, south, above, and below.[31]

Before continuing the biblical passage, we insert a non-biblical phrase (*baruch Shem* ["blessed be the Name"]). The Talmud teaches that when our forefather Jacob's twelve sons, the progenitors of the tribes of Israel, declared their faith in G-d by reciting the Shema, Jacob expressed his happiness by reciting this passage in response.[32] *Baruch Shem* is recited quietly to distinguish it from the Shema itself, to avoid confusing passages of biblical and non-biblical origin.[33]

The third paragraph of the Shema (p. 43) contains the biblical commandment of *tsitsit*. Before reciting this paragraph, it is customary for men to transfer the *tstisit* that they are holding in their left hand to their right hand. Those who are left-handed do the opposite. The strings of the *tsitsit* are then kissed each time the word *tsitsit* is read—and once more at the word *emet* ("truth"), which is appended to the conclusion of the Shema (p. 44).[34]

31 *Shulchan Aruch HaRav, Orach Chayim*, 61:5–7.

32 Talmud, Pesachim 56a.

33 *Shulchan Aruch HaRav, Orach Chayim*, 61:13.

34 See Talmud, Berachot 14a.

When praying in private, before adding the word *emet* ("truth"), the last three words of the Shema are repeated. These are the words *Ado-nai Elo-heichem emet*, thereby bringing the total of the words of the Shema to 248, corresponding to the number of positive commandments in the Torah. When praying with a *minyan*, this is not necessary because the *chazan* repeats these three words on behalf of the congregation.

In the *Ashkenaz* custom, when praying without a *minyan*, one recites three alternate words *before* the Shema.

5. Final Blessing of *Birchot Keriat Shema*

The Shema is followed by a blessing of praise for the wondrous miracles that G-d performed during the Exodus and at the Sea of Reeds (pp. 44–45), in fulfillment of our obligation to praise G-d each morning for the miracles He performs.[35] The blessing concludes with a declaration of our faith that G-d is our redeemer.

6. Amidah

The Amidah begins on page 45 and concludes on page 54. On Shabbat, it begins on page 211 and concludes on page 217.[36]

This most important prayer, the pinnacle of our morning devotion, is recited standing upright, feet together, preferably in front of a wall, and facing in the direction of Jerusalem.[37] The tradition of facing Jerusalem dates back to King Solomon, who taught that all the prayers in the world make their way to the Temple Mount and from there ascend to G-d.[38]

Before beginning, it is customary to take three steps forward to demonstrate that we are approaching G-d in direct, personal prayer.[39] When standing in front of a table or wall, take three steps back and then three steps forward.

It is ancient tradition to take a number of bows during the Amidah as follows: at the very start of the initial blessing, we bend the knees at the word *baruch* ("blessed"), then bow forwards from the waist at the word *atah* ("You"), and then stand erect once more before continuing. This procedure is repeated at the end of the first blessing as well. It is repeated once more at the conclusion of

35 Psalms 92:3; Rashi, Berachot 12a.

36 The Amidah for festivals appears on pages 331–337.

37 Shulchan Aruch, *Orach Chayim* 90:21 and 94:1.

38 Ibid., 94:1.

39 *Shulchan Aruch HaRav* 95:2.

the eighteenth blessing. In addition, at the start of the eighteenth blessing, at the words *modim anachnu Lach she'Atah Hu* ("we thankfully acknowledge that You"), we bow from the waist.[40]

After completing the Amidah, we take three steps backward (moving the left foot first as a symbol of reluctance to depart from G-d's presence). We do so with the head bowed toward the chest, as if departing humbly from a king. After taking three steps, we straighten our posture and bow the head to the left, to the right, and forward as we recite the phrase *oseh shalom* ("He Who makes peace"). Finally, we take three steps forward to our original position. Some have a custom of rising slightly on their toes to express a desire to draw closer to G-d.

On Shabbat and festivals, only the first three blessings of the Amidah and its final blessing remain the same. The entire middle section of the Amidah is replaced so that instead of reciting a series of thirteen blessings, we offer a single blessing that depicts the nature and theme of the occasion.

In a congregational prayer with a *minyan*, the leader repeats the Amidah aloud once the congregation has concluded their muted prayers. The congregation listens attentively, responds *amen* at the conclusion of each blessing, and participates in the recital of *kedushah*. This will be explained further below.

7. Special Inserts into the Amidah

Havdalah: On Saturday nights, a prayer to mark the end of Shabbat, known as Havdalah ("distinction"), is inserted into the fourth blessing (p. 125) to distinguish between Shabbat and the weekdays. It is included in the prayer for knowledge because our

40 Shulchan Aruch, *Orach Chayim* 113:1 and 121:1.

sages taught that knowledge is a prerequisite to our ability to make appropriate distinctions.[41]

Fast Days: The ninth day of the month of Av (a day known as Tishah Be'Av) marks the destruction of the Holy Temples. On this day, an urgent prayer for the rebuilding of Jerusalem and the Holy Temple is inserted into the fourteenth blessing (p. 106).

On all fast days, a plea for G-d to transform our tragedies into joyous occasions is inserted into the sixteenth blessing (p. 108).

Festivals: On Rosh Chodesh (the start of each Jewish month) and the intermediate days of the Passover and Shavuot festivals, a passage beginning *Elokeinu . . . yaaleh veyavo* ("our G-d . . . may there ascend") is inserted into the seventeenth blessing (p. 108). This prayer asks G-d to remember us for good, provide for us, and protect us on this auspicious day.

Several additional prayers are inserted into the Amidah during the first ten days of the Jewish year, from the start of Rosh Hashanah until the conclusion of Yom Kippur (pp. 46–47, 49, 52–53).

Seasons: The texts of the second and ninth blessings of the Amidah (pp. 46 and 48) are slightly modified to account for the changes of the natural seasons. Each of these prayers has a summer and a winter phase. The shift to the summer version is introduced on the first day of Passover. The shift to the winter version is completed in two steps: the blessing on p. 46 is modified on the festival of Shemini Atseret, while the modification on p. 48 is made on the fifth of December.

41 Jerusalem Talmud, Berachos 5:2.

8. *Tachanun*—Supplications

On weekdays, the Amidah is immediately followed by *tachanun* (pp. 54–55, 59–60), in which we seek forgiveness from G-d.[42] On Monday and Thursday mornings, additional supplications are recited (pp. 56–59). None of these are recited on Shabbat, Jewish festivals, or days of special joy in the Jewish calendar or communal/personal experience.

In a congregational prayer with a *minyan*, the "half Kaddish" (p. 60) is recited after *tachanun*. On Monday and Thursday mornings, this is followed by a brief Torah reading (pp. 61–65). These are explained further below.

9. *Kedushah* and the Song of the Day

The next section (pp. 66–68) is a combination of passages culled from a variety of sources. We repeat Psalm 145 (p. 66) and the *kedushah* (pp. 67–68)—in which we echo the loving and reverential prayers sung by the angels. This entire section is omitted on Shabbat.

In a congregational prayer with a *minyan*, the complete Kaddish (p. 69) is recited after the completion of this section.

Our next prayer is the Song of the Day (pp. 71–75). A different psalm is recited for each day of the week. These were the psalms chanted by the Levitical choir each day in the Holy Temple.

42 When *tachanun* is recited with a *minyan*, the congregation chants the thirteen attributes of G-d's name (p. 55) in unison. When *tachanun* is recited without a *minyan*, these attributes are omitted. (These attributes are not chanted in the Ashkenazic tradition.) After this point, one sits and reads the rest of the *tachanun*. When *tachanun* is recited in a house where a Torah scroll is present, we lower the head onto the left arm while reciting *tachanun*. One who is wearing *tefilin* on the left arm lowers the head onto the right arm.

In a congregational prayer with a *minyan*, the Mourners' Kaddish is recited at this point (p. 77).

On Shabbat, the order of prayers following the Amidah is modified so that we immediately recite the Song of the Day for Shabbat (pp. 218–219), followed by a second Amidah referred to as *musaf* ("additional"—pp. 230–246).[43]

In a congregational prayer with a *minyan* on Shabbat, the entire weekly Torah portion is read before *musaf* (see pp. 222–230).

10. Conclusion

The next prayer (pp. 78–79 in the weekday prayers) is a hymn of praise, followed by a description of the incense offering that was brought in the Holy Temple.

In a congregational prayer with a *minyan*, *Rabbanan Kaddish* is recited at this point (p. 79).

Our morning prayers conclude with *aleinu* (p. 88), a famous prayer that many congregations sing to a widely familiar tune. This is an ancient prayer regarding G-d's sovereignty and our subservience to G-d's Kingship, authored by Joshua as he led the Jews into Israel some 3300 years ago.[44]

This final prayer is recited while standing. As we reach the words *vaanachnu kore'im* ("but we bend the knee"), we bend at the knees. At the word *umishtachavim* ("bow down"), we bow from the waist. We then stand erect for the rest of the prayer.

43 The *musaf* Amidah for Rosh Chodesh appears on pp. 313–320. The *musaf* Amidah for Rosh Chodesh that coincides with Shabbat appears on pp. 320–326. The *musaf* Amidah for festivals is on pages 340–350.

44 *Teshuvas Hage'onim, Shaarei Teshuvah* 44. See also *Kol Bo*, chapter 16.

In a congregational prayer with a *minyan*, the Mourners' Kaddish is recited at this point (p. 81).

C. *MINCHAH*—AFTERNOON PRAYER

It is preferable to recite the afternoon service (pp. 101–117) in the later part of the day. It is comprised of Psalm 145, the Amidah, supplications for forgiveness, and *aleinu*.

D. *ARVIT*—EVENING PRAYER

The evening prayer (pp. 118–135) may be recited after nightfall, preferably before midnight. It consists of the Shema and its surrounding blessings (two before the Shema and another two subsequent to the Shema), followed by the Amidah and *aleinu*. Although the themes of the blessings surrounding the Shema in the evening prayer are similar to those surrounding the Shema in the morning prayer, their texts are by no means identical.

III. Congregational Prayer

A. CHAZAN—LEADER

When a *minyan* gathers for communal prayer, one of those present is chosen to serve as the prayer leader (referred to as the *chazan*) for that prayer service. The *chazan* stands at the front of the group and chants aloud the beginning and end of each prayer. The *chazan* also leads entire congregational portions such as the repetition of the Amidah, Kaddish, *kedushah*, and *barchu*. On Shabbat and Jewish festivals, when the congregation is less hurried due to the prohibition against working on those days, the *chazan* often incorporates melodies into the service, and the congregation joins together in song.

B. CHAZARAT HASHATS—REPETITION OF THE AMIDAH

When praying with a *minyan*, the *chazan* repeats the entire Amidah aloud after the congregation has completed their silent reading of same text. Listening to this repetition and answering *amen* after each blessing allows those who cannot pray on their own to fulfill their obligation.[45] It is imperative that the congregants pay attention to the *chazan*'s prayers; chatting or even studying Torah is prohibited during the repetition.[46]

As the *chazan* pronounces G-d's name toward the end of each blessing, the congregation honors G-d by responding: *baruch Hu uvaruch Shemo* ("blessed is He and blessed is His name"). As the *chazan* concludes each blessing, the congregation responds with

45 Shulchan Aruch, *Orach Chayim* 124:1.
46 Ibid., 124:4.

amen, thereby affirming their belief that the words of the prayer are true. *Amen* also expresses the congregation's confidence that G-d will receive their prayers and grant their petitions.[47]

C. *KEDUSHAH*

This prayer echoes the reverential prayers of the angels in heaven, as described by the prophets. During the *chazan*'s repetition of the Amidah, this prayer is inserted immediately after the conclusion of the third blessing.

While reciting or singing these praises with the *chazan*, we strive to emulate the immense joy and reverence experienced by the heavenly angels as they recite these same phrases.[48] At the start of each stanza, we raise our eyes heavenward and rise lightly on our toes. This is done to mimic the angels' constant spiritual rise[49] and to indicate our desire to draw higher and closer to G-d.[50]

D. *BARCHU*—"BLESS G-D"

With this prayer, the *chazan* invites the congregation to bless G-d aloud, in unison. The *chazan* bows from the waist and proclaims: *barchu et Ado-nai Hamevorach* ("Bless G-d Who is blessed!") The congregation responds by similarly bowing from the waist and exclaiming: *barchu et Ado-nai Hamevorach le'olam va'ed* ("Blessed be G-d Who is blessed forever!") The *chazan* bows a second time and echoes the congregation's response.

This brief but powerful prayer summons us to pause and consider the tremendous significance of the prayer that we are about to

47 *Shulchan Aruch HaRav* 124:9.

48 *Anaf Yosef* on *kedushah* in the name of *Yaaros Devash.*

49 *Magen Avraham, Orach Chayim* 125:2.

50 *Shulchan Aruch HaRav, Orach Chayim* 125:3.

begin—the morning and evening Shema and its blessings. (An identical exchange is conducted before reading from the Torah.[51])

E. TORAH READING

When praying with a *minyan* on Mondays and Thursdays, as well as on Shabbat mornings and afternoons, the Torah scroll is removed from its ark and a portion is read.

The Torah is divided into large portions, and on each subsequent Shabbat morning, a successive portion is read so that the entire Torah is completed in the course of a year. Far briefer selections are read on Shabbat afternoons and on Monday and Thursday mornings. On those occasions, a number of opening verses from the upcoming Shabbat portion are read in advance.

The Torah is read on additional days, including Rosh Chodesh, fast days, Jewish festivals, and the High Holidays. On these dates, the selections are directly related to the theme of the day.

As the Torah is being read, each congregant should follow in a printed copy of the Torah. It is important to refrain from conversation during the reading.

After the reading, the scroll is raised high and held open for all to see. It is then lowered, closed, dressed in its mantel, and returned respectfully to its ark.

On Shabbat, Jewish festivals, and other special occasions, the last person summoned to the Torah reading chants the *haftarah*—a reading from the prophets—subsequent to the Torah reading.

51 Rabbi Nissan Mindel, *My Prayer* (Brooklyn, N.Y.: Merkos L'Inyonei Chinuch, 2000), p. 139.

F. KADDISH

Kaddish is a moving declaration of faith in G-d that petitions G-d to fully reveal His presence on earth. It is most familiar as the special prayer recited by mourners during the first eleven months following the passing of a parent. It is also recited annually on a *yahrzeit*—anniversary of a loved one's passing. The Mourners' Kaddish is recited at various points of the prayer service, as well as at a gravesite, at the conclusion of a funeral or unveiling, provided that ten Jewish men are present. With this prayer, mourners express their faith in the ultimate truth and justice of G-d's judgment, and they thereby continue the sacred mission of the deceased.

Nevertheless, the Kaddish is not restricted to mourners. At a number of junctures in the prayer services, the *chazan* recites the Kaddish.

Whenever it is recited, the congregation responds with *amen* in the appropriate places. The third *amen* (second in the Ashkenazic tradition) is followed by the words: *yehe Shmey rabbah mevarech le'alam ule'almei almaya yitbarech* ("May His great Name be blessed forever and to all eternity!"). These words are recited aloud. Our sages taught that reciting these words aloud and with complete concentration can overturn the severest of Heaven's decrees.[52]

There are four variations of Kaddish:

a. *The Half Kaddish* is recited by the *chazan* at specific points in the service. These serve to distinguish the various sections of the prayers.

b. *The Complete Kaddish* is recited by the *chazan* upon concluding the Amidah, for it includes a prayer that G-d grant all of our petitions, and the Amidah is replete with petitions.

52 *Shulchan Aruch HaRav, Orach Chayim* 69:2.

c. *Rabbanan Kaddish* ("the Kaddish for the rabbis") includes an additional prayer for Torah students and scholars. It is recited after a passage of rabbinical teachings (Mishnah or Talmud) is studied or recited in the presence of a *minyan*.

d. *The Mourners' Kaddish*, as described earlier.

AFTERWORD

Life skills are not acquired overnight, and the art of sincere and successful prayer is certainly no different. Rather, it must be approached, practiced, and perfected one step at a time. Add fresh insights and directions at a gradual pace into your prayer routine, and keep practicing. The more frequently you pray, the more familiar you will be with the nuanced customs and laws. Soon enough, it will all become routine, allowing you to advance to the next stage of inspiration and bonding with G-d, for prayer is a ladder that allows you to climb continuously higher into the heavens, rung after rung, bringing ever greater attachment and blessings down to its feet, which are firmly planted on earth.

Acknowledgments

"Prayer is for the soul what nourishment is for the body."

—RABBI YEHUDAH HALEVI, *KUZARI* 3:5

Deliberately or spontaneously, vocally or mentally, it is undeniable that humans are hardwired to pray. Perhaps a glad heart soaring on wings of gratitude or a reflexive response to tragedy or personal crisis; longing for a brighter future or solace to a lonely soul; an atheist in a foxhole or a card-carrying worshipper traveling an oft-journeyed highway to the Creator's throne room; amid joy at a wedding, tears at a funeral, or the ancient blast of a ram's horn on Rosh Hashanah: for endless reasons, humans pray.

It is also true that many find the concept of prayer, particularly formal prayer, distant and mysterious. In our era of high-tech self-absorption, prayer services are often seen as bewildering or daunting. The assumed tool of prayer, the prayer book, is a closed book for the uninitiated, each page inspiring further bafflement. Some find prayer boring, others confusing, and yet others archaic or senseless.

The Rohr Jewish Learning Institute (JLI) has set for itself the ambitious goal of tackling these challenges and restoring prayer, one of the Jewish nation's most precious and potent treasures, to its rightful place: the vibrant hearts and inspired minds of Jews worldwide. *With All My Heart* seeks to remove the barriers that prevent people from enjoying the gifts of meaningful and rewarding communication with their G-d whenever they need it most.

We are grateful to the following individuals for helping shape this innovative course:

Rabbis Mordechai Dinerman and **Naftali Silberberg,** who codirect the JLI Curriculum Department and the Flagship editorial team; **Rabbi Dr. Shmuel Klatzkin,** JLI's senior editor; and **Rabbi Zalman Abraham,** who skillfully provides the vision for strategic branding and marketing of JLI course offerings.

Rabbi Yosi Wolf played a leading role in designing and authoring this course. **Rabbi Lazer Gurkow** authored Lesson Five and "The How of Jewish Prayer," and **Rabbi Baruch Shalom Davidson** authored Lesson Six. **Rabbis Avrohom Bergstein** and **Yakov Gershon**—of JLI's Machon Shmuel: The Sami Rohr Research Institute—provided extensive research. **Shmuel Gomes** also assisted with writing some of the lessons.

Rabbi Leibel Fajnland, Rabbi Shmuel Kaplan, Rabbi Mordechai Newman, Rabbi Sholom Raichik, Rabbi Yosef Chaim Sufrin, and **Rabbi Avrohom Sternberg,** members of the JLI Editorial Board, spent many hours reviewing the course materials with the JLI team and provided numerous useful suggestions that have enhanced the course and ensured its suitability for a wide range of students.

Rivki Mockin streamlined the curriculum process and ensured the smoothness and timeliness of the product, and **Chana Dechter,** JLI Flagship's administrator, contributed immeasurably to the production and professionalism of the entire project. **Mushka Backman** provided editorial assistance, and **Rakefet Orobona, Mimi Palace, Rabbi Shmuel Super, Shmuel Telsner,** and **Ya'akovah Weber** enhanced the quality and accuracy of the writing with their proofreading. **Mushka Backman, Rivky Fieldsteel, Rabbi Zalman Korf,** and **Shternie Zaltzman** designed the textbooks with taste and expertise, and the textbook images were researched and selected by **Rabbi Zalman Abraham.**

Rabbi Mendel Sirota directed the book's publication and distribution.

Mushka Backman, Chany Block, and **Rivka Rapoport** designed the aesthetically pleasing PowerPoint presentations, and **Moshe Raskin** and **Getzy Raskin** produced the videos. Special thanks to **Rabbi Dr. Laibl Wolf**, noted lecturer and spiritual mentor, for his contribution to the meditative videos for this course. **Baila Goldstein** illustrated the artistic comics in Lesson Three. **Chaya Mushka Kanner** and **Shifra Tauber** tastefully designed the course marketing materials.

We are immensely grateful for the encouragement of JLI's visionary chairman, and vice-chairman of *Merkos L'Inyonei Chinuch*—Lubavitch World Headquarters, **Rabbi Moshe Kotlarsky**. Rabbi Kotlarsky has been highly instrumental in building the infrastructure for the expansion of Chabad's international network and is also the architect of scores of initiatives and services to help Chabad representatives across the globe succeed in their mission. We are blessed to have the unwavering support of JLI's principal benefactor, **Mr. George Rohr**, who is fully invested in our work, continues to be instrumental in JLI's monumental growth and expansion, and is largely responsible for the Jewish renaissance that is being spearheaded by JLI and its affiliates across the globe.

The commitment and sage direction of JLI's dedicated Executive Board—**Rabbis Chaim Block, Hesh Epstein, Ronnie Fine, Yosef Gansburg, Shmuel Kaplan, Yisrael Rice**, and **Avrohom Sternberg**—and the countless hours they devote to the development of JLI are what drive the vision, growth, and tremendous success of the organization.

Finally, JLI represents an incredible partnership of more than 1,400 *shluchim* and *shluchot* in more than 1,000 locations across the globe, who contribute their time and talent to further Jewish adult education. We thank them for generously sharing feedback and making suggestions that steer JLI's development and growth. They are our most valuable critics and our most cherished contributors.

Inspired by the call of the **Lubavitcher Rebbe**, of righteous memory, it is the mandate of the Rohr JLI to **provide a community of learning** for all Jews throughout the world where they can participate in their precious heritage of Torah learning and experience its rewards. May this course succeed in fulfilling this sacred charge!

On behalf of the Rohr Jewish Learning Institute,

RABBI EFRAIM MINTZ
Executive Director

RABBI YISRAEL RICE
Chairman, Editorial Board

10 Shevat, 5779

The Rohr Jewish Learning Institute

AN AFFILIATE OF MERKOS L'INYONEI CHINUCH,
THE EDUCATIONAL ARM OF THE CHABAD-LUBAVITCH MOVEMENT
822 EASTERN PARKWAY, BROOKLYN, NY 11213

CURRICULUM DEVELOPMENT

Rabbi Mordechai Dinerman
Rabbi Naftali Silberberg
EDITORS IN CHIEF

Rabbi Shmuel Klatzkin, PhD
Rabbi Yanki Tauber
SENIOR EDITORS

Rabbi Baruch Shalom Davidson
Rabbi Binyomin Bitton
Mr. Shmuel Gomes, M.A.
Rabbi Eliezer Gurkow
Rabbi Michoel Lipskier
Rabbi Ahrele Loschak
Rabbi Zalman Margolin
Rabbi Berry Piekarski
Rabbi Mendel Rubin
Rabbi Michoel Shapiro
Rabbi Shmuel Super
Rabbi Benyomin Walters
Rabbi Boruch Werdiger
Rabbi Yosi Wolf
CURRICULUM TEAM

Mrs. Rivki Mockin
CONTENT COORDINATOR

MARKETING AND BRANDING

Rabbi Zalman Abraham
DIRECTOR

Ms. Mashie Feldman
ADMINISTRATOR

Mrs. Chaya Mushka Kanner
Mrs. Shevi Rivkin
Mrs. Shifra Tauber
Mrs. Rikkie Wolf
GRAPHIC DESIGN

Mrs. Chany Block
Mrs. Rivky Fieldsteel
Rabbi Zalman Korf
Mrs. Shternie Zaltzman
PUBLICATION DESIGN

Lazer Cohen
SOCIAL MEDIA

Yisroel Beenstock
MARKETING FOR RESULTS

Rabbi Yaakov Paley
WRITER

Rabbi Yossi Grossbaum
Rabbi Mendel Lifshitz
Rabbi Mendel Teldon
Rabbi Shraga Sherman
Rabbi Ari Sollish
MARKETING COMMITTEE

MARKETING CONSULTANTS

JJ Gross
Israel

Warren Modlin
MEDNETPRO, INC.
Orange County, CA

Alan Rosenspan
ALAN ROSENSPAN & ASSOCIATES
Sharon, MA

Gary Wexler
PASSION MARKETING
Los Angeles, CA

Joseph Jaffe
EVOL8TION
New York, NY

JLI CENTRAL

Ms. Rochel Karp
Ms. Devorah Kotlarsky
Mrs. Aliza Mayteles
Ms. Adina Posner
Mrs. Mussie Sputz
ADMINISTRATION

Rabbi Mendel Sirota
AFFILIATE SUPPORT

Rabbi Shlomie Tenenbaum
PROJECT MANAGER

Mrs. Mindy Wallach
AFFILIATE ORIENTATION

Ms. Mushka Backman
Mrs. Chany Block
Mrs. Bunia Chazan
Mrs. Mushka Druk
Mrs. Baila Goldstein
Mendel Laine
Getzy Raskin
Moshe Raskin
MULTIMEDIA DEVELOPMENT

Rabbi Sholom Cohen
Rabbi Mendy Elishevitz
Mendel Grossbaum
Mrs. Rochie Rivkin
Mrs. Chana Weinbaum
ONLINE DIVISION

Dr. Rakefet Orobona
Ms. Mimi Palace
Mrs. Ya'akovah Weber
PROOFREADERS

Rabbi Mendel Sirota
PRINTING AND DISTRIBUTION

Mrs. Musie Liberow
Mrs. Shaina B. Mintz
Mrs. Shulamis Nadler
ACCOUNTING

Rabbi Zalman Abraham
Ms. Mushka Backman
Mrs. Shulamis Nadler
Mrs. Mindy Wallach
Mr. Yehuda Wengrofsky
DEVELOPMENT

Mrs. Musie Liberow
Mrs. Mindy Wallach
CONTINUING EDUCATION

JLI FLAGSHIP

Rabbi Yisrael Rice
CHAIRMAN

Mrs. Chana Dechter
PROJECT MANAGER

Rabbi Yisroel Altein
Rabbi Hesh Epstein
Rabbi Sholom Raichik
Mrs. Michla Schanowitz
Rabbi Shraga Sherman
Mrs. Rivkah Slonim
Rabbi Ari Sollish
Rabbi Avraham Steinmetz
Rabbi Avrohom Sternberg
EDITORIAL BOARD

JLI INTERNATIONAL

Rabbi Avrohom Sternberg
CHAIRMAN

Rabbi Dubi Rabinowitz
DIRECTOR

Rabbi Berry Piekarski
ADMINISTRATOR

Rabbi Yosef Yitzchok Noyman
ADMINISTRATOR, JLI ISRAEL
IN PARTNERSHIP WITH
MIVTZA TORAH—ISRAEL

Rabbi Eli Wolf
ADMINISTRATOR, JLI IN THE CIS
IN PARTNERSHIP WITH
THE FEDERATION OF JEWISH
COMMUNITIES OF THE CIS

Rabbi Shevach Zlatopolsky
EDITOR, JLI IN THE CIS

Rabbi Nochum Schapiro
REGIONAL REPRESENTATIVE,
AUSTRALIA

Rabbi Avraham Golovacheov
REGIONAL REPRESENTATIVE,
GERMANY

Rabbi Shmuel Katzman
REGIONAL REPRESENTATIVE,
NETHERLANDS

Rabbi Avrohom Steinmetz
REGIONAL REPRESENTATIVE,
BRAZIL

Rabbi Bentzi Sudak
REGIONAL REPRESENTATIVE,
UNITED KINGDOM

Rabbi Mendel Edelman
LIAISON TO FRENCH-SPEAKING
COUNTRIES

NATIONAL JEWISH RETREAT

Rabbi Hesh Epstein
CHAIRMAN

Mrs. Shaina B. Mintz
DIRECTOR

Bruce Backman
HOTEL LIAISON

Rabbi Menachem Klein
PROGRAM COORDINATOR

Rabbi Shmuly Karp
SHLUCHIM LIAISON

Rabbi Mendel Rosenfeld
LOGISTIC COORDINATOR

Ms. Rochel Karp
Mrs. Aliza Mayteles
Mrs. Mussie Sputz
SERVICE AND SUPPORT

JLI LAND & SPIRIT

ISRAEL EXPERIENCE

Rabbi Shmuly Karp
DIRECTOR

Mrs. Shaina B. Mintz
ADMINISTRATOR

Rabbi Yechiel Baitelman
Rabbi Dovid Flinkenstein
Rabbi Chanoch Kaplan
Rabbi Levi Klein
Rabbi Mendel Lifshitz
Rabbi Mendy Mangel
Rabbi Sholom Raichik
Rabbi Ephraim Silverman
STEERING COMMITTEE

SHABBAT IN THE HEIGHTS

Rabbi Shmuly Karp
DIRECTOR

Mrs. Shulamis Nadler
SERVICE AND SUPPORT

Rabbi Chaim Hanoka
CHAIRMAN

Rabbi Mordechai Dinerman
Rabbi Zalman Marcus
STEERING COMMITTEE

MYSHIUR

ADVANCED LEARNING INITIATIVE

Rabbi Shmuel Kaplan
CHAIRMAN

Rabbi Levi Kaplan
DIRECTOR

TORAHCAFE.COM

ONLINE LEARNING

Rabbi Mendy Elishevitz
WEBSITE DEVELOPMENT

Moshe Levin
CONTENT MANAGER

Avrohom Shimon Ezagui
FILMING

MACHON SHMUEL

THE SAMI ROHR RESEARCH INSTITUTE

Rabbi Avrohom Bergstein
DEAN

Rabbi Zalman Korf
ADMINISTRATOR

Rabbi Gedalya Oberlander
Rabbi Chaim Rapoport
Rabbi Levi Yitzchak Raskin
Rabbi Chaim Schapiro
Rabbi Moshe Miller
RABBINIC ADVISORY BOARD

Rabbi Yakov Gershon
RESEARCH FELLOW

FOUNDING DEPARTMENT HEADS

Rabbi Mendel Bell
Rabbi Zalman Charytan
Rabbi Mendel Druk
Rabbi Menachem Gansburg
Rabbi Meir Hecht
Rabbi Levi Kaplan
Rabbi Yoni Katz
Rabbi Chaim Zalman Levy
Rabbi Benny Rapoport
Dr. Chana Silberstein
Rabbi Elchonon Tenenbaum
Rabbi Mendy Weg

Faculty Directory

ALABAMA

BIRMINGHAM
Rabbi Yossi Friedman 205.970.0100

MOBILE
Rabbi Yosef Goldwasser 251.265.1213

ALASKA

ANCHORAGE
Rabbi Yosef Greenberg
Rabbi Mendy Greenberg 907.357.8770

ARIZONA

CHANDLER
Rabbi Mendy Deitsch 480.855.4333

FLAGSTAFF
Rabbi Dovie Shapiro 928.255.5756

FOUNTAIN HILLS
Rabbi Mendy Lipskier 480.776.4763

ORO VALLEY
Rabbi Ephraim Zimmerman 520.477.8672

PHOENIX
Rabbi Zalman Levertov
Rabbi Yossi Friedman 602.944.2753

SCOTTSDALE
Rabbi Yossi Levertov 480.998.1410

TUCSON
Rabbi Yehuda Ceitlin 520.881.7956

ARKANSAS

LITTLE ROCK
Rabbi Pinchus Ciment 501.217.0053

CALIFORNIA

AGOURA HILLS
Rabbi Moshe Bryski
Rabbi Yisroel Levine 818.991.0991

BAKERSFIELD
Rabbi Shmuli Schlanger
Mrs. Esther Schlanger 661.331.1695

BEL AIR
Rabbi Chaim Mentz 310.475.5311

BERKELEY
Rabbi Yosef Romano 510.396.4448

BURBANK
Rabbi Shmuly Kornfeld 818.954.0070

CARLSBAD
Rabbi Yeruchem Eilfort
Mrs. Nechama Eilfort 760.943.8891

CHATSWORTH
Rabbi Yossi Spritzer 818.718.0777

CONTRA COSTA
Rabbi Dovber Berkowitz 925.937.4101

CORONADO
Rabbi Eli Fradkin 619.365.4728

ENCINO
Rabbi Aryeh Herzog 818.784.9986
Chapter founded by Rabbi Joshua Gordon, OBM

FOLSOM
Rabbi Yossi Grossbaum 916.608.9811

FREMONT
Rabbi Moshe Fuss 510.300.4090

GLENDALE
Rabbi Simcha Backman 818.240.2750

HUNTINGTON BEACH
Rabbi Aron David Berkowitz 714.846.2285

LA JOLLA
Rabbi Baruch Shalom Ezagui 858.455.5433

LOMITA
Rabbi Eli Hecht
Rabbi Sholom Pinson 310.326.8234

LONG BEACH
Rabbi Abba Perelmuter 562.621.9828

LOS ANGELES
Rabbi Leibel Korf 323.660.5177

MALIBU
Rabbi Levi Cunin 310.456.6588

MARINA DEL REY
Rabbi Danny Yiftach-Hashem
Rabbi Dovid Yiftach 310.859.0770

NORTH HOLLYWOOD
Rabbi Nachman Abend 818.989.9539

NORTHRIDGE
Rabbi Eli Rivkin 818.368.3937

OJAI
Rabbi Mordechai Nemtzov 805.613.7181

PACIFIC PALISADES
Rabbi Zushe Cunin 310.454.7783

PALO ALTO
Rabbi Yosef Levin
Rabbi Ber Rosenblatt 650.424.9800

PASADENA
Rabbi Chaim Hanoka
Rabbi Sholom Stiefel 626.539.4578

PLEASANTON
Rabbi Josh Zebberman 925.846.0700

POWAY
Rabbi Mendel Goldstein 858.208.6613

RANCHO MIRAGE
Rabbi Shimon H. Posner 760.770.7785

RANCHO PALOS VERDES
Rabbi Yitzchok Magalnic 310.544.5544

RANCHO S. FE
Rabbi Levi Raskin 858.756.7571

REDONDO BEACH
Rabbi Yossi Mintz
Rabbi Zalman Gordon 310.214.4999

RIVERSIDE
Rabbi Shmuel Fuss 951.329.2747

S. CLEMENTE
Rabbi Menachem M. Slavin 949.489.0723

S. CRUZ
Rabbi Yochanan Friedman 831.454.0101

S. DIEGO
Rabbi Rafi Andrusier 619.387.8770
Rabbi Motte Fradkin 858.547.0076

S. FRANCISCO
Rabbi Shlomo Zarchi 415.752.2866

S. LUIS OBISPO
Rabbi Chaim Leib Hilel 805.229.1836

S. MONICA
Rabbi Boruch Rabinowitz 310.394.5699

S. RAFAEL
Rabbi Yisrael Rice 415.492.1666

SACRAMENTO
Rabbi Mendy Cohen 916.455.1400

SOUTH LAKE TAHOE
Rabbi Mordechai Richler 530.314.7677

SUNNYVALE
Rabbi Yisroel Hecht 408.720.0553

TUSTIN
Rabbi Yehoshua Eliezrie 714.508.2150

VENTURA
Rabbi Yakov Latowicz 805.658.7441

WEST HOLLYWOOD
Rabbi Mordechai Kirschenbaum 310.275.1215

WEST LOS ANGELES
Rabbi Mordechai Zaetz 424.652.8742

YORBA LINDA
Rabbi Dovid Eliezrie 714.693.0770

COLORADO

ASPEN
Rabbi Mendel Mintz 970.544.3770

DENVER
Rabbi Yossi Serebryanski 303.744.9699

FORT COLLINS
Rabbi Yerachmiel Gorelik 970.407.1613

HIGHLANDS RANCH
Rabbi Avraham Mintz 303.694.9119

LONGMONT
Rabbi Yakov Borenstein 303.678.7595

VAIL
Rabbi Dovid Mintz 970.476.7887

WESTMINSTER
Rabbi Benjy Brackman 303.429.5177

CONNECTICUT

FAIRFIELD
Rabbi Shlame Landa 203.373.7551

GLASTONBURY
Rabbi Yosef Wolvovsky 860.659.2422

GREENWICH
Rabbi Yossi Deren
Rabbi Menachem Feldman 203.629.9059

MILFORD
Rabbi Schneur Wilhelm 203.887.7603

NEW LONDON
Rabbi Avrohom Sternberg 860.437.8000

STAMFORD
Rabbi Yisrael Deren
Rabbi Levi Mendelow 203.3.CHABAD

WEST HARTFORD
Rabbi Shaya Gopin 860.232.1116

WESTPORT
Rabbi Yehuda L. Kantor 203.226.8584

DELAWARE

WILMINGTON
Rabbi Chuni Vogel 302.529.9900

DISTRICT OF COLUMBIA

WASHINGTON
Rabbi Levi Shemtov
Rabbi Shua Hecht 202.332.5600

FLORIDA

ALTAMONTE SPRINGS
Rabbi Mendy Bronstein 407.280.0535

BAL HARBOUR
Rabbi Dov Schochet 305.868.1411

BOCA RATON
Rabbi Zalman Bukiet
Rabbi Arele Gopin 561.994.6257
Rabbi Moishe Denburg 561.526.5760
Rabbi Ruvi New 561.394.9770

BOYNTON BEACH
Rabbi Yosef Yitzchok Raichik 561.732.4633

BRADENTON
Rabbi Menachem Bukiet 941.388.9656

SOUTHWEST BROWARD COUNTY
Rabbi Aryeh Schwartz 954.252.1770

CAPE CORAL
Rabbi Yossi Labkowski 239.963.4770

CORAL GABLES
Rabbi Avrohom Stolik 305.490.7572

CORAL SPRINGS
Rabbi Yankie Denburg 954.471.8646

DELRAY BEACH
Rabbi Sholom Ber Korf 561.496.6228

FISHER ISLAND
Rabbi Efraim Brody 347.325.1913

FLEMING ISLAND
Rabbi Shmuly Feldman 904.290.1017

FORT LAUDERDALE
Rabbi Yitzchok Naparstek 954.568.1190

FORT MYERS
Rabbi Yitzchok Minkowicz
Mrs. Nechama Minkowicz 239.433.7708

HALLANDALE BEACH
Rabbi Mordy Feiner 954.458.1877

HOLLYWOOD
Rabbi Leizer Barash 954.965.9933
Rabbi Leibel Kudan 954.801.3367

KENDALL
Rabbi Yossi Harlig 305.234.5654

LAKELAND
Rabbi Moshe Lazaros 863.510.5968

LONGWOOD
Rabbi Yanky Majesky 407.636.5994

MAITLAND
Rabbi Sholom Dubov
Rabbi Levik Dubov 470.644.2500

MIAMI
Rabbi Yakov Fellig 305.445.5444

MIAMI BEACH
Rabbi Yisroel Frankforter 305.534.3895

N. MIAMI BEACH
Rabbi Eli Laufer 305.770.4412

OCALA
Rabbi Yossi Hecht 352.330.4466

ORLANDO
Rabbi Yosef Konikov 407.354.3660

ORMOND BEACH
Rabbi Asher Farkash 386.672.9300

PALM BEACH GARDENS
Rabbi Dovid Vigler 561.624.2223

PALM CITY
Rabbi Shlomo Uminer 772.288.0606

PALM HARBOR
Rabbi Pinchas Adler 727.789.0408

PALMETTO BAY
Rabbi Zalman Gansburg 786.282.0413

PARKLAND
Rabbi Mendy Gutnick 954.796.7330

PEMBROKE PINES
Rabbi Mordechai Andrusier 954.874.2280

PLANTATION
Rabbi Pinchas Taylor 954.644.9177

PONTE VEDRA BEACH
Rabbi Nochum Kurinsky 904.543.9301

S. AUGUSTINE
Rabbi Levi Vogel 904.521.8664

S. PETERSBURG
Rabbi Alter Korf 727.344.4900

SARASOTA
Rabbi Chaim Shaul Steinmetz 941.925.0770

SATELLITE BEACH
Rabbi Zvi Konikov 321.777.2770

SOUTH PALM BEACH
Rabbi Leibel Stolik 561.889.3499

SOUTH TAMPA
Rabbi Mendy Dubrowski 813.922.1723

SUNNY ISLES BEACH
Rabbi Alexander Kaller 305.803.5315

TALLAHASSEE
Rabbi Schneur Oirechman 850.523.9294

VENICE
Rabbi Sholom Ber Schmerling 941.493.2770

WELLINGTON
Rabbi Mendy Muskal 561.333.4663

WESLEY CHAPEL
Rabbi Mendy Yarmush
Rabbi Mendel Friedman 813.731.2977

WESTON
Rabbi Yisroel Spalter 954.349.6565

WEST PALM BEACH
Rabbi Yoel Gancz 561.659.7770

GEORGIA

ALPHARETTA
Rabbi Hirshy Minkowicz 770.410.9000

ATLANTA
Rabbi Yossi New
Rabbi Isser New 404.843.2464

ATLANTA: INTOWN
Rabbi Eliyahu Schusterman
Rabbi Ari Sollish 404.898.0434

CUMMING
Rabbi Levi Mentz 310.666.2218

GWINNETT
Rabbi Yossi Lerman 678.595.0196

MARIETTA
Rabbi Ephraim Silverman 770.565.4412

IDAHO

BOISE
Rabbi Mendel Lifshitz 208.853.9200

ILLINOIS

CHICAGO
Rabbi Mendy Benhiyoun 312.498.7704
Rabbi Meir Hecht 312.714.4655
Rabbi Dovid Kotlarsky 773.495.7127
Rabbi Yosef Moscowitz 773.772.3770
Rabbi Levi Notik 773.274.5123

DES PLAINES
Rabbi Lazer Hershkovich 224.392.4442

ELGIN
Rabbi Mendel Shemtov 847.440.4486

GLENVIEW
Rabbi Yishaya Benjaminson 847.910.1738

HIGHLAND PARK
Mrs. Michla Schanowitz 847.266.0770

NORTHBROOK
Rabbi Meir Moscowitz 847.564.8770

OAK PARK
Rabbi Yitzchok Bergstein 708.524.1530

PEORIA
Rabbi Eli Langsam 309.692.2250

ROCKFORD
Rabbi Yecheskel Rothman 815.596.0032

SKOKIE
Rabbi Yochanan Posner 847.677.1770

VERNON HILLS
Rabbi Shimmy Susskind 847.984.2919

WILMETTE
Rabbi Dovid Flinkenstein 847.251.7707

INDIANA

INDIANAPOLIS
Rabbi Avraham Grossbaum
Rabbi Dr. Shmuel Klatzkin 317.251.5573

IOWA

BETTENDORF
Rabbi Shneur Cadaner 563.355.1065

KANSAS

OVERLAND PARK
Rabbi Mendy Wineberg 913.649.4852

KENTUCKY

LOUISVILLE
Rabbi Avrohom Litvin 502.459.1770

LOUISIANA

BATON ROUGE
Rabbi Peretz Kazen 225.267.7047

METAIRIE
Rabbi Yossie Nemes
Rabbi Mendel Ceitlin 504.454.2910

MARYLAND

BALTIMORE
Rabbi Velvel Belinsky 410.764.5000
Classes in Russian

BEL AIR
Rabbi Kushi Schusterman 443.353.9718

BETHESDA
Rabbi Sender Geisinsky 301.913.9777

CHEVY CHASE
Rabbi Zalman Minkowitz 301.260.5000

CLARKSBURG
Rabbi Yehuda Glick 301.337.0514

COLUMBIA
Rabbi Hillel Baron
Rabbi Yosef Chaim Sufrin 410.740.2424

FREDERICK
Rabbi Boruch Labkowski 301.996.3659

GAITHERSBURG
Rabbi Sholom Raichik 301.926.3632

OLNEY
Rabbi Bentzy Stolik 301.660.6770

OWINGS MILLS
Rabbi Nochum H. Katsenelenbogen 410.356.5156

POTOMAC
Rabbi Mendel Bluming 301.983.4200
Rabbi Mendel Kaplan 301.983.1485

ROCKVILLE
Rabbi Moishe Kavka 301.836.1242

MASSACHUSETTS

ANDOVER
Rabbi Asher Bronstein 978.470.2288

BOSTON
Rabbi Yosef Zaklos 617.297.7282

BIGHTON
Rabbi Dan Rodkin 617.787.2200

CAPE COD
Rabbi Yekusiel Alperowitz 508.775.2324

HINGHAM
Rabbi Levi Lezell 617.862.2770

LONGMEADOW
Rabbi Yakov Wolff 413.567.8665

NEWTON
Rabbi Shalom Ber Prus 617.244.1200

SUDBURY
Rabbi Yisroel Freeman 978.443.0110

SWAMPSCOTT
Rabbi Yossi Lipsker
Rabbi Yisroel Baron 781.581.3833

MICHIGAN

ANN ARBOR
Rabbi Aharon Goldstein 734.995.3276

BLOOMFIELD HILLS
Rabbi Levi Dubov 248.949.6210

GRAND RAPIDS
Rabbi Mordechai Haller 616.957.0770

WEST BLOOMFIELD
Rabbi Elimelech Silberberg 248.855.6170

MINNESOTA

MINNETONKA
Rabbi Mordechai Grossbaum
Rabbi Shmuel Silberstein 952.929.9922

S. PAUL
Rabbi Shneur Zalman Bendet 651.998.9298

MISSOURI

S. LOUIS
Rabbi Yosef Landa 314.725.0400

NEVADA

LAS VEGAS
Rabbi Yosef Rivkin 702.217.2170

SUMMERLIN
Rabbi Yisroel Schanowitz
Rabbi Tzvi Bronchtain 702.855.0770

NEW JERSEY

BASKING RIDGE
Rabbi Mendy Herson
Rabbi Mendel Shemtov 908.604.8844

CHERRY HILL
Rabbi Mendel Mangel 856.874.1500

CLINTON
Rabbi Eli Kornfeld 908.623.7000

FAIR LAWN
Rabbi Avrohom Bergstein 201.362.2712

FORT LEE
Rabbi Meir Konikov 201.886.1238

FRANKLIN LAKES
Rabbi Chanoch Kaplan 201.848.0449

GREATER MERCER COUNTY
Rabbi Dovid Dubov
Rabbi Yaakov Chaiton 609.213.4136

HASKELL
Rabbi Mendy Gurkov 201.696.7609

HOLMDEL
Rabbi Shmaya Galperin 732.772.1998

MADISON
Rabbi Shalom Lubin 973.377.0707

MANALAPAN
Rabbi Boruch Chazanow
Rabbi Levi Wolosow 732.972.3687

MEDFORD
Rabbi Yitzchok Kahan 609.451.3522

MOUNTAIN LAKES
Rabbi Levi Dubinsky 973.551.1898

MULLICA HILL
Rabbi Avrohom Richler 856.733.0770

OLD TAPPAN
Rabbi Mendy Lewis 201.767.4008

ROCKAWAY
Rabbi Asher Herson
Rabbi Mordechai Baumgarten 973.625.1525

RUTHERFORD
Rabbi Yitzchok Lerman 347.834.7500

SCOTCH PLAINS
Rabbi Avrohom Blesofsky 908.790.0008

SHORT HILLS
Rabbi Mendel Solomon
Rabbi Avrohom Levin 973.725.7008

SOUTH BRUNSWICK
Rabbi Levi Azimov 732.398.9492

TENAFLY
Rabbi Mordechai Shain 201.871.1152

TOMS RIVER
Rabbi Moshe Gourarie 732.349.4199

VENTNOR
Rabbi Avrohom Rapoport 609.822.8500

WAYNE
Rabbi Michel Gurkov 973.694.6274

WEST ORANGE
Rabbi Mendy Kasowitz 973.325.6311

WOODCLIFF LAKE
Rabbi Dov Drizin 201.476.0157

NEW MEXICO

LAS CRUCES
Rabbi Bery Schmukler 575.524.1330

NEW YORK

BAY SHORE
Rabbi Shimon Stillerman 631.913.8770

BEDFORD
Rabbi Arik Wolf 914.666.6065

BINGHAMTON
Mrs. Rivkah Slonim 607.797.0015

BRIGHTON BEACH
Rabbi Moshe Winner 718.946.9833

CEDARHURST
Rabbi Zalman Wolowik 516.295.2478

COMMACK
Rabbi Mendel Teldon 631.543.3343

DOBBS FERRY
Rabbi Benjy Silverman 914.693.6100

EAST HAMPTON
Rabbi Leibel Baumgarten
Rabbi Mendy Goldberg 631.329.5800

ELLENVILLE
Rabbi Shlomie Deren 845.647.4450

FOREST HILLS
Rabbi Yossi Mendelson 917.861.9726

GREAT NECK
Rabbi Yoseph Geisinsky 516.487.4554

KINGSTON
Rabbi Yitzchok Hecht 845.334.9044

LARCHMONT
Rabbi Mendel Silberstein 914.834.4321

LITTLE NECK
Rabbi Eli Shifrin 718.423.1235

LONG BEACH
Rabbi Eli Goodman 516.897.2473

NYC KEHILATH JESHURUN
Rabbi Elie Weinstock 212.774.5636

NYC UPPER EAST SIDE
Rabbi Uriel Vigler 212.369.7310

NYACK
Rabbi Chaim Zvi Ehrenreich 845.356.6686

OCEANSIDE
Rabbi Levi Gurkow 516.764.7385

OSSINING
Rabbi Dovid Labkowski 914.923.2522

OYSTER BAY
Rabbi Shmuel Lipszyc
Rabbi Shalom Lipszyc 347.853.9992

PARK SLOPE
Rabbi Menashe Wolf 347.957.1291

PORT WASHINGTON
Rabbi Shalom Paltiel 516.767.8672

PROSPECT HEIGHTS
Rabbi Mendy Hecht 347.622.3599

ROCHESTER
Rabbi Nechemia Vogel 585.271.0330

ROSLYN
Rabbi Yaakov Reiter 516.484.8185

SEA GATE
Rabbi Chaim Brikman 917.975.2792

SOUTHAMPTON
Rabbi Chaim Pape 917.627.4865

STATEN ISLAND
Rabbi Mendy Katzman 718.370.8953

STONY BROOK
Rabbi Shalom Ber Cohen 631.585.0521

SUFFERN
Rabbi Shmuel Gancz 845.368.1889

YORKTOWN HEIGHTS
Rabbi Yehuda Heber 914.962.1111

NORTH CAROLINA

ASHEVILLE
Rabbi Shaya Susskind 828.505.0746

CARY
Rabbi Yisroel Cotlar 919.651.9710

CHARLOTTE
Rabbi Yossi Groner
Rabbi Shlomo Cohen 704.366.3984

GREENSBORO
Rabbi Yosef Plotkin 336.617.8120

RALEIGH
Rabbi Pinchas Herman
Rabbi Lev Cotlar 919.637.6950

OHIO

BEACHWOOD
Rabbi Shmuli Friedman 216.282.0112

BLUE ASH
Rabbi Yisroel Mangel 513.793.5200

COLUMBUS
Rabbi Yitzi Kaltmann 614.294.3296

DAYTON
Rabbi Nochum Mangel
Rabbi Shmuel Klatzkin 937.643.0770

OKLAHOMA

OKLAHOMA CITY
Rabbi Ovadia Goldman 405.524.4800

TULSA
Rabbi Yehuda Weg 918.492.4499

OREGON

PORTLAND
Rabbi Mordechai Wilhelm 503.977.9947

SALEM
Rabbi Avrohom Yitzchok Perlstein 503.383.9569

PENNSYLVANIA

AMBLER
Rabbi Shaya Deitsch 215.591.9310

BALA CYNWYD
Rabbi Shraga Sherman 610.660.9192

LAFAYETTE HILL
Rabbi Yisroel Kotlarsky 484.533.7009

LANCASTER
Rabbi Elazar Green 717.368.6565

MONROEVILLE
Rabbi Mendy Schapiro 412.372.1000

NEWTOWN
Rabbi Aryeh Weinstein 215.497.9925

PHILADELPHIA: CENTER CITY
Rabbi Yochonon Goldman 215.238.2100

PITTSBURGH
Rabbi Yisroel Altein .... 412.422.7300 EXT. 269

PITTSBURGH: SOUTH HILLS
Rabbi Mendy Rosenblum 412.278.3693

RYDAL
Rabbi Zushe Gurevitz 267.536.5757

WYNNEWOOD
Rabbi Moishe Brennan 610.529.9011

PUERTO RICO

CAROLINA
Rabbi Mendel Zarchi 787.253.0894

RHODE ISLAND

WARWICK
Rabbi Yossi Laufer 401.884.7888

SOUTH CAROLINA

COLUMBIA
Rabbi Hesh Epstein
Rabbi Levi Marrus 803.782.1831

MYRTLE BEACH
Rabbi Doron Aizenman 843.448.0035

TENNESSEE

CHATTANOOGA
Rabbi Shaul Perlstein 423.490.1106

MEMPHIS
Rabbi Levi Klein 901.754.0404

TEXAS

ARLINGTON
Rabbi Levi Gurevitch 817.451.1171

BELLAIRE
Rabbi Yossi Zaklikofsky 713.839.8887

DALLAS
Rabbi Mendel Dubrawsky
Rabbi Moshe Naparstek 972.818.0770

FORT WORTH
Rabbi Dov Mandel 817.263.7701

FRISCO
Rabbi Mendy Kesselman 214.460.7773

HOUSTON
Rabbi Dovid Goldstein
Rabbi Zally Lazarus 281.589.7188
Rabbi Moishe Traxler 713.774.0300

HOUSTON: RICE UNIVERSITY AREA
Rabbi Eliezer Lazaroff 713.522.2004

LEAGUE CITY
Rabbi Yitzchok Schmukler 281.724.1554

MISSOURI CITY
Rabbi Mendel Feigenson 832.758.0685

PLANO
Rabbi Mendel Block
Rabbi Yehudah Horowitz 972.596.8270

S. ANTONIO
Rabbi Chaim Block
Rabbi Levi Teldon 210.492.1085

THE WOODLANDS
Rabbi Mendel Blecher 281.719.5213

UTAH

SALT LAKE CITY
Rabbi Benny Zippel 801.467.7777

VERMONT

BURLINGTON
Rabbi Yitzchok Raskin 802.658.5770

VIRGINIA

ALEXANDRIA/ARLINGTON
Rabbi Mordechai Newman 703.370.2774

FAIRFAX
Rabbi Leibel Fajnland 703.426.1980

GAINESVILLE
Rabbi Shmuel Perlstein 571.445.0342

NORFOLK
Rabbi Aaron Margolin
Rabbi Levi Brashevitzky 757.616.0770

TYSONS CORNER
Rabbi Chezzy Deitsch 703.829.5770
Chapter founded by Rabbi Levi Deitsch, OBM

WASHINGTON

BELLINGHAM
Rabbi Yosef Truxton 360.224.9919

MERCER ISLAND
Rabbi Elazar Bogomilsky 206.527.1411

OLYMPIA
Rabbi Yosef Schtroks 360.867.8804

SPOKANE COUNTY
Rabbi Yisroel Hahn 509.443.0770

WISCONSIN

BAYSIDE
Rabbi Cheski Edelman 414.439.5041

KENOSHA
Rabbi Tzali Wilschanski 262.359.0770

MADISON
Rabbi Avremel Matusof 608.231.3450

MILWAUKEE
Rabbi Mendel Shmotkin 414.961.6100

WAUKESHA
Rabbi Levi Brook 925.708.4203

ARGENTINA

BUENOS AIRES
Mrs. Chani Gorowitz 54.11.4865.0445
Rabbi Mendi Mizrahi 54.11.4963.1221
Rabbi Mendy Gurevitch 55.11.4545.7771
Rabbi Pinhas Sudry 54.1.4822.2285
Rabbi Shloimi Setton 54.11.4982.8637
Rabbi Shiele Plotka 54.11.4634.3111
Rabbi Yosef Levy 54.11.4504.1908

SALTA
Rabbi Rafael Tawil 54.387.421.4947

AUSTRALIA

NEW SOUTH WALES

DOUBLE BAY
Rabbi Yanky Berger
Rabbi Yisroel Dolnikov 612.9327.1644

QUEENSLAND

BRISBANE
Rabbi Levi Jaffe 617.3843.6770

DOVER HEIGHTS
Rabbi Motti Feldman 614.0400.8572

NORTH SHORE
Rabbi Nochum Schapiro
Mrs. Fruma Schapiro 612.9488.9548

VICTORIA

MOORABBIN
Rabbi Elisha Greenbaum 614.0349.0434

WESTERN AUSTRALIA

PERTH
Rabbi Shalom White 618.9275.2106

AZERBAIJAN

BAKU
Mrs. Chavi Segal 994.12.597.91.90

BELARUS

BOBRUISK
Mrs. Mina Hababo 375.29.104.3230

MINSK
Rabbi Shneur Deitsch
Mrs. Bassie Deitsch 375.29.330.6675

BRAZIL

CURITIBA
Rabbi Mendy Labkowski 55.41.3079.1338

S. PAULO
Rabbi Avraham Steinmetz 55.11.3081.3081

CANADA

ALBERTA

CALGARY
Rabbi Mordechai Groner 403.281.3770

EDMONTON
Rabbi Ari Drelich
Rabbi Mendy Blachman 780.200.5770

BRITISH COLUMBIA

KELOWNA
Rabbi Shmuly Hecht 250.575.5384

RICHMOND
Rabbi Yechiel Baitelman 604.277.6427

VANCOUVER
Rabbi Dovid Rosenfeld 604.266.1313

VICTORIA
Rabbi Meir Kaplan 250.595.7656

MANITOBA

WINNIPEG
Rabbi Shmuel Altein 204.339.8737

ONTARIO

LAWRENCE/EGLINTON
Rabbi Menachem Gansburg 416.546.8770

MAPLE
Rabbi Yechezkel Deren 647.883.6372

MISSISSAUGA
Rabbi Yitzchok Slavin 905.820.4432

NIAGARA FALLS
Rabbi Zalman Zaltzman 905.356.7200

OTTAWA
Rabbi Menachem M. Blum 613.843.7770

RICHMOND HILL
Rabbi Mendel Bernstein 905.770.7700

GREATER TORONTO REGIONAL OFFICE & THORNHILL
Rabbi Yossi Gansburg 905.731.7000

THORNHILL WOODS
Rabbi Chaim Hildeshaim 905.881.1919

WATERLOO
Rabbi Moshe Goldman 226.338.7770

WHITBY
Rabbi Tzali Borenstein 905.493.9007

YORK MILLS
Rabbi Levi Gansburg 416.551.9391

QUEBEC

HAMPSTEAD
Rabbi Moshe New
Rabbi Berel Bell 514.739.0770

MONTREAL
Rabbi Ronnie Fine
Pesach Nussbaum 514.738.3434

S. LAZARE
Rabbi Nochum Labkowski 514.436.7426

TOWN OF MOUNT ROYAL
Rabbi Moshe Krasnanski
Rabbi Shneur Zalman Rader 514.342.1770

WESTMOUNT
Rabbi Yossi Shanowitz
Mrs. Devorah Leah Shanowitz 514.937.4772

SASKATCHEWAN

REGINA
Rabbi Avrohom Simmonds 306.585.1359

SASKATOON
Rabbi Raphael Kats 306.384.4370

CAYMAN ISLANDS

GRAND CAYMAN
Rabbi Berel Pewzner 717.798.1040

COLOMBIA

BOGOTA
Rabbi Chanoch Piekarski 57.1.635.8251

COSTA RICA

S. JOSÉ
Rabbi Hershel Spalter
Rabbi Moshe Bitton 506.4010.1515

CROATIA

ZAGREB
Rabbi Pinchas Zaklas 385.1.4812227

DENMARK

COPENHAGEN
Rabbi Yitzchok Loewenthal 45.3316.1850

ESTONIA

TALLINN
Rabbi Shmuel Kot 372.662.30.50

FRANCE

BOULOGNE
Rabbi Michael Sojcher 33.1.46.99.87.85

DIJON
Rabbi Chaim Slonim 33.6.52.05.26.65

MARSEILLE

Rabbi Eliahou Altabe 33.6.11.60.03.05
Rabbi Menahem Mendel Assouline 33.6.64.88.25.04
Rabbi Emmanuel Taubenblatt 33.4.88.00.94.85

PARIS

Rabbi Avraham Barou'h Pevzner 33.6.99.64.07.70
Rabbi Asher Marciano 33.1.45.26.87.60

PONTAULT COMBAULT

Rabbi Yossi Amar 33.6.61.36.07.70

VILLIERS-SUR-MARNE

Rabbi Mendy Mergui 33.6.31.19.94.92

GEORGIA

TBILISI

Rabbi Meir Kozlovsky 995.32.2429770

GERMANY

BERLIN

Rabbi Yehuda Tiechtel 49.30.2128.0830

DUSSELDORF

Rabbi Chaim Barkahn 49.173.2871.770

HAMBURG

Rabbi Shlomo Bistritzky 49.40.4142.4190

HANNOVER

Rabbi Binyamin Wolff 49.511.811.2822

GREECE

ATHENS

Rabbi Mendel Hendel 30.210.323.3825

GUATEMALA

GUATEMALA CITY

Rabbi Shalom Pelman 502.2485.0770

ISRAEL

ASHKELON

Rabbi Shneor Lieberman 054.977.0512

BALFURYA

Rabbi Noam Bar-Tov 054.580.4770

CAESAREA

Rabbi Chaim Meir Lieberman 054.621.2586

EVEN YEHUDA

Rabbi Menachem Noyman 054.777.0707

GANEI TIKVA

Rabbi Gershon Shnur 054.524.2358

GIV'ATAYIM

Rabbi Pinchus Bitton 052.643.8770

KARMIEL

Rabbi Mendy Elishevitz 054.521.3073

KFAR SABA

Rabbi Yossi Baitch 054.445.5020

KIRYAT BIALIK

Rabbi Pinny Marton 050.661.1768

KIRYAT MOTZKIN

Rabbi Shimon Eizenbach 050.902.0770

KOCHAV YAIR

Rabbi Dovi Greenberg 054.332.6244

MACCABIM-RE'UT

Rabbi Yosef Yitzchak Noiman 054.977.0549

NES ZIYONA

Rabbi Menachem Feldman 054.497.7092

NETANYA

Rabbi Schneur Brod 054.579.7572

RAMAT GAN-KRINITZI

Rabbi Yisroel Gurevitz 052.743.2814

RAMAT GAN-MAROM NAVE

Rabbi Binyamin Meir Kali 050.476.0770

RAMAT YISHAI

Rabbi Shneor Zalman Wolosow 052.324.5475

RISHON LEZION

Rabbi Uri Keshet 050.722.4593

ROSH PINA

Rabbi Sholom Ber Hertzel 052.458.7600

TEL AVIV

Rabbi Shneur Piekarski 054.971.5568

JAPAN

TOKYO

Rabbi Mendi Sudakevich 81.3.5789.2846

KAZAKHSTAN

ALMATY
Rabbi Shevach Zlatopolsky 7.7272.77.59.49

KYRGYZSTAN

BISHKEK
Rabbi Arye Raichman 996.312.68.19.66

LATVIA

RIGA
Rabbi Shneur Zalman Kot
Mrs. Rivka Glazman 371.6720.40.22

LITHUANIA

VILNIUS
Rabb Sholom Ber Krinsky 370.6817.1367

LUXEMBOURG

LUXEMBOURG
Rabbi Mendel Edelman 352.2877.7079

NETHERLANDS

ALMERE
Rabbi Moshe Stiefel 31.36.744.0509

AMSTERDAM
Rabbi Yanki Jacobs 31.644.988.627
Rabbi Jaacov Zwi Spiero 31.652.328.065

EINDHOVEN
Rabbi Simcha Steinberg 31.63.635.7593

HAGUE
Rabbi Shmuel Katzman 31.70.347.0222

HEEMSTEDE-HAARLEM
Rabbi Shmuel Spiero 31.23.532.0707

MAASTRICHT
Rabbi Avrohom Cohen 32.48.549.6766

NIJMEGEN
Rabbi Menachem Mendel Levine 31.621.586.575

ROTTERDAM
Rabbi Yehuda Vorst 31.10.265.5530

PANAMA

PANAMA CITY
Rabbi Ari Laine
Rabbi Gabriel Benayon 507.223.3383

RUSSIA

ASTRAKHAN
Rabbi Yisroel Melamed 7.851.239.28.24

BRYANSK
Rabbi Menachem Mendel Zaklas 7.483.264.55.15

CHELYABINSK
Rabbi Meir Kirsh 7.351.263.24.68

MOSCOW: MARINA ROSHA
Rabbi Mordechai Weisberg 7.495.645.50.00

NIZHNY NOVGOROD
Rabbi Shimon Bergman 7.920.253.47.70

OMSK
Rabbi Osher Krichevsky 7.381.231.33.07

PERM
Rabbi Zalman Deutch 7.342.212.47.32

ROSTOV
Rabbi Chaim Danzinger 7.8632.99.02.68

S. PETERSBURG
Rabbi Zvi Pinsky 7.812.713.62.09

SAMARA
Rabbi Shlomo Deutch 7.846.333.40.64

SARATOV
Rabbi Yaakov Kubitshek 7.8452.21.58.00

TOGLIATTI
Rabbi Meier Fischer 7.848.273.02.84

UFA
Rabbi Dan Krichevsky 7.347.244.55.33

VORONEZH
Rabbi Levi Stiefel 7.473.252.96.99

SINGAPORE

SINGAPORE
Rabbi Mordechai Abergel 656.337.2189
Rabbi Netanel Rivni 656.336.2127
Classes in Hebrew

SOUTH AFRICA

CAPE TOWN
Rabbi Levi Popack 27.21.434.3740

JOHANNESBURG
Rabbi Dovid Masinter
Rabbi Ari Kievman 27.11.440.6600

SWEDEN

MALMO
Rabbi Shneur Kesselman 46.707.366.770

STOCKHOLM
Rabbi Chaim Greisman 468.679.7067

SWITZERLAND

BASEL
Rabbi Zalmen Wishedsky 41.41.361.1770

LUZERN
Rabbi Chaim Drukman 41.41.361.1770

THAILAND

BANGKOK
Rabbi Yosef C. Kantor 6681.837.7618

UKRAINE

DNEPROPETROVSK
Rabbi Dan Makagon 380.504.51.13.18

NIKOLAYEV
Rabbi Sholom Gotlieb 380.512.37.37.71

ODESSA
Rabbi Avraham Wolf
Rabbi Yaakov Neiman .... 38.048.728.0770 EXT. 280

ZHITOMIR
Rabbi Shlomo Wilhelm 380.504.63.01.32

UNITED KINGDOM

BOURNEMOUTH
Rabbi Bentzion Alperowitz 44.749.456.7177

CHEADLE
Rabbi Peretz Chein 44.161.428.1818

LEEDS
Rabbi Eli Pink 44.113.266.3311

LONDON
Rabbi Mendel Cohen 44.777.261.2661
Rabbi Nissan D. Dubov 44.208.944.1581
Rabbi Dovid Katz 44.207.624.2770
Rabbi Yisroel Lew 44.207.060.9770
Rabbi Gershon Overlander
Rabbi Hillel Gruber 44.208.202.1600
Rabbi Shlomo Odze 44.791.757.3558
Rabbi Yossi Simon 44.208.458.0416
Rabbi Bentzi Sudak 44.207.078.7469

MANCHESTER
Rabbi Levi Cohen 44.161.792.6335
Rabbi Shmuli Jaffe 44.161.766.1812

URUGUAY

MONTEVIDEO
Rabbi Mendy Shemtov 598.2628.6770

THE JEWISH LEARNING MULTIPLEX

Brought to you by the Rohr Jewish Learning Institute

In fulfillment of the mandate of the Lubavitcher Rebbe, of blessed memory, whose leadership guides every step of our work, the mission of the Rohr Jewish Learning Institute is to transform Jewish life and the greater community through the study of Torah, connecting each Jew to our shared heritage of Jewish learning.

While our flagship program remains the cornerstone of our organization, JLI is proud to feature additional divisions catering to specific populations, in order to meet a wide array of educational needs.

THE ROHR JEWISH LEARNING INSTITUTE,
a subsidiary of *Merkos L'Inyonei Chinuch*,
is the adult education arm of the Chabad-Lubavitch Movement.

Torah Studies provides a rich and nuanced encounter with the weekly Torah reading.

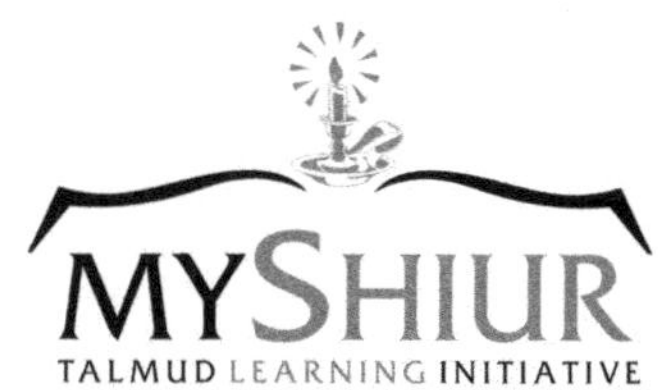

MyShiur courses are designed to assist students in developing the skills needed to study Talmud independently.

IN PARTNERSHIP WITH CHABAD ON CAMPUS

This rigorous fellowship program invites select college students to explore the fundamentals of Judaism.

IN PARTNERSHIP WITH CTEEN: CHABAD TEEN NETWORK

Jewish teens forge their identity as they engage in Torah study, social interaction, and serious fun.

The Rosh Chodesh Society gathers Jewish women together once a month for intensive textual study.

TorahCafe.com provides an exclusive selection of top-rated Jewish educational videos.

This yearly event rejuvenates mind, body, and spirit with a powerful synthesis of Jewish learning and community.

Participants delve into our nation's rich past while exploring the Holy Land's relevance and meaning today.

Select affiliates are invited to partner with peers and noted professionals, as leaders of innovation and excellence.

THE SAMI ROHR
RESEARCH INSTITUTE

Machon Shmuel is an institute providing Torah research in the service of educators worldwide.